Racial Coalition Building in Local Elections

This book examines racial and ethnic coalition building in local elections and considers Black and Latino political incorporation more broadly. Although many argue that Black and Latino voters have much to gain from alliances that advance shared interests, coalitions between the two groups have not always formed easily or been stable over time. Recent mayoral elections across the country show different patterns of out-group candidate support. This book seeks to explain these variations and the specific conditions under which Blacks and Latinos vote for the same candidate. Drawing on large-n observational data, survey experiments, and qualitative case studies, Andrea Benjamin develops a theory of co-ethnic endorsements, which points to the significance of elite cues from Black and Latino leaders. This book demonstrates that voters use elite co-ethnic endorsements to help inform their votes, that they do so particularly when race is salient in an election, and that this has real implications for representation and access to political benefits.

Andrea Benjamin is Assistant Professor of Political Science at the University of Missouri, Columbia. She received her Ph. D. from the University of Michigan. Her research interests include Black and Latino politics, local politics, and coalitions. She teaches courses on race and politics, identity politics, and urban politics.

Racial Coalition Building in Local Elections

Elite Cues and Cross-Ethnic Voting

ANDREA BENJAMIN
University of Missouri, Columbia

CAMBRIDGE
UNIVERSITY PRESS

University Printing House, Cambridge CB2 8BS, United Kingdom

One Liberty Plaza, 20th Floor, New York, NY 10006, USA

477 Williamstown Road, Port Melbourne, VIC 3207, Australia

4843/24, 2nd Floor, Ansari Road, Daryaganj, Delhi – 110002, India

79 Anson Road, #06–04/06, Singapore 079906

Cambridge University Press is part of the University of Cambridge.

It furthers the University's mission by disseminating knowledge in the pursuit of education, learning, and research at the highest international levels of excellence.

www.cambridge.org
Information on this title: www.cambridge.org/9781108415415
DOI: 10.1017/9781108233644

© Andrea Benjamin 2017

This publication is in copyright. Subject to statutory exception and to the provisions of relevant collective licensing agreements, no reproduction of any part may take place without the written permission of Cambridge University Press.

First published 2017

Printed in the United States of America by Sheridan Books, Inc.

A catalogue record for this publication is available from the British Library.

ISBN 978-1-108-41541-5 Hardback

Cambridge University Press has no responsibility for the persistence or accuracy of URLs for external or third-party internet websites referred to in this publication and does not guarantee that any content on such websites is, or will remain, accurate or appropriate.

*This book is dedicated to my parents,
Herman and Joan Benjamin*

Contents

List of Figures	*page* viii
List of Tables	x
Acknowledgments	xii
Introduction	1
1 The Co-ethnic Elite Cues Theory	24
2 An Experimental Test of the Co-ethnic Elite Cues Theory	54
3 The Co-ethnic Elite Cues Theory and Elite Black–Latino Coalitions	99
4 The Co-ethnic Elite Cues Theory and Racial Attitudes	123
Conclusion	144
Elections Appendix	153
References	168
Index	178

Figures

0.1	The Co-ethnic Elite Cues Theory	page 10
2.1	Support for Candidate 2 among Blacks, by Treatment	67
2.2	Perceived Sympathy by Candidate 2 among Blacks, by Treatment	71
2.3	Support for Candidate 2 among Latinos, by Treatment	73
2.4	Perceived Sympathy by Candidate 2 among Latinos, by Treatment	75
2.5	Support for Garcetti (Marginal Effects)	80
2.6	Support for Greuel among Blacks (Marginal Effects)	81
2.7	Support for Garcetti among Blacks (Marginal Effects)	82
2.8	Support for Greuel among Latinos (Marginal Effects)	83
2.9	Support for Garcetti among Latinos (*La Opinion*) (Marginal Effects)	84
2.10	Support for Garcetti among Latinos (Salma Hayek) (Marginal Effects)	84
3.1	Support for Candidate 2 among Latinos	107
3.2	Support for Candidate 2 among Blacks	109
3.3	Support for Candidate 2 among Whites	110
3.4	Support for Candidate 2 among Whites	111
4.1	Latinos' Racial Attitudes towards Blacks (Priming)	129
4.2	Blacks' Racial Attitudes towards Latinos (Priming)	131
4.3	Whites' Racial Attitudes towards Latinos (Priming)	134

4.4 Whites' Racial Attitudes towards Blacks (Priming)   136
4.5 Whites' Racial Attitudes towards Latinos when Reading about Black Candidates (Priming)   139
4.6 Whites' Racial Attitudes towards Blacks when Reading about Latino Candidates (Priming)   141

Tables

0.1	Percent White, Black, and Latino Populations in the Year 2000	*page* 12
0.2	Foreign Populations by City	16
0.3	Citizenship Estimates by City	17
0.4	Voter Turnout by City	18
0.1A	Top 10 Metropolitan Areas for Latinos	20
0.2A	Top 10 Metropolitan Areas for Blacks	21
0.3A	Top Six Cities with Latinos and Blacks	21
0.4A	Population Projections	22
1.1	Newspaper Circulation	39
1.2	Relationship between Endorsements and Vote Choice by Racial/Ethnic Salience in Mayoral Elections	40
1.1A	Racial/Ethnic Newspaper Coverage and Racial/Ethnic Issues	51
2.1	Black Sample Demographics	65
2.2	Latino Sample Demographics	66
2.1A	Logistic Regression Analysis of Support for Candidate 2 among Blacks, by Treatment	87
2.2A	Logistic Regression Analysis of Support for Candidate 2 among Latinos, by Treatment	88
2.3A	Logistic Regression Analysis of Support for Garcetti	89
2.4A	Logistic Regression Analysis of Candidate Support (Greuel) among Black voters	91
2.5A	Logistic Regression Analysis of Candidate Support (Garcetti) among Black voters	92

List of Tables

2.6A	Logistic Regression Analysis of Candidate Support (Greuel) among Latino voters	93
2.7A	Logistic Regression Analysis of Candidate Support (Garcetti) among Latino voters	94
3.1	Experimental Treatments	105
3.1A	Logistic Regression Analysis of Support for Candidate 2 among Latinos	115
3.2A	Logistic Regression Analysis of Support for Candidate 2 among Blacks	115
3.3A	Logistic Regression Analysis of Support for Candidate 2 among Whites	116
3.4A	Logistic Regression Analysis of Support for Candidate 2 among Whites	117
4.1	Regression Analysis of Latinos' Racial Attitudes toward Blacks (Priming)	128
4.2	Regression Analysis of Blacks' Racial Attitudes toward Latinos (Priming)	130
4.3	Regression Analysis of Whites' Racial Attitudes toward Latinos (Priming)	133
4.4	Regression Analysis of Whites' Racial Attitudes toward Blacks (Priming)	135
4.5	Regression Analysis of Whites' Racial Attitudes towards Latinos when Reading about Black Candidates (Priming)	138
4.6	Regression Analysis of Whites' Racial Attitudes toward Blacks when Reading about Latino Candidates (Priming)	140
C.1	Current minority mayors in the 100 largest U.S. cities by population	148
EA 0.1	Los Angeles Election Results (% Vote)	153
EA 0.2	New York Election Results (% Vote)	154
EA 0.3	Houston Election Results (% Vote)	154
EA 0.4	Chicago Election Results (% Vote)	156
EA 0.5	Los Angeles Poll	156
EA 0.6	Relationship between Endorsements and Vote Choice by Racial/Ethnic Salience in Mayoral Elections	158

Acknowledgments

This book is for my parents, Herman and Joan Benjamin. While neither of them is here to enjoy this moment, I hope they both are proud of me. I am a living example that parents want their children to achieve more than they achieved (Dad) and that unconditional love can make all the difference in the world (Mom). I am thankful you never told me my dreams were too big!

I started working on this project long before most of us knew the name Barack Obama. In many ways, the yearning of Black voters to elect a Black president overshadowed the perceived need for this project; the issue of minority mayors seemed limited and naïve. Yet, at the time, the media was interested in the potential to elect Latino mayors in places like New York and Los Angeles. In the years it has taken me to complete this book, in which national elections have revolved around race in an unprecedented way, I stand by my decision to focus on municipal elections. I believe this work is even more relevant today as we try to make sense of what is happening to Black and Brown people in our cities and towns. My hope is that this book provides communities and candidates with a plan to gain the representation they desire. This might seem too ambitious, but it is my one wish for this book.

I could not have completed this book without the help of many people. I would like to thank my family and friends for their support. Some of you have been here from the beginning; some of you joined the party late, but you have all been crucial in reminding me that I am more than my work. Thank you for letting me be your sister, your aunt, your godmother, your cousin, your niece, your granddaughter, and your friend.

Vince Hutchings, you are a great mentor, advisor, teacher, and friend. From day one, you guided me, encouraged me, and nudged me in the right direction. I always knew that your support would make the difference for me and that has been proven time and time again. My hope is that I can one day be the mentor and advisor that you are. Cara Wong, thank you for all your timely advice and words of wisdom. You always select your words wisely and I know that you always have my best interests at heart. Thank you for your continued support, long after it was expected. John Stewart, you are my mentor and my friend. I am so thankful that you are a part of my life and I count you among my many blessings. Your support, guidance, and love mean the world to me. Thank you for showing me what was possible, when I couldn't see it myself. Frank Baumgartner, thank you for all of your guidance and support in the past five years. I appreciate it more than I can express. Finally, I wish Hanes Walton Jr. was here to celebrate this moment with us. He is truly missed.

To the Benjamin family, I am so thankful for you. Mathew, Lucy, Alyssa, and Madalyn, I could not have finished this book without your love and support. You kept me grounded. Thank you for believing in me and pushing me when I needed it the most.

To my friends who are like sisters to me, Nicky Allen, Liza Carwile, Meredith Clark, Brighid Dwyer, Ashley Jardina, Allison Mathews, Michelle Montenegro, Dani Parker-Moore, Candice Powell, LaFleur Stephens-Dougan, Jeniffer Urquilla, Ricki Wells and Natalie Whitfield, I cannot imagine my life without each of you. You have helped me with this book in different ways. From writing sessions, to feedback, to just asking how the book was coming along; thank you for lending your ear, cheering me on, and just being my friend.

Thank you to my extended family: Erva Stock, Aunt Frances, Sonja, Dan, Jurrell, Jocelyn, Aunt Cecilia, Diana, Colleen, Pam, Vanessa, Cherelle, Moses, Schonze, Cherish, Donnie, Uncle Russell, Paul, Russ, and my godparents, Sue and Spence Leslie.

Thank you to the many friends who helped along the way: Christine Acham, Michelle Allendoerfer, Luis Alvarez, Amanda Barnes Cook, the Carwile family, Vanessa Cruz, Erica Dixon and the ladies at Zumba, Katherine Drake, the Estrera family, Gena Flynn, the Gailey family, Eric Groenendyk, Steven M. Harris, Lynette Hoelter, the Iniguez family, the Kuhl family, Frederique Laubepin, Eric McDaniel, the Urquilla family, Neill Mohammad, the Montenegro family, the Perez family, Tasha

Philpot, the Potter family, Matthew L. Rodgers, Laura Schram, Maria R. Tucker, Patricia Turner, Jessica Trounstine, and Esmeralda Zendejas.

To my godchildren, Bryan Estrera, Illiana Montenegro, Kaleb Carwile, and Donovan Ajunwa: my hope for each of you is that you find your passion and follow it.

Thank you to the Department of Political Science at the University of Michigan, the Horace H. Rackham School of Graduate Studies, and the Umphenhour-Stock Family Trust for the financial support needed to complete this early part of this project. Thank you to the College of Arts and Sciences at the University of North Carolina, Chapel Hill for the financial support to collect the additional data for this book. Thank you to my students at Carolina for inspiring me to complete this book. Finally, thank you to Agnes Ezekwesili for helping with the cover.

As many of you know, I live my life by one rule: focus on your own path. I believe when you focus on your own path, you will always be where you belong.

Introduction

> I don't know what taking an endorsement means.
> – *Michael Bloomberg*[1]

> In many ways, the candidates' policy ideas were in sync on transportation, flooding, economic development and other issues, leading voters to pay more attention to endorsements and attacks.
> – *Mayoral race voters delve into hopefuls' personalities. Campaign that ends Saturday pits Locke, Parker in tight contest [for] voters: election is Saturday.* Houston Chronicle[2]

This book is primarily concerned with voting behavior in local elections. More specifically, it examines Black and Latino voting behavior in mayoral elections. I ask, what explains voting behavior in these elections? In many recent mayoral elections, there does not appear to be a consistent pattern of vote choice for Blacks or Latinos. In local elections, the race and ethnicity of voters help explain vote choice very well. In some elections, there is evidence of high levels of co-ethnic voting: Blacks and Latinos support candidates from their own racial and ethnic groups at high rates. However, when Black and Latino voters do not have the option to support a candidate from their own racial/ethnic groups, the pattern is less consistent. In order to win an election, candidates must outreach to all potential voters, and one strategy to do this effectively is to build a coalition. Yet, there are many barriers to coalition formation. One barrier is co-ethnic voting itself. That is, if there is a co-ethnic candidate on the ballot, the other candidate may find it hard to get support from that group. In addition, there is evidence that Blacks and Latinos do not always feel positively about one another, which makes a coalition seem less likely.

Finally, changing demographics in cities create varied incentives for coalition formation. When groups are large in a city, they may decide it's not worth it to work with other groups. When groups are smaller, larger groups may reach out to them to join their coalition, but the smaller group may have to give up some of its preferences and power to work with that group.

How do voters decide which candidate to support when there is not a co-ethnic candidate on the ballot? I argue that co-ethnic cues can help us better understand vote choice in local elections. In addition to the race or ethnicity of the candidates, co-ethnic elite cues (endorsements) can help us better understand *when* Blacks and Latinos will engage in cross-ethnic voting. This book adds to our knowledge about elite cues and helps us better understand Black and Latino vote choice in local elections. Co-ethnic cues provide voters with a low-cost piece of information about which candidate will best represent the interests of the group in office, when there is not a co-ethnic on the ballot. The endorsers take on the burden of researching the candidates, so the voters only have to know about the endorsement to make an informed decision on Election Day. While many elites (elected official and organizations, for example) may endorse candidates in an election, voter awareness and responses toward these endorsements will vary. The relationship between the voters and endorsements will be strong if the voters perceive a connection between themselves and the endorser. That connection might come from membership in the organization offering the endorsement, through mutually shared beliefs with the endorser, or through shared racial and ethnic group membership. If this relationship is strong, then the voters may translate this endorsement into votes for the endorsed candidate. However, if this relationship is weak, then the voters may cast support for the opposing candidate, or abstain from voting altogether. In the case of Blacks and Latinos, the context of the campaign – the extent to which race and ethnicity become a part of the campaign – will remind Blacks and Latinos about this identity, making co-ethnic endorsements more important in that election and cross-ethnic voting more likely.

RACE, ETHNICITY, AND VOTING BEHAVIOR IN LOCAL ELECTIONS

In the past 20 years, mayoral elections in New York, Los Angeles, Chicago, and Houston demonstrate this mixed pattern among Black and Latino voters. I selected these cities because of their large Black and Latino populations – in fact, these cities are in the top five locales where Blacks *and* Latinos reside. These are the places where we *might* observe Black and Latino cross-ethnic voting in electoral coalitions. The racial and ethnic diversity of the mayoral candidates in these cities provides a unique opportunity to explore Black and Latino cross-ethnic coalitions. Yet, there are limitations to the generalizability of these cases. In cities where the Black or Latino populations are not as large, we might expect each group to form coalitions with Whites instead. Further, in cities and towns where the Black and Latino populations are smaller, there might be greater incentives for these two groups to compete with one another.

In many of the elections in New York, Los Angeles, Chicago, and Houston, voters faced the same candidates, but support for those candidates was not fixed. In some cases, Blacks and Latinos supported the same candidates, but this was not always the case. In some elections, candidates formed Black–Latino coalitions, while in other cases, Blacks and Latinos supported the same candidates without any coalitions. I argue that voter preferences are better understood when we consider the presence or absence of co-ethnic elite endorsements. These cues have the potential to help Black and Latino voters select candidates that will represent the interests of their group (Grossman and Helpman 1999). These cues, much like cues from partisans, ideological organizations, and newspapers, serve as a shortcut that allows voters to distinguish between candidates. However, co-ethnic endorsements will not matter in every election. The racial and ethnic salience of each campaign and the race and ethnicity of both the candidates and the voters also matter. In this way, this book expands what we know about cues and helps us understand racial and ethnic politics more fully. These co-ethnic elite cues work most effectively when voters are thinking about their own racial and ethnic identities. To the extent that a campaign or a candidate does not highlight these identities, voters will not rely on co-ethnic elite cues. However, if race and ethnicity are salient, then these cues become useful to voters. Once we account for these factors, we can better understand why Blacks and Latinos supported the same candidate in some elections and not in others.

Recent mayoral elections in Los Angeles, New York, Houston, and Chicago reveal a mixed pattern in voter behavior among Blacks and Latinos.[3] Two mayoral contests in Los Angeles illustrate this mixed pattern well. In 2001, Jim Hahn, a White candidate, was elected mayor of Los Angeles against Latino opponent Antonio Villaraigosa. Black voters overwhelmingly supported Hahn (80%); Latino voters overwhelmingly supported Villaraigosa (82%). But in 2005, Villaraigosa defeated

Hahn in a rematch of their 2001 mayoral contest, with a majority of Blacks (58%) voting for Villaraigosa. Latino support for Villaraigosa remained stable and exceptionally high across both contests. What happened between 2001 and 2005 that made Blacks more supportive of Villaraigosa? Some commentators have suggested that Hahn lost the support of Blacks because he did not appoint Bernard Parks, an African American, for a second term as police chief. *Los Angeles Times* poll data, however, suggest that many Black voters chose Villaraigosa because they believed he was better suited to the office of mayor (as determined by policy preferences) – fewer than half of Blacks attributed their votes to the Parks situation. That is, Blacks did not vote for Villaraigosa solely because of Parks' dismissal. Black elites in Los Angeles were clear, though, that the Parks firing drove their support for Villaraigosa over Hahn in 2005. Why did a Black–Latino electoral coalition emerge in 2005 but not in 2001?[4]

After a successful first term, Villaraigosa ran virtually uncontested in 2009, but, due to term limits, the 2013 race was wide open. In 2001 and 2005, the race and ethnicity of the voters were important. Latinos supported the Latino candidate in each election, while the Black votes shifted from one candidate to another.

The mayoral race in 2013 started with a diverse set of four candidates: Eric Garcetti, a Latino and Jewish candidate; Wendy Greuel, a White candidate; Kevin James, a White candidate; and Jan Perry, a Black candidate. In this election, 56% of Black voters supported Jan Perry and 49% of Latino voters supported Eric Garcetti (Guerra and Gilbert 2013). No one candidate won the race outright, so Garcetti and Greuel vied for the office in a runoff election. While Garcetti was poised to be the first Jewish mayor and the only consecutive Latino mayor, Greuel was poised to be the first female mayor of Los Angeles. In the runoff, there was evidence of racial and ethnic voting blocs as a majority of Latinos, Whites, and Asians supported Garcetti, while a majority of Blacks voted for Greuel (Guerra and Gilbert 2013).

The volatility of Black and Latino votes in local elections is not confined to Los Angeles. In New York City, for example, Blacks and Latinos often vote for the same mayoral candidate, but the levels of support vary across elections. When Latino candidate Fernando Ferrer ran for mayor against an incumbent in 2005, most Blacks and Latinos voted for him (at 53% and 63%, respectively). But only four years earlier, the 2001 mayoral contest featured two White candidates, and the vast majority (75%) of Blacks supported the Democratic candidate, Mark Green, whereas Latinos were almost evenly divided between Green and the Republican candidate, Michael Bloomberg. This division among Latino voters was most likely due to what many regarded as Green's ethnically inflammatory campaign against Fernando Ferrer during the Democratic primary.

In 2009, Blacks and Latinos supported Bill Thompson, a Black candidate, in his losing bid against Michael Bloomberg, a two-term incumbent who received permission to run for a third term from voters. Thompson lost the election by four percentage points. In 2013, there was no incumbent candidate and the Democratic primary was quite competitive. Bill Thompson put his hat back in the ring, and he faced an Asian American candidate, John Liu; two White candidates, Bill de Blasio and Christine Quinn; and a Jewish candidate, Anthony Weiner. Thompson and de Blasio split the Black vote, while Latinos gave de Blasio a slight advantage over Thompson. Overall, the Democratic primary was close, but Thompson conceded the election and de Blasio earned the party's nomination. Bill de Blasio went on to easily win the general election (73% to 24%), with support from all racial and ethnic groups (*New York Times* exit poll).

An even starker racial divide emerged in Houston. In 1997, the mayoral election produced four contenders in a nonpartisan contest: Lee Brown, a Black candidate; Rob Mosbacher, a White candidate; Gracie Saenz, a Latina candidate; and George Greanias, another White candidate. Blacks overwhelmingly supported Brown (97%), while Latinos gave the majority of their support to Saenz (69%), and Whites split their votes between Mosbacher (51%) and Greanias (30%). The election was forced into a runoff, which pitted Brown against Mosbacher. This time, Blacks and Latinos supported Brown (97% and 66%, respectively), while 77% of Whites voted for Mosbacher. Brown became the first Black mayor of Houston. In 1999, he was easily reelected. However, in a 2001 runoff election, Brown faced a Republican candidate of Cuban descent, Orlando Sanchez. Blacks and Latinos each overwhelmingly supported the candidate from their own group (97% and 70%, respectively), but Brown was able to get close to 28% of the Latino vote, while Sanchez received only 10% of the Black vote. Brown defeated Sanchez in a close race, 52% to 48% in overall votes. The next mayor, Bill White, served three terms from 2003 to 2009, and race was less of an issue in those campaigns. In 2009, Bill White reached the term limit and Annise Parker was elected mayor in a race that focused more on her sexual orientation than on her race or ethnicity. She was easily reelected in 2011 and 2013.

In Chicago, Richard M. Daley served as mayor from 1989 to 2011. Prior to the Daley reign, Blacks and Latinos worked together to elect the city's first Black mayor, Harold Washington, in 1983 (Muñoz and Henry 1986). In 2011, Daley did not run for reelection and so for the first time, the race for mayor of Chicago was open. Four candidates vied to be the next mayor of Chicago: Carol Moseley Braun, a Black candidate; Gery Chico and Miguel del Valle, both Latino candidates; and Rahm Emanuel, a Jewish candidate. Polls leading up to the election showed that the race was not close at all; Emanuel led the way with 49% of voters saying they planned to vote for him.[5] Emanuel won that election with 55% of the votes to become Chicago's first Jewish mayor. In 2015, Emanuel was back and faced a viable Latino candidate, Jesus "Chuy" Garcia. Garcia forced Emanuel into the city's first runoff election, but he did not win. He tried to build an Elite Black–Latino Coalition, but was not successful. Emanuel was reelected in the runoff election.

These elections illustrate the variance in voting patterns among Blacks and Latinos in mayoral elections. These elections featured White, Black, and Latino candidates, and provide some insight into how groups vote when they have the option to support a co-ethnic candidate and how they vote when they do not (cross-ethnic voting). While co-ethnic voting is important, this book is concerned with cross-ethnic voting – the situations where groups do not have the option to support a co-ethnic candidate. In the next section, I discuss electoral coalitions to lay the foundation for how the race of the candidate, the electoral context around racial and ethnic issues, and the presence of co-ethnic elite cues (endorsements) help or hinder the likelihood of cross-ethnic voting among Blacks and Latinos.

MINORITY COALITIONS: A BRIEF HISTORICAL PERSPECTIVE

In order to best understand coalitions, one must first understand the process of incorporation. This book owes a great debt to previous work on political incorporation (Browning, Marshall, and Tabb 1984). By asking how groups gain access to positions of power in local governments, Browning, Marshall, and Tabb demonstrated that groups who were once excluded from positions of power were more likely to gain access to power by working together (ibid.). In their seminal study of 10 cities in Northern California, they observe one instance of a biracial electoral alliance, where liberal Whites and Blacks were equal partners in the coalition to elect the first Black mayor, in Berkeley (ibid.). Browning, Marshall, and Tabb highlighted the importance of the coalition or electoral alliance as a successful strategy to gain access to the mayoral office. Prior to the scholarship on the success of the biracial alliance as a route to winning office, racial and ethnic groups assumed that it was best to present a united front and support their own co-racial or co-ethnic candidates (Dahl 1962). However, as cities grew more diverse, it became clear that working with other groups might be the best route to political power. But which groups? The answer was simple: racial and ethnic groups should seek out partners that share similar interests and ideology (Browning, Marshall, and Tabb 1984; Ture and Hamilton [1967] 1992). Some scholars even suggested that leaders matter in solidifying these group connections (Sonenshein 1993). Many cities were studied to assess how minorities gained access to the mayor's office: Berkeley, Oakland, San Francisco, Los Angeles, Chicago, Philadelphia, and New York (Browning et al. 1984; Kaufmann 2003a; Keiser 2003; Mollenkopf 2003; Pinderhughes 2003; and Sonenshein 2003a).

As elections took place in many of the larger and more diverse cities, however, observers began to lose faith in the strength of the biracial liberal coalition like the one observed in Berkeley. The increased diversity in many cities, coupled with some early success in getting minorities into the mayor's office, seems to have lessened the commitment among minority groups to working toward shared political goals. In addition to the evidence that minority group members were not supporting the same candidates in elections, surveys that measured feelings about out-group members found that minorities were not always fond of one another (Jackson, Gerber, and Cain 1994; Kaufmann 2003a; McClain et al. 2006; Orr and West 2006). When feelings were positive, there was support for coalitions with other racial and or ethnic[6] groups, but when feelings were negative, it was unlikely that successful coalitions could emerge (Jackson et al. 1994; Orr and West 2006). I will return to this question in Chapter 4, but the data presented here will show that elite cues are largely ineffective at moving voters to feel more positively toward out-group members.

TOWARD A BROAD THEORY OF ETHNIC POLITICS IN LOCAL ELECTIONS

In this book, when I use the term *coalition*, I mean an electoral coalition, where the goal of the coalition is to elect your preferred candidate to office. I contend that when a simple majority of voters from two racial or ethnic groups supports the same candidate, we have evidence of support for such a coalition. Voters, then, are crucial to ensure victory and translate preferences into outcomes. So, how do voters learn which candidate to support? I argue that leaders or elites are an important part of this story as they provide the information to voters about the coalition. In the context of local elections, elites may be other local politicians, state and national politicians, leaders of local or national organizations, clergy, unions, or prominent businesspeople. These elites may endorse a particular candidate, which is then announced to the voters via newspapers. To the extent that voters feel that they share particular traits with the endorsers, these endorsements will be persuasive. The endorsements serve as a cue to voters to know which candidate to support. In the case of Black and Latino voters, the endorsements from Black and Latino elites have the potential to provide the voters with information about the coalition and tell voters which candidate has agreed to help their racial or ethnic group in this particular election. However, I do not think endorsements from co-ethnics matter in each and every election. The levels of racial and ethnic discourse or racial/ethnic salience around the campaign will determine how effective co-ethnic elite cues are among voters. That is, voters are more likely to rely on co-ethnic elite endorsements when some aspects of the campaign have highlighted race/ethnicity or made these identities salient in the minds of voters. This book contributes to the source cues literature by showing that co-ethnic elite endorsements are a very important source cue that can explain candidate preferences under certain conditions. This book contributes to the coalition literature by showing the link between elite-level coalition formation and voter support.

THE CO-ETHNIC ELITE CUES THEORY

In order to win elections, candidates must appeal to a variety of voters; in this project, I am interested in appeals to Black and Latino voters. To account for the development of Black–Latino voting blocs, I present the Co-ethnic Elite Cues Theory: when partisan cues are absent and race/ethnicity is salient in an election, co-ethnic endorsements should prompt minority group members to vote for that candidate, even if the candidate is from another ethnic group.[7] I expect that whenever a Black or Latino candidate is running, Black and Latino voters will overwhelmingly support the candidate belonging to their racial/ethnic group, regardless of leader endorsements (co-ethnic voting). But if there is one White candidate and one Latino candidate, I expect the Black vote will be determined largely by Black leader/organization endorsements. Thus, when an Elite Black–Latino Coalition has formed, I hypothesize that this has occurred because of electoral cues sent by co-ethnic leaders, and I expect to find a preponderance of local Black leaders and organizations endorsing the Latino candidate and to observe a high level of cross-ethnic voting among Black voters. Similarly, if there is one White candidate and one Black candidate, I expect the Latino vote will be determined largely by Latino leader and organization endorsements. And, as with the previous example, when Black and Latino voters coalesce behind a Black candidate, my theory holds that this is due to co-ethnic elite cues indicating that Latinos should support this candidate, and I expect to observe a high level of cross-ethnic voting among Latinos. When minority voters are confronted with two White candidates, I expect Latino votes to be determined by Latino leader and organization endorsements and Black votes to be determined by Black leader and organization endorsements. The campaign context is an important factor in my theory: when racial/ethnic issues are particularly salient in the campaign, then elite endorsements should be especially influential. If race/ethnicity is not salient in an election, then endorsements will be less effective (see Figure 0.1).

Previous research on biracial coalitions has mostly been limited to the study of Whites and Blacks – and to a much lesser extent, Latinos – in cities where the Black population ranged from 5% to 45% and the Latino population ranged from 5% to 21% (Browning et al. 1984, 21). But today, Blacks and Latinos make up about 28% of the population of the United States.[8] According to the Census Bureau, Latinos are now the largest minority group in the United States, and in many major cities, Blacks and Latinos comprise a plurality or majority of the population.[9] Cities, therefore, are the ideal sites for a study of potential minority coalitions (for details on the distribution of Black and Latino populations, see Appendices 0.1 and 0.2).[10] Indeed, in metropolitan areas like New York, Los Angeles, Chicago, and Houston, Blacks and Latinos compose 37% to 56% of the population, significantly more than the nationwide average of 28% (see Appendix Table 0.3 in this Introduction). In light of these demographic changes, this project seeks to understand the prospects for coalitions between Blacks and Latinos. It is often assumed that Blacks and Latinos should work together – that is, that they are natural allies – because of their shared experience as disadvantaged minorities relative to Whites. I will show, however, that when Blacks and Latinos make up a plurality of the population, they exhibit only a mixed pattern of electoral alliances.

Why is it that Elite Black–Latino Coalitions emerge in some cities but not others – in some elections but not others? There seems to be no clear pattern from one election to the next, even when voters are faced with the same candidates (e.g., the Los Angeles mayoral elections of 2001 and

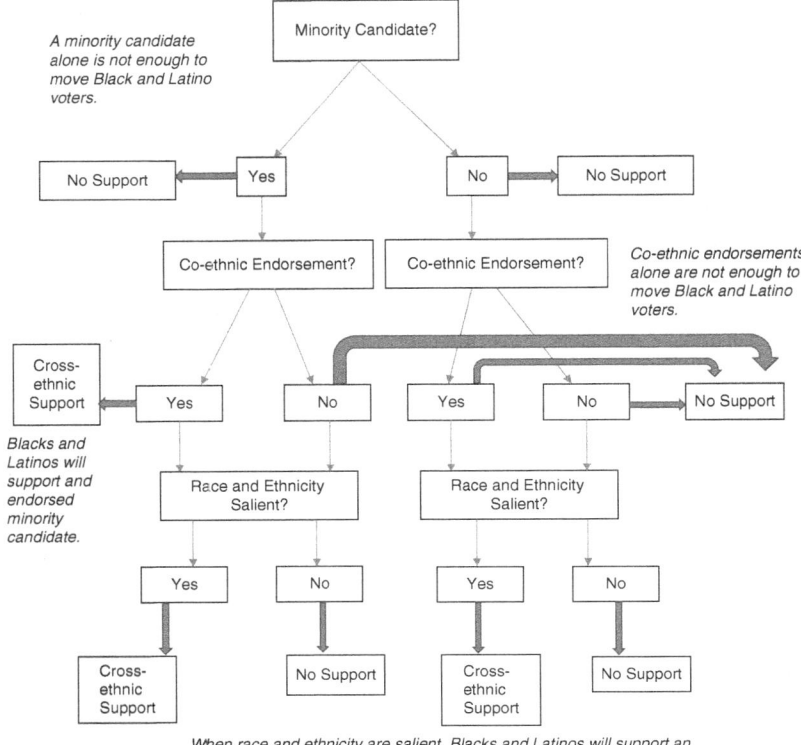

FIGURE 0.1 The Co-ethnic Elite Cues Theory
When Blacks and Latinos do not have the option to support a co-ethnic candidate

2005). In the next chapters, I demonstrate that the extant literature has failed to provide a satisfactory answer to these questions. I argue that this is primarily due to researchers overlooking the important role that elite cues, in the form of endorsements from ethnic and racial group organizations and elites, provide in explaining the variation in voting patterns among Blacks and Latinos. In this book, I explore the relationship between endorsements and candidate preferences. More specifically, I examine the circumstances under which elite cues are persuasive enough to voters to encourage them to support the endorsed candidate. I introduce and provide evidence to support the Co-ethnic Elite Cues Theory. This book seeks to explain what happens when a Black–Latino co-ethnic leadership coalition is formed and publicized to voters.

BROAD PATTERNS IN LOCAL ELECTIONS

Before I lay out the structure for the rest of this book, I want to consider Black, White, and Latino voting behavior in mayoral elections in some of the nation's largest and most diverse cities. I rely on Hajnal and Trounstine's "Mayoral Elections Data Set" (2014, 69).[11] Hajnal and Trounstine's Mayoral Elections Data Set provides rich detail about racial and ethnic voting patterns in local elections. According to the authors, they amassed "a data set with the aggregate vote by race for 254 candidates in 96 elections that represent a fairly wide range of cities and electoral contexts" (ibid.).[12] Here, I am interested in two observable outcomes: how often voters of the same race or ethnic group support the same candidate and how often a majority of voters from more than one race or ethnic group supports the same candidate. Hajnal and Trounstine find that in local elections, the race and ethnicity of the voters is the most important factor in vote choice, even when they control for partisanship, ideology, and class (Hajnal and Trounstine 2014). The answer to the first question, about how often voters of the same race or ethnic group support the same candidate, is most of the time. These voting patterns are the foundation for this book as I move beyond this finding that racial or ethnic groups vote in blocs. To answer the second question, about how often a majority of voters from more than one race or ethnic group supports the same candidate, I define this type of electoral coalition using the 50%+1 rule: in order to classify an election as having a coalition, more than 50%+1 of two or more racial/ethnic groups need to support a the same candidate.[13] The 50%+1 threshold is ideal because it is not so low a threshold that I observe too many "electoral coalitions" and it is not so high that no electoral coalitions emerge.[14] How often do more than 50% of Blacks and more than 50% of Latinos support the same candidate? Does that candidate win? Are Whites and Latinos more likely to support the same candidate? Or do Whites and Blacks team up to get their preferred candidate into office? As it turns out, the answer to all of these questions is: it depends.

I used the Hajnal and Trounstine Mayoral Elections Data Set to quantify possible coalitions (2014). In Table 0.1, I provide demographic information – the population of the city and the racial/ethnic composition of the city – for the cities in the data set. I only consider elections in the data set where the mayor is elected. This includes general elections, runoff elections, elections where no runoff was needed, and special elections, but excludes primary elections. This yields data on 60 elections

TABLE 0.1 *Percent White, Black, and Latino Populations in the Year 2000*

City	Population	%White	%Black	%Latino
Baltimore, MD	651,154	31	64	2
Boston, MA	589,141	50	25	14
Charlotte, NC	540,828	55	33	7
Chicago, IL	2,896,016	31	37	26
Cleveland, OH	478,403	39	51	7
Columbus, OH	711,470	67	3	25
Dallas, TX	1,188,580	35	26	36
Denver, CO	554,636	52	11	32
Detroit, MI	951,270	11	82	5
Houston, TX	1,953,631	31	25	37
Indianapolis, IN	781,870	68	26	4
Jacksonville, FL	735,617	55	31	8
Los Angeles, CA	3,694,820	30	11	47
Memphis, TN	650,100	37	59	3
Milwaukee, WI	596,974	45	37	12
New York, NY	8,008,278	35	27	27
Philadelphia, PA	1,517,550	43	43	9
Phoenix, AZ	1,321,045	56	5	34
San Antonio, TX	1,144,646	31	7	58
San Diego, CA	1,223,400	49	8	25
San Francisco, CA	776,733	44	8	14
San Jose, CA	894,943	38	4	30
Tucson, AZ	486,699	54	4	36
Washington, DC	572,059	28	60	8

Data from the Census website. I used the year 2000 because it was the midpoint for many of the elections (www.census.gov/statab/ccdb/cit1020r.txt).

that put a mayor in office. Because some no-runoff elections feature more than two candidates, however, there are 69 losing candidates. I include the losing candidates in order to show that not all alliances are successful. Perhaps unsurprisingly, some alliances are consistently unsuccessful. As it turns out, in this data set, there are only two instances where a majority of Blacks, Latinos, and Whites support the same winning candidate. In one case, they successfully elected the mayor (Dallas 1989). In the other election, San Francisco 1991, they were unsuccessful; this is most likely because the candidate supported by Asian Americans in the city won.[15] The most successful alliances were found among Whites and Latinos. At the 50%+1 threshold, Whites and Latinos supported the same winning candidate in 12 elections (Chicago 1989, 1991, 1995;

Dallas 2002; Houston 1991; Jacksonville 2003; Los Angeles 1997; Milwaukee 2004; New York 1997; Phoenix 1999; San Antonio 2001; and San Jose 2002). In contrast, Whites and Latinos supported a losing candidate only three times (Houston 1997, 2001 and San Francisco 2003). There are five instances of Black and Latino winning alliances (Boston 1993; Denver 1995; New York 1989; Philadelphia 2003; and San Diego special election 2005). There are seven instances where Blacks and Latinos supported the same losing candidate (Dallas 2007; Los Angeles 1993; New York 1993, 2001; San Antonio 2005; San Diego 2000; and Tucson 2003). Finally, a majority of Blacks and Whites supported the same winning candidate five times (Denver 2003; Houston 2003; Indianapolis 2003; Los Angeles 2001; and San Antonio 1991). There are no instances where Blacks and Whites supported the same losing candidate at the 50%+1 level.

In terms of the elections that do not show any patterns of coalition formation, there are five instances where racial/ethnic groups did not cooperate at all to elect the mayor in this data set. In Houston in 2003, each group had a co-ethnic candidate and each group supported that candidate. In the end, the White candidate, backed by White voters, won the election. In the Dallas 1991 election, Blacks and Whites supported different candidates, while Latinos split their votes. In Dallas in 1995, again, each group had a co-ethnic candidate, but votes did not neatly follow ethnic lines. Latinos supported the White candidate, while Whites' votes were split between the Black and the White candidates. Black voters supported the Black candidate at a level of 97%, and the Black candidate won the race. In the San Diego 2004 election, Blacks, Whites, and Latinos each voted for their co-ethnic candidate. In Philadelphia in 2003, Black voters supported the Black candidate and White voters supported the White candidate. The Latino vote was split, and the Black candidate won the race.

Finally, 22 elections do not provide enough information to determine if there was a cross-racial coalition. In most of these cities, there are no data on how Latinos voted (Baltimore 1991; Charlotte 2001; and Cleveland 1989). Many of these cities did not have large Latino populations at the time of these elections – a fact that is verified by the data, as Blacks and Whites seemed to be at extreme odds in these elections. In the remaining elections, data are missing from the dataset, so I cannot analyze the voting behavior of groups (Detroit 2005; Houston 1989, 1999; Los Angeles 1989; Los Angeles 2005; New York 2005; and San Jose 2006).

DIVERSE COALITIONS: DIVERSE CANDIDATES?

There is an interesting pattern here. Whites and Latinos support the same candidate in 15 elections and they are quite successful, electing their preferred candidate in 12 elections. On the other hand, Blacks and Latinos often support the same candidate but are not very successful, electing their preferred candidate in only 5 of 12 elections. When we shift our attention to the race of the candidate, we see a different pattern emerge. While White and Latino alliances are the most common and the most successful in the data set, they elected 10 White candidates and only two Latino candidates. Black and Latino alliances elected two White candidates, two Black candidates, and one Latino candidate. In five elections, Black and White alliances only elected White candidates. Even the losing coalitions show that Black and Latino alliances often support a diverse set of candidates (four White, one Black, one Asian American, and one Latino). White and Latino losing coalitions supported one White and two Latino candidates. So while cross-ethnic coalitions between different minority groups support candidates of diverse races, there is evidence that cross-ethnic coalitions between Whites and a minority group tend to elect White candidates.

Of course, these patterns are not causal and do not take account of all the possible reasons a voter may prefer one candidate to another. We know that the following factors are quite important: candidate traits, money spent, issue positions, and elite cues all help explain vote choice. Unfortunately, most candidates are not willing to let researchers run his or her campaign in order to test various theories about electoral coalitions. The next best solution is an experimental research design based on surveys. This allows the researcher to control factors such as candidate charisma, campaign spending, and issue positions. The bulk of the evidence I provide in this book comes from survey experiments. The experiments I designed were modeled after elections in major cities since the late 1990s. The goal of a survey experiment is to isolate the causal mechanisms through the random assignment of treatments. The experimental data used in this book rely on fictitious candidates in fictitious elections, where I manipulate small details about the candidates, such as their race, ethnicity, or their position on issues. Then, I compare levels of support for each candidate and I attribute the differences I observe to the changes I made in the treatment. The experimental data largely confirm the Co-ethnic Elite Cues Theory, and I replicate these findings in the real world as well.

DEMOGRAPHIC CHANGES AND THE POLITICAL LANDSCAPE

The population of the United States is changing: in many places, non-Hispanic Whites are no longer the clear majority and Blacks are no longer the *only* minority.[16] Over the past few decades, immigration from Latin American and Asian countries has risen dramatically (Frey 2006, 2014). As these population changes continue, it is imperative to understand how Whites, Latinos,[17] Blacks,[18] and Asians relate to one another and how these groups vary with respect to levels of political incorporation, racial attitudes, voting behavior, policy preferences, and the development of electoral coalition partnerships. This book focuses on mayoral elections at the local level, but the political dynamics under consideration certainly affect state and national politics as well.

According to Walton, "politics is concerned primarily with the distribution of advantages and disadvantages among people. It is also concerned with the behavior of individuals and groups as they vie for a favorable distribution of these advantages" (1972, 1). It is the role of governments to decide which groups get which resources. These groups may form based on partisanship, they may form based on race or ethnicity, they may form based on neighborhood, or they may form to support or oppose a local ordinance. If multiple groups are competing, one factor that is important is the size of each group. In our majoritarian system, the group that can mobilize its membership to translate preferences into policy receives the favorable distribution of political benefits. If one group does not constitute the numerical majority in the city, political elites may rely on coalitions as one route to ensure their group or someone who will help their group has access to the political arena and the political benefits of that arena.

The population trends in major cities in the United States demonstrate that Blacks and Latinos together have the potential to constitute such a majority if they work together. In cities like Chicago, Houston, Los Angeles, and New York, the population growth has been steady. Immigrants contribute to this growth, which contributes to the growth of these minority populations (see Table 0.2). When we consider noncitizen populations in these cities, we see that as a proportion of the city population, the numbers are fairly stable in recent years. In Table 0.3, we see that in Chicago, the noncitizen population is about 12%. In Los Angles and New York, noncitizens constitute roughly 22% and 18% of the population, respectively. Finally, the noncitizen population in Houston is about 17% of the population. This is important, because it

TABLE 0.2 *Foreign Populations by City*

	1990	2000	2010
Los Angeles	3,485,398	3,694,820	3,792,657
Foreign Born	1,336,665	1,512,720	1,471,551
Percent Foreign Born	38.35%	40.94%	38.80%
New York	7,322,564	8,008,288	8,174,959
Foreign Born	2,082,931	2,871,032	3,024,735
Percent Foreign Born	28.45%	35.85%	37.00%
Chicago	2,783,911	2,893,666	2,695,598
Foreign Born	469,187	628,903	566,076
Percent Foreign Born	16.85%	21.73%	21.00%
Houston	1,631,766	1,953,631	2,096,661
Foreign Born	290,374	516,105	593,355
Percent Foreign Born	17.80%	26.42%	28.30%

1990: Gibson, Campbell J. and Emily Lennon. "Historical Census Statistics on the Foreign-Born Population of the United States: 1850–1990."
2000: Malone, Nolan, Kaari F. Baluja, Joseph M. Costanzo, and Cynthia J. Davis. 2003. "The Foreign-Born Population: 2000. Census 2000 Brief."
2010: City Facts.

has real implications for both Blacks and Latinos in terms of political participation. Noncitizens cannot participate in all aspects of our political system. While there are no restrictions preventing noncitizens from donating money to campaigns, canvassing for candidates, or placing signs in their lawns, they cannot vote. Given the emphasis on elections in this book, it is important to note even as cities have grown more diverse, thanks in part to an increase in foreign-born populations, not all new inhabitants can participate in politics as conceived in this book. Still, even those who can participate may not be as engaged as we might hope. Data on voter turnout in these cities are rather low when compared to national elections. In Table 0.4, we can see that voter turnout in recent elections in these cities ranges from a high of 42% in Chicago in 2011 to a low of 13% in Houston in 2007. With roughly a quarter to a third of voters turning out in these mayoral elections, it means that each vote really does count. How can candidates and groups capitalize on this? Coalitions may provide one route for candidates to receive the support they need from voters to win an election, but the size of the group is only one factor that influences coalition formation. The race of the candidate, co-ethnic endorsements, and the electoral context also help explain coalition formation.

TABLE 0.3 *Citizenship Estimates by City*

	2009	2010	2011	2012	2013
Los Angeles	3,796,840	3,772,486	3,782,544	3,804,503	3,827,261
Noncitizen	922,914	902,463	891,153	877,606	869,614
Percent Noncitizen	24.31%	23.92%	23.56%	23.07%	22.72%
New York	8,302,659	8,078,471	8,128,980	8,199,221	8,268,999
Noncitizen	1,454,639	1,443,008	1,447,982	1,455,533	1,460,623
Percent Noncitizen	17.52%	17.86%	17.81%	17.75%	17.66%
Chicago	2,824,064	2,703,466	2,700,741	2,702,471	2,706,101
Noncitizen	354,507	340,051	339,056	341,225	336,565
Percent Noncitizen	12.55%	12.58%	12.55%	12.63%	12.44%
Houston	2,191,400	2,068,026	2,089,090	2,107,449	2,134,707
Noncitizen	444,481	427,659	433,039	433,313	437,979
Percent Noncitizen	20.28%	20.68%	20.73%	20.56%	20.52%

Los Angeles Source: 2008–2012 American Community Survey 5-Year Estimates.
New York Source: U.S. Census Bureau, 2009–2013 5-Year American Community Survey.
Chicago Source: U.S. Census Bureau, 2006–2010 American Community Survey.
Houston Source: U.S. Census Bureau, 2009–2013 5-Year American Community Survey.

WHAT'S NEXT? AN OVERVIEW OF THE CHAPTERS

In many ways, this book is about candidates, but they are only one part of the story. Candidates want to win elections, and this book provides real strategies for candidates to win the mayor's office in diverse cities. These cities are more diverse than ever before, and the data indicate that this will continue to be the case. As Hajnal and Trounstine note, racial and ethnic identity are very important in local elections (2014). In local elections, voters tend to vote with members of their racial and ethnic groups fairly consistently (ibid.). But as the data discussed earlier show, very few candidates have been elected without the support of more than one racial/ethnic group. So regardless of their own race or ethnicity, White, Black, and Latino candidates must appeal to voters from all groups. One way to make these appeals effectively is through shared interests and issues. From there, a candidate can gain favor and support from various community leaders and organizations. Specifically, when these

TABLE O.4 *Voter Turnout by City*

Los Angeles

	1997	2001 General	2001 Runoff	2005 General	2005 Runoff	2009 General	2013 General	2013 Runoff
Registered Voters	1,339,036	1,525,350	1,538,229	1,474,186	1,469,296	1,596,165	1,817,107	1,797,318
Voters	424,653	511,521	579,408	420,570	498,729	285,658	377,881	419,592
Percent Voter Turnout	31.71%	33.53%	36.67%	28.53%	33.94%	17.90%	20.79%	23.34%

New York

	1997	2001	2005	2009	2013
Registered Voters	N/A	4,104,923	4,383,276	4,462,657	4,609,905
Voters	N/A	1,520,443	1,289,935	1,154,802	1,087,710
Percent Voter Turnout	N/A	37.04%	29.43%	25.88%	23.60%

Houston

	1997	1999	2001	2003 General	2003 Runoff
Registered Voters	1,212,937	N/A	1,006,301	955,205	954,713
Voters	342,099	N/A	284,748	298,110	241,525
Percent Voter Turnout	28.20%	N/A	28.30%	31.21%	25.30%

	2005	2007	2009 General	2009 Runoff	2011	2013
Registered Voters	964,551	912,888	935,073		920,172	953,380
Voters	189,046	123,413	178,777	154,975	121,468	174,620
Percent Voter Turnout	19.60%	13.52%	19.12%	16.57%	13.20%	18.32%

Chicago

	1999	2003	2007	2011	2015 General	2015 Runoff
Registered Voters	N/A	1,436,286	1,407,979	1,406,037	1,421,430	1,441,637
Voters	N/A	463,145	456,765	590,357	478,204	590,733

Chicago Board of Elections, Harris County Board of Elections (Houston), Los Angeles Board of Elections, and New York Board of Elections.

community leaders and organizations reflect the preferences of racial and ethnic groups, it is likely that these endorsements provide useful information to voters. This book, then, demonstrates when and why voters are receptive to the suggestions of their co-ethnics.

In Chapter 1, I consider the conditions under which Blacks and Latinos vote for out-group candidates and the conditions under which Blacks and Latinos are willing to support an Elite Black–Latino Coalition. I provide the theoretical foundation of this project: the Co-ethnic Elite Cues Theory: that elite cues, heuristics, and endorsements from local ethnic and racial leadership and organizations matter to Black and Latino voters. That is, when information about candidates is low, Blacks and Latinos use elite cues when casting their votes. Additionally, the Co-ethnic Elite Cues Theory is useful in explaining Black and Latino cross-ethnic support for candidates in the context of an Elite Black–Latino Coalition. After I present my theory, I look back at some of the recent elections in Los Angeles, New York, Houston, and Chicago over the past 20 years. Using newspaper articles and exit poll data, I investigate the relationship between racial and ethnic salience in campaigns, endorsements from co-ethnic leaders and organizations, and vote choice in Los Angeles, New York, Houston, and Chicago. I find that that under the right conditions, co-ethnic elite cues matter. Taken together, these data provide evidence that my theory has applications in the real world. These data, however, are not causal. I address this limitation in Chapter 2 using a survey experiment.

In Chapter 2, I rely on experimental data to isolate the three main factors of interest – endorsements, race of the candidate, and racial/ethnic salience – and show that when race and ethnicity are salient in an election, cues and endorsements from co-ethnic leaders provide Black voters with important information about vote choice. However, when race and ethnicity are not salient in the election, these cues matter less. Latinos exhibit a different pattern. Endorsements are not very persuasive when it comes to candidate preferences. However, when it comes to assessing whether the candidate is sympathetic to Latinos, endorsements from co-ethnic leaders can move Latinos to believe this is true about Black candidates, regardless of ethnic salience. They also believe the endorsed Whites candidate is sympathetic to Latinos when ethnicity is salient. This is consistent with the data from Hajnal and Trounstine's Mayoral Data Set. I close the chapter with a test of the Co-ethnic Elite Cues Theory in the real world. I collected data on endorsements and vote choice in the 2013 Los Angeles mayoral election and find that the real world largely confirms the experimental data.

In Chapter 3, I present data from another survey experiment that shows that Blacks and Latinos are supportive of out-group minority candidates when endorsements are provided and in the context of an Elite Black–Latino Coalition. In this chapter, I also consider the relationship between minority candidates and White voters. The data show that Whites are not supportive of Black candidates on their own, but they do not seem to punish Latino candidates, regardless of Black endorsements or participation in an Elite Black–Latino Coalition.

In Chapter 4, I return to the question of racial attitudes and show that endorsements and calls to support Elite Black–Latino Coalitions prime Blacks to feel more slightly more favorably toward Latinos, but Latinos do not express these feelings. Similarly, Whites' racial attitudes appear fairly stable. On the other hand, Whites express more negative feelings towards Blacks when a Black candidate calls on voters to support him in an Elite Black–Latino Coalition.

Finally, in the Conclusion, I consider the current national climate around police–community relations and show why political incorporation at the local level is still important. I offer some final thoughts on the Co-ethnic Elite Cues Theory: endorsements, out-group candidate support, racial/ethnic salience candidate calls to support Elite Black–Latino Coalitions, and racial attitudes. I offer a summary of how these factors help explain the variation we see in Black and Latino vote choice in mayoral elections and connect these findings to the broader literature on racial and ethnic politics.

One final note: I created an Elections Appendix, which provides vote return data for the elections discussed in Chicago, Houston, Los Angeles, and New York. The Elections Appendix also has more detailed discussions of elections that I reference in the text.

APPENDIX

TABLE 0.1A *Top 10 Metropolitan Areas for Latinos*

Metropolitan Area/City	Metro Area 2004 Population	(%)
Los Angeles-Long Beach-Santa Ana, CA	5,587,692	43.2
New York-Northern New Jersey-Long Island, NY-NJ-PA	3,882,817	20.8
Miami-Fort Lauderdale-Miami Beach, FL	1,982,641	37

(continued)

TABLE 0.1A *(continued)*

Metropolitan Area/City	Metro Area 2004 Population	(%)
Chicago-Naperville-Joliet, IL-IN-WI	1,725,685	18.4
Houston-Baytown-Sugar Land, TX	1,637,992	31.6
Riverside-San Bernardino-Ontario, CA	1,580,457	41.7
Dallas-Fort Worth-Arlington, TX	1,423,020	25
Phoenix-Mesa-Scottsdale, AZ	1,056,145	28.4
San Antonio, TX	965,745	52.1
San Diego-Carlsbad-San Marcos, CA	849,771	29

Frey, William H. 2006. "Diversity Spreads Out: Metropolitan Shifts in Hispanic, Asian, and Black Populations since 2000." *Living Cities Census Series*, The Brookings Institution. March 2006, pp. 1–28.

TABLE 0.2A *Top 10 Metropolitan Areas for Blacks*

Metropolitan Area/City	Metro Area 2004 Population	(%)
New York-Northern New Jersey-Long Island, NY-NJ-PA	3,202,808	17.1
Chicago-Naperville-Joliet, IL-IN-WI	1,694,518	18
Atlanta-Sandy Springs-Marietta, GA	1,406,290	29.9
Washington-Arlington-Alexandria, DC-VA-MD-WV	1,335,823	26
Philadelphia-Camden-Wilmington, PA-NJ-DE-MD	1,162,847	20
Miami-Fort Lauderdale-Miami Beach, FL	1,044,406	19.5
Detroit-Warren-Livonia, MI	1,026,048	22.8
Los Angeles-Long Beach-Santa Ana, CA	947,351	7.3
Houston-Baytown-Sugar Land, TX	848,221	16.4
Dallas-Fort Worth-Arlington, TX	789,807	13.9

TABLE 0.3A *Top Six Cities with Latinos and Blacks*

Cities with Latinos and Blacks	Black–Latino Population	%Black and Latino
New York-Northern New Jersey-Long Island, NY-NJ-PA	7,085,625	37.9
Los Angeles-Long Beach-Santa Ana, CA	6,535,043	50.5
Chicago-Naperville-Joliet, IL-IN-WI	3,420,203	36.4
Miami-Fort Lauderdale-Miami Beach, FL	3,027,047	56.5
Houston-Baytown-Sugar Land, TX	2,486,213	48
Dallas-Fort Worth-Arlington, TX	2,212,827	38.9

TABLE 0.4A *Population Projections*

Percent Race and/or Hispanic Origin	2000	2010	2020	2030	2040	2050
White alone	81.0	79.3	77.6	75.8	73.9	72.1
Black alone	12.7	13.1	13.5	13.9	14.3	14.6
Asian Alone	3.8	4.6	5.4	6.2	7.1	8.0
All other races	2.5	3.0	3.5	4.1	4.7	5.3
Hispanic (of any race)	12.6	15.5	17.8	20.1	22.3	24.4
White alone, not Hispanic	69.4	65.1	61.3	57.5	53.7	50.1

U.S. Census Bureau. 2004. "U.S. Interim Projections by Age, Sex, Race, and Hispanic Origin." www.census.gov/ipc/www/usinterimproj/. Internet Release Date: March 18, 2004.

NOTES

1. "Bloomberg is said to get nod from mayor." *New York Times*. October 27, 2001.
2. "Mayoral race voters delve into hopefuls' personalities. Campaign that ends Saturday pits Locke, Parker in tight contest voters: election is Saturday." *Houston Chronicle*. December 11, 2009.
3. All of the exit poll data discussed in this section can be found in the Elections Appendix.
4. At least part of the reason that Black voters abandoned Hahn in his reelection bid was because he did not reappoint the African American chief of police. This was not, however, the only factor as pre-election polls also showed that Blacks preferred Villaraigosa on some policy domains. Less than half of Blacks attributed their vote to the Parks situation.
5. "Emanuel at 49%, Chico at 19% in Tribune/WGN poll." *Chicago Tribune*, February 11, 2011.
6. I use the terms *racial* and/or *ethnic groups* and *racial/ethnic* interchangeably in this book.
7. While partisanship is often available as a cue in national elections, local elections often lack these cues. More than 61% of local elections lack partisan cues (DeSantis and Renner 2002).
8. Source: U.S. Census Bureau. 2004. "U.S. Interim Projections by Age, Sex, Race, and Hispanic Origin." www.census.gov/ipc/www/usinterimproj/. Internet Release Date: March 18, 2004. See Appendix 0.4.
9. Although new estimates indicate that Asian Americans will claim that title by 2055.
10. Source: U.S. Census Bureau. 2011. "U.S. Hispanic Population Surpasses 45 Million Now 15 Percent of Total." www.census.gov/newsroom/releases/archives/population/cb08-67.html.

11. These data were generously provided by Zoltan Hajnal and Jessica Trounstine. I can only imagine the amount of work it took to compile this data set. I am very grateful to these two scholars for sharing these data with me.
12. This includes the following elections: Baltimore 1991; Boston 1993; Charlotte 2001; Chicago 1989, 1991, 1995; Cleveland 1989, 2001; Columbus 1991, 1995, 1999; Dallas 1989, 1991, 1995, 2002, 2007; Denver 1995, 2003; Detroit 2001, 2005; Houston 1989, 1991, 1997, 1999, 2001, 2003; Indianapolis 2003; Jacksonville 2003; Los Angeles 1989, 1993, 1997, 2001, 2005; Memphis 1991, 1995; Milwaukee 1996, 2004; New York 1989, 1993, 1997, 2001, 2005; Philadelphia 1999, 2003; Phoenix 1999; San Antonio 1991, 2001, 2005; San Diego 2000, 2004, 2005; San Francisco 1991, 1995, 1999, 2003; San Jose 1998, 2002, 2006; Tucson 2003; and Washington, DC, 1994.
13. This is in line with the notion of the absolute majority used in the first ballot in France (Lijphart 1999, 146).
14. The choice of threshold is important. When I use 40%+1, I find coalitions everywhere: there are 37 winning coalitions and 27 losing coalitions. When I use 45%+1, there are 30 winning coalitions and 16 losing coalitions. When I use 55%+1, there are 18 winning coalitions and 10 losing coalitions. Finally, when I use 60%+1, there are 12 winning coalitions and five losing coalitions.
15. Of course, Asian Americans are important voters in many other cities as well. Future iterations should consider their contributions to biracial coalitions.
16. Yet, none of these groups should be thought of as monolithic. There is a lot of in-group variation. See J. Jennings (Ed.), *Blacks, Latinos, and Asians in Urban America: Status and Prospects for Politics and Activism* (Westport, CT: Praeger Press, 1994). Additionally, work has been done that looks at how West Indians and Blacks identify in the United States. See T. Thomas and K. Deaux (2006). "Black Immigrants to the United States: Confronting and Constructing Ethnicity and Race." In R. Mahalingam (Ed.), *Cultural Psychology of Immigrants*. Mahwah, NJ: Lawrence Erlbaum; M. Waters, *Black Identities: Immigrant Dreams and American Realities* (Cambridge, MA: Harvard University Press, 1999).
17. In this book, I use the term *Latinos* to mean people who come from the Spanish-speaking Caribbean and Latin America. Though, where needed, I also use national origin terms (Masuoka 2008).
18. I use the terms *Black* and *African American* to refer to groups who are of African descent.

1

The Co-ethnic Elite Cues Theory

Are Elite Cues Meaningful? How Co-ethnic Elite Cues Provide Information to Voters

In this chapter, I rely on content analysis data to show the correlation between co-ethnic elite endorsements and vote choice in real-world mayoral elections. The data show that, for the most part, when race and ethnicity are made salient in a campaign, the number and direction of co-ethnic leader endorsements are associated with candidate preference among Black and Latino voters.[1] Alternatively, when race and ethnicity are not salient in a campaign, co-ethnic leader cues typically matter less.[2] Recent mayoral elections in Los Angeles, New York, Houston, and Chicago demonstrate that there are cases in which Blacks and Latinos vote for the same candidate and other cases in which they do not support the same candidate. While Whites and Latinos are slightly more likely to support the same candidate than Blacks and Latinos, the candidates Whites and Latinos support are more likely to be White candidates (73% compared to 45%) (Hajnal and Trounstine 2014). In national and state-level elections, most Blacks and Latinos vote for Democratic candidates (Hajnal and Lee 2011). However, local elections offer a different perspective on voting behavior because they are often either nonpartisan (Los Angeles and Houston) or dominated by one-party rule (Chicago and, until recently, New York) (DeSantis and Renner 1991; Kaufmann 2004; Oliver and Ha 2007). Thus, for the most part, partisanship alone cannot explain voting patterns in local elections.

In the Introduction, I asked: how do we account for the varying degree of shared candidate support among Blacks and Latinos in local elections? One subset of the previous literature suggests that we should consider factors such as commonality of interests, compatible ideologies, and entrepreneurial leadership (Browning, Marshall, and Tabb 1984;

Sonenshein 1993), while yet another subset of the literature suggests that levels of racial antagonism between Blacks and Latinos can explain the variation in voting (Gay 2006; Kaufmann 2003a; McClain et al. 2006; Orr and West 2006). While important, neither approach has been able to fully explain the voting patterns observed in mayoral elections. One problem with explanations that rely on commonality of interests, compatible ideologies, and entrepreneurial leadership is that these variables are relatively static (Hajnal and Trounstine 2014). In other words, when focusing on different elections within the same city, it is not likely that ideology, interests, or leaders change much from one contest to the next – they cannot account for the ebb and flow of biracial coalitions. Thus, it seems unlikely that these factors alone can explain the changes in voting patterns among Blacks and Latinos. But studies that focus on ideology and racial attitudes are not compelling either, as these attitudes are also fairly stable from election to election, even as voting patterns are not (Kaufmann 2004). Factors such as candidate charisma, campaign money, issue positions, and endorsements vary more, and are therefore more likely to explain variation in candidate preference (Krebs 1998; Lieske 1989).

Building on the incorporation literature and the racial attitudes literature, this book seeks to understand and clarify the conditions under which Black and Latino voters are responsive to Black–Latino political collaborations in local elections. That is, what are the prospects for Blacks and Latinos to make political gains in local politics together? Can Blacks and Latinos go it alone, without liberal Whites? Perhaps the better question is, should they? I offer an explanation for Black and Latino voting patterns in local elections, drawing on both the incorporation literature, which explains coalition formation through population, interests, and ideology, and the racial attitudes literature, which explains coalition formation by focusing on the way Blacks and Latinos feel about one another. A satisfactory explanation for Black and Latino voting patterns needs to be dynamic enough to account for short-term changes in electoral coalitions. While population, ideology, interests, and racial attitudes are fairly stable, leader endorsements and candidates are dynamic. In fact, different leaders may respond to different candidates based on a number of factors, including issues or community perceptions of the candidate. As noted in the Introduction, Latino populations are on the rise and Blacks and Latinos are now the plurality, if not the majority, of many large cities (see the Appendix in the Introduction). Yet it is unclear if the literature exploring Black–White coalitions can be applied to Elite Black–Latino Coalitions. Indeed, there are reasons to believe that Elite Black–Latino

Coalitions might form under a different set of conditions. Elite Black–Latino Coalitions depend on leader endorsements, the racial/ethnic characteristics of candidates, and the racial context of an election. The goal of this book is to understand the conditions that enable cross-ethnic voting among Blacks and Latinos.

GROUP POLITICS: ELITES, ENDORSEMENTS, CANDIDATES, AND THE POLITICAL CONTEXT

Groups form the foundation of politics: the process of deciding who gets what and for how long is the basis for many studies of politics. One's preference for which groups gets what resources may be influenced by elites, though researchers have shown that racial and ethnic groups often share these preferences absent elite cues (Walsh 2004). The Co-ethnic Elite Cues Theory *is* about elites *and* group politics. The theory sheds light on the ways in which groups can access the local political arena and have a say in how resources will be distributed. Of particular interest here are instances of cross-ethnic voting – cases where a co-ethnic group member is not an option to represent one's group in the political arena. Researchers have demonstrated that when politics are framed with reference to groups, people are very knowledgeable about who should get what and for how long (Brady and Sniderman 1985; Campbell et al. 1960; Converse 1964; Key 1949; Kinder and Kam 2005; Kinder and Sanders 1996; Nelson and Kinder 1996; Walsh 2003; and Walton 1984). The Co-ethnic Elite Cues Theory builds on this research in that it requires racial and ethnic group identity to be salient in the minds of voters. Then, if elites have formed a coalition to gain access to the political arena, they will inform voters of this coalition via endorsements. Electoral coalitions have a short-term goal: to elect the preferred candidate to office. In this book, I am interested in the cases where a simple majority of voters from two groups supports the same candidate (Browning et al. 1984; Hero 1992; Hero and Preuhs 2013; Kaufmann 2003a; Lijphart 1999; and Sonenshein 1993). I argue that the context of the campaign has the potential to make co-ethnic elite endorsements more important to voters as they vote. Specifically, when race and ethnicity become salient in a campaign, Blacks and Latinos look to Black and Latino elites to help interpret the campaign environment. In these conditions, the endorsements offered to a candidate will be much more persuasive. Now that we have a sense of why groups matter and what their goal is, let's turn to a more in-depth discussion of the moving parts of the theory.

BEYOND THE PARTISAN CUE: ALTERNATIVE CUES AND HEURISTICS

In many local elections, voters are unable to rely on partisanship to make voting choices, so they may look for other sources of information (cues): the co-ethnic elite cue. While racial and ethnic group identity has been linked to political behavior, we have not adequately explored how cues from leaders in one's racial and ethnic group or racial and ethnic organizations might influence candidate preferences. Voters are often competent enough to use pieces of information, such as known elite preferences and knowledge of group positions, to produce vote choices that appear to be in line with their own preferences. For example, Kuklinski and Hurley demonstrate that it matters who gives the cue, as well as the information contained in the cue (1994). In fact, they found that for Blacks, the race of the person giving the message matters. That is, Black respondents think Black leaders (as cue-givers) will generally have their best interest at heart (749; see also Campbell et al. 1960; Zaller 1992). Research on Latino voting behavior shows that Latinos are more likely to be persuaded by endorsements from organizations that work to the benefit of the Latino community (Latino Decisions 2008).[3]

Further research shows that when voters have low levels of information about an issue, knowing where particular groups stand on the issue acts as a cue, allowing voters to vote as though they were fully informed (Gerber and Phillips 2003; Lupia 1994). Other studies have shown that voters are able to identify where various groups in society stand on political issues with great accuracy (Brady and Sniderman 1985). Voters, then, are only required to know how they feel about a particular group – their feeling about the group guides how they should feel about the issue. Despite all of this research on cues, most studies have not focused on co-ethnic elite cues as a potential source cue that sends important information to voters. This book seeks to fill that gap, but first, let me discuss who constitutes an elite in the context of local elections.

ELITES – WHO CONSTITUTES AN ELITE IN THE POLITICAL ARENA?

Throughout this book, *elites* are people who are knowledgeable about politics and in a position to *influence* politics. In many ways, I adopt Zaller's definition of elites: "politicians, higher level government officials, journalists, some activists and many kinds of experts and policy specialists" (Zaller 1992, 6). Lee offers a complementary, although perhaps more nuanced, definition of elites; he argues that when groups are not a part of the mainstream political system, yet want to influence that political system, they may not start out as "elites" in the traditional sense, though they move into that position as they make changes to the political system (2002, 10). Though Lee's work considers times of political unrest, it is applicable to Blacks and Latinos insofar as Black and Latino elites are working to get candidates elected into offices that are historically White.[4] Lee says, "elites are best identified not by who they are ... but rather by what they do (that is, by their leadership, their ability to persuade and mobilize, and their flexible adaptation to and exploitation of rapidly changing circumstances)" (2002, 10). Hero and Preuhs (2013) rely on a very specific definition of elites to mean those elected officials in Congress and those who have access to these members (via interest and advocacy groups). Members of Congress may weigh in on local politics, but it is much more likely that state-level representatives will get involved in these elections. Taken together, these definitions provide a sense of who might influence politics in minority communities: ministers, people active in community organizations, politicians at all levels, racial/ethnic news outlets, and other prominent members of the community (Rogers 2006; Wong 2006). I do not want to go so far as to say that everyone is an elite. I am interested in people and organizations that influence others in political contexts.

It is important to note that elites may have their own incentives in seeking to influence other people in political contexts. While elites are sometimes acting based on the good of the community, there are also instances when elites feel that they are competing with one another for influence. Harris-Lacewell suggests that "black ideological elites perceive themselves as competitors in a marketplace of ideas and they attempt to sell their ideological product to African American masses" (2004, 205). Admittedly, Harris-Lacewell is not referring to endorsements, but her conceptualization of elites as competitors is important when we think about the election cycle and the ways in which elites compete with one another to win the favor of candidates and voters. In any given election, some Black leaders will endorse one candidate while other Black leaders will endorse another. The same is true for Latino leaders. It is up to the voters to decide which endorsements, if any, are persuasive.

ENDORSEMENTS – WHY IS THIS CUE USEFUL?

In this book, an *endorsement* is a formal, public announcement of support for a particular candidate by a community leader or organization.[5] Returning to the recent mayoral elections in Houston, Los Angeles, Chicago, and New York (discussed in the Introduction), we know that Blacks and Latinos do not always agree on candidates from one election to the next. One possible explanation for the various shifts in Black and Latino voting behavior is that Black and Latino elites offer their support via endorsements to different candidates from one election the next. For elections in which Blacks and Latinos supported the same candidate, it is possible that Black and Latino elites endorsed *the same* candidate. For elections in which Blacks and Latinos did not support the same candidate, it is possible that Black and Latino elites supported a *different candidate* in those elections. According to Downs, in an ideal world, voters would have full information about candidates and make decisions based on their perceptions of the benefits of one candidate over another (1957, 37). Yet we know that voters are not well informed (Delli, Carpini, and Keeter 1996). Therefore, without full information, elite cues such as endorsements can fill the information gap for voters. Endorsements may serve as a cue to voters and may allow voters to update their candidate preferences, without researching all of the information about the candidate (Lodge, Steenbergen, and Brau 1995).

Previous research on the effectiveness of endorsements has been inconclusive. It is unclear what endorsements actually mean to voters and whether or not voters find them persuasive. Indeed, as the quote at the beginning of the Introduction suggests, even candidates are not sure what endorsements mean. But there is evidence that group membership increases the effectiveness of endorsements. Rappaport, Stone, and Abramowitz (1991) found that during the Democratic caucuses in 1984, endorsements from labor and teachers' unions mattered for in-group members: labor and teachers' union members were more likely to support the endorsed candidate. Endorsements from women's groups, however, were not as persuasive. One major benefit of this research is that it focuses on the Democratic caucuses, allowing us to move beyond partisanship as a cue. Moreover, the salience of group memberships (which can vary depending on the circumstances) may also be important. That is, when group identity (here, labor and teachers' union membership) is salient, we would expect cues or endorsements to be more persuasive.

It is not clear from this research whether endorsements from racial/ethnic leaders will be persuasive. Are racial/ethnic endorsements more like union endorsements or endorsements from a women's group? It is difficult to know when racial and ethnic identities become important in local elections, because candidate evaluation is influenced by many factors other than endorsements (incumbency, campaign spending, issue positions). Work done at the national level provides some support for the notion that endorsements matter. Erickson found that the endorsements provided by newspapers for Johnson in 1964 led to roughly a 5% increase in votes for Johnson (1976, 217). Liu saw similar results in New Orleans (2001, 2003). Overall, there is some evidence to suggest that endorsements can influence voter preferences, but what is less clear is when to expect this. In a later section, I return to the relationship between group membership and identity salience in local elections.

Building on previous endorsement research, McDermott (2006) found that endorsements from the American Federation of Labor and Congress of Industrial Organizations (AFL–CIO)[6] encouraged self-identified liberals to vote for the endorsed Democratic candidate, but made self-identified conservatives less likely to support the candidate. This suggests that endorsements can send messages to in-group members about whom to vote for, as well as messages to out-group members about whom to avoid. McDermott also found that labor endorsements for Republican candidates did not seem to influence candidate preferences in liberal or conservative voters. This is most likely because the message did not match the messenger (Kuklinski and Hurley 1994). This suggests that several conditions must be met for endorsements to be persuasive.

Most importantly, there is much to learn about co-ethnic elite endorsements. With the exception of Campbell and colleagues (1960), who mostly hypothesized about the relationship between Black endorsements and Black votes in the 1950s, Kuklinski and Hurley (1994), who found that Blacks are receptive to cues from Black leaders (regardless of the ideology of the leader), and Barreto and colleagues (2008), who found that Latinos were responsive to Latino endorsements for Hillary Clinton, there has been no systematic study of the influence of co-ethnic elite endorsements on vote choice among Blacks and Latinos. This project adds to this research by testing these claims directly using experiments and survey data.

RACIAL AND ETHNIC SALIENCE IN THE POLITICAL ARENA

The political context, as defined by Walton, is "a thesis which postulates that political behavior at either the individual or the group level is not independent of the political environment (a particular time period and a particular place) in which it occurs" (1997, 7). Indeed, it would be difficult to study Black–Latino voting blocs absent the context of each election. Though it would be easy to consider the factors that make each election unique and offer an explanation for voting behavior in that election, it would not add to our understanding of Black and Latino voting preferences generally, nor would it provide us with rules or conditions that could be applied to future elections. The goal is to think about the context of elections collectively and move beyond candidate-specific attributes in a particular election, campaign spending in a given year, and campaign issues that are important at the time of the election (Abrajano, Nagler, and Alvarez 2005; Krebs 1998; Lieske 1989; Oliver 2012; Oliver and Ha 2007; Schaffner, Streb, and Wright 2002; and Squire and Smith 1988). This is not to say that these factors are unimportant, but if we want to be able to make informed predictions about how Blacks and Latinos will respond to candidates in local elections, we have to think about contextual factors more generally.

Kaufmann uses the political context in local elections to explain voter preferences. She seeks to "identify the contextual factors that tend to trigger racially and ethnically polarized voting within the domain of local elections and to use these insights to construct a theory of local voting behavior" (2004, 9). Kaufmann is less interested in Black–Latino voting blocs, but she uses survey data about racial attitudes and attitudes about race relations more generally to show that "during periods of heightened conflict – especially when minority groups challenge status quo power relations – members of dominant groups become more attuned to group-based competition and are more likely to coalesce on this basis" (39). This work is excellent in explaining how White voters respond to shifting perceptions of racial conflict, but given that these perceptions are far more stable among racial minorities, this theory is less conclusive about Black and Latino voting patterns in local elections. Consequently, it may be that highlighting race is sufficient to prompt Blacks and Latinos to rely on group-based voting criteria. Taking this idea of racial salience in campaigns a step further, sociologist Paul Luebke says, "racial appeals 'are present in a campaign if one candidate calls attention to the race of his or her opponent or opponent's supporters or if the news media covering a campaign disproportionately calls attention to the race of one candidate or of that candidate's supporters'" (Grofman, Handley, and Niemi 1994, 107; Reeves 1997, 21). This definition moves beyond the conflict-focused definition derived from Kaufmann's work and permits race and ethnicity to become salient in a wider variety of contexts. This definition also helps explain when race and ethnicity are salient in any electoral contest.

While this book focuses on local electoral contexts, race and ethnicity can become salient in state and national elections as well. In fact, much of the research on the subject focuses on state- and national-level elections. Mendelberg finds that racial images can cue race implicitly (2001). Further, McIlwain and Caliendo tackle race-based appeals in congressional, senate, and presidential elections (2011). They find that minority candidates can also use race-based appeals to gain support from co-ethnic voters. They also show how the media contribute to racial and ethnic saliency by what they report in any given campaign (McIlwain and Caliendo 2011). Finally, in experiments, Valentino and colleagues show that it is more than just racial images that cue stereotypes – the message must be consistent with the stereotype (2002). Taken together, I expect local elections to work in a similar fashion. The candidates may highlight race and ethnicity (via issues, through their own race and ethnicity, and by the groups they choose to focus on in their outreach). The media can highlight race and ethnicity by reporting on the race and ethnicity of the candidates and of their supporters, and by covering racial and ethnic issues. Finally, images of the candidates or their supporters may also cue race and ethnicity, though the messages associated with those images also matter.

In order to test the claim that heightened media attention to race or racial issues may lead to increased racial/ethnic bloc voting, I must classify whether race and ethnicity were salient in each campaign. This enables us to look at voting preferences for Blacks and Latinos in these two types of elections to see if any patterns emerge. For this project, race and ethnicity become salient in a campaign a number of ways: when there is a Black or Latino candidate *and* the media draws attention to the race of the candidates while reporting the news, when the media highlights the race or ethnicity of the supporters of a particular candidate, or when candidates take sides on racial and ethnic issues.

CANDIDATE CHARACTERISTICS: WHY DOES THE CANDIDATE'S RACE AND ETHNICITY MATTER?

Endorsements alone cannot explain vote choice. The electoral context, as discussed earlier, helps set the tone for these endorsements to be persuasive. Additionally, the traits and positions of the candidates are important factors. Indeed, candidates are relevant when assessing the efficacy of elite endorsements. In the recent elections in Houston, Los Angeles, and New York, we have the benefit of several cases in which one or more of the same candidates ran in different elections, and in which Black and Latino voters did not always respond to the candidates in a consistent manner. This suggests that there are several criteria that voters use when evaluating candidates, and that voters may call on different criteria at different times. Previous research suggests that voters often think Black and female candidates are more liberal than men and non-Blacks (McDermott 1998). Based on evidence from actual mayoral elections, the only consistent pattern that emerges is that when there is a Black candidate, Black voters invariably support that candidate, and when there is a Latino candidate, Latino voters routinely support their co-ethnic candidate. What is less clear is what prompts Black voters to support Latino candidates and Latino voters to support Black candidates. Taken as a whole, there are three moving parts that might explain Black–Latino voting blocs in local elections: elites and possible endorsements, candidates (race and/or ethnicity), and context.

A COMPARATIVE PERSPECTIVE OF ETHNIC POLITICS BEYOND THE UNITED STATES

Sociologists, anthropologists, and political scientists have all sought to understand the relationship between national, ethnic, racial, religious, and linguistic identities and political systems (Anderson 1991; Deutsch 1966; and Gellner 1983). In some countries, this relationship has manifested as the development of ethnic, linguistic, or religious political parties (Horowitz 1985; Varshney 2002). Indeed, the foundation of consociational democracies is to reinforce the social cleavages of the country by allocating seats to groups based on population size or some other arrangement. This system is largely about the relationship between elites, who must cooperate with one another, and the relationship between elites and the masses. That is, the masses trust the elites to manage potential societal conflict through political office. Though local elections in the United States are not consociational, these types of arrangements highlight the mechanism by which ethnic, religious, linguistic, or racial identities are a part of the electoral process. That is, if the masses trust that elites have their best interests at heart (Kuklinski and Hurley 1994), then we can expect the masses to trust the political arrangements elites make.

Another way that societies can manage potential ethnic, racial, linguistic, and religious conflict is to have electoral rules that make it impossible for one group to win an election without support from out-group members (Horowitz 1991). This is very different from consociational democracies because, in these types of systems, candidates and party leaders must seek out support from members of all groups, not just from members of their own racial, ethnic, religious, or linguistic group. Most mayoral elections in the United States are winner take all, so this is much closer to what we might see in local elections in cities in the United States. The question then becomes: how do members of one group appeal to voters in another group, *if* group identity is an important factor? Although cities in the United States are not full of outright ethnic conflict, voters may rely on ethnic or racial identities to guide candidate preferences when partisanship is not an easy cue or heuristic. If racial and ethnic identities become important in any given election, then we would expect candidates to find ways to obtain support from their own racial/ethnic group as well as from members of other racial/ethnic groups.

BLACK POLITICAL BEHAVIOR: A LESSON IN POLITICAL COHESIVENESS

Previous research on Black political behavior has been quite conclusive: conceptions of Blackness or group consciousness are a strong predictor of Black political participation, and Blacks tend to vote fairly cohesively at the national level (Dawson 1994; Tate 1993; Walton 1985; and White 2007). Walton found that at the individual level, levels of group consciousness among Blacks are a major explanation for Black voting behavior (1985). Verba and Nie concur that, for Blacks, group consciousness can overcome socioeconomic explanations for voting behavior (1987). Miller and colleagues found that group consciousness is associated with higher levels of participation when group members realize their status relative to other groups (1981). Black voters will typically support Black candidates; work by Bobo and Gilliam found that Blacks that have Black mayors are more politically active than Blacks who live in areas where Blacks are not in positions of power (1990). That is, having a Black mayor increases political activity among Blacks. At the local level, Hajnal and Trounstine find that Blacks vote in blocs more consistently than any other group (2014). Finally, church membership has been found to increase Black political participation (Tate 1993).

As a result of the research that emphasizes the cohesive nature of Black political behavior, this book recognizes that Blacks may be open to taking cues from Black leaders (Dawson 1994; White 2007). Yet there are instances when Blacks do not behave in such a cohesive manner (Cohen 1999; Rogers 2006). Cohen finds that several issues related to sexuality and health have not been incorporated into the "Black Agenda," even though the issues may have real implications for the Black community (1999). Rogers finds that once we account for immigration from the Caribbean, there is less support among native-born Black voters for immigrant candidates in New York City (2006). At the core of this research is the notion that conceptions of Blackness may need to be more flexible. It also suggests, however, that elites may need to set the tone for changes within the community. Hajnal and Lee show that local elections are one political venue where Blacks are likely to vote differently than a majority of other Blacks (2011, 271). They find that 26% of Blacks vote differently than other Blacks for the mayor in local elections (ibid.). Black political cohesion is well documented, but the same is not true for Latinos.

LATINO POLITICAL BEHAVIOR: THE POTENTIAL FOR POLITICAL COHESIVENESS

With the increase in the Latino population in the United States over the past three decades, more work has been done analyzing Latino voting patterns (Colby and Ortman 2004). One of the early studies of Mexican Americans found that, much like African Americans, they professed overwhelming support for the national Democratic Party (Garcia and Arce 1988). But, unlike most African Americans, a sizable proportion of Latinos face barriers to political participation: citizenship status and language (Jones-Correa 1998; Tam Cho 1999).[7] Although some types of political participation require a particular residency status, Bean and colleagues found that children of Mexican immigrants can incorporate into the political process in the United States (2006). Leal found that noncitizens did participate in non-electoral-related activities, but not at the same levels as citizens (2002). Campaign contributions and volunteering do not require Latinos to be eligible to vote, so there are realms in which Latinos can be politically active – these activities may ease the transition from political volunteer to political participant.

The literature on Latino politics finds that Latinos can and do behave like a voting bloc under certain conditions. In the mayoral elections discussed in the previous chapter, we saw that when there were Latino candidates, Latino voters overwhelmingly supported these candidates. Barreto found that when Latino candidates run for office, Latino voter turnout increases (2007). Barreto states, "Latinos are more likely to side with other Latinos on matters of political significance, even ones whom they have only the term 'Latino' in common" (427; see also Barreto 2009). Yet Latino candidates are not the only way to increase Latino vote turnout. Michelson found that when Latino campaign workers contact potential Latino voters, Latinos are more likely to turn out in elections (2006). That is, like Blacks, there is a sense of shared experience (see also Leal 2002). This sense of group consciousness not only leads to increased voter turnout for co-ethnic candidates, it also influences Latino political attitudes about political issues that are related to ethnicity (Sanchez 2006). Hajnal and Trounstine also found that Latinos vote in blocs. They note that the average level of support among Latino voters for the Latinos' preferred candidate is 67% (2014). Finally, Barreto and colleagues (2008) found that one of the reasons Hillary Clinton did so well among Latino voters during the 2008 Democratic primary was "endorsements from major Latino officials" (Barreto et al. 2008, 755). This research provides evidence that, under certain conditions, Latinos are receptive to endorsements from Latinos.

THE CO-ETHNIC ELITE CUES THEORY

In order to win elections, candidates must appeal to a variety of voters: in this project, I am interested in appeals to Black and Latino voters. In order to account for the development of Black–Latino electoral coalitions, I rely on the Co-ethnic Elite Cues Theory: if partisan cues are absent and race/ethnicity is salient in an election, candidate endorsements by co-ethnic leaders should prompt minority group members to vote for that candidate, even if the candidate is from another ethnic group.[8] I still expect co-ethnic voting to be strong, such that when a Black or Latino candidate is running, Black and Latino voters will overwhelmingly support the candidate belonging to their racial/ethnic group, regardless of leader endorsements. When Blacks do not have a co-ethnic candidate to support and are faced with one White candidate and one Latino candidate, I expect the Black cross-ethnic voting will be determined largely by Black leader/organization endorsements. Thus, when an Elite Black–Latino Coalition has formed, I hypothesize that this has occurred because of electoral cues sent by co-ethnic leaders and I expect to find a preponderance of local Black leaders and organizations endorsing the Latino candidate. Similarly, if Latinos do not have a co-ethnic candidate to support and are faced with one White candidate and one Black candidate, I expect

Latino cross-ethnic voting will be determined largely by Latino leader and organization endorsements. And, as with the previous example, when Black and Latino voters coalesce behind a Black candidate, my theory holds that this is due to co-ethnic elite cues indicating that Latinos should support this candidate. When minority voters are confronted with two White candidates, I expect Latino votes to be determined by Latino leader and organization endorsements and Black votes to be determined by Black leader and organization endorsements. The campaign context is an extremely important factor in my theory: when racial/ethnic mentions are high and candidates discuss racial and ethnic issues, then elite endorsements should be especially influential. If race and ethnicity are not salient in an election, voters will rely on endorsements less.

The notion of "Latino identity" is challenging. Latinos have multiple identity choices ranging from a pan-ethnic identity to a national origin identity, or may select Latino as a racial group identity (Masuoka 2008). Scholars have even asked if there is such a thing as Latino politics (Hero 1992). As I mentioned earlier, context plays a large role in this project. I do not expect that those who *can* identify as Latino will always select this identity. However, if my theory is correct, then they will respond accordingly to the co-ethnic elite cue. If they do not identify with the term *Latino*, then the cues will not be persuasive. I will return to this discussion after the empirical chapters.

PATTERNS FROM RECENT ELECTIONS: A CLOSER LOOK BACK

As we saw in the previous chapter, cities like Los Angeles, Houston, New York, and Chicago are ideal places to explore the possibility of Black–Latino voting coalitions because of the size of these groups in these locations. According to the Co-ethnic Elite Cues Theory, three factors might explain the variations in Black and Latino voting patterns in local elections: elites and their endorsements; the quality and demographic characteristics of the candidates; and the political context (racial/ethnic salience). The remainder of this chapter will focus on the three potential determinants. Specifically, I consider the correlation between local racial/ethnic elite endorsements and Black–Latino voting preferences, and whether heightened racial salience makes endorsements more influential. Given that these elections take place in the real world, I cannot control the race of the candidates or the other factors (co-ethnic elite cues or the racial/ethnic salience), but I still discuss the ways in which the race of the candidate may be important for Black and Latino voters. What can we learn from recent city elections that show a mixed record of Black and Latino voters supporting the same candidates? By examining real-world elections and the voting preferences of Blacks and Latinos in those elections, I specify voting preferences on the basis of elites and their endorsements, the candidates, and the role of racial salience. The ensuing discussion of local elections will be largely descriptive, but will build the foundation for two survey experiments designed to test the relationship between these three factors and vote choice in a more rigorous manner.

CO-ETHNIC ELITE CUES, RACIAL/ETHNIC SALIENCE, AND CANDIDATE PREFERENCES IN RECENT MUNICIPAL ELECTIONS

In order to assess the campaign environment in multiple local mayoral contests to determine whether endorsements might account for the pattern of levels of candidate support from Black and Latino voters, I consider elections in New York, Los Angeles, Houston, and Chicago. These cities were selected because their Black and Latino populations range from a plurality to a majority. They are also among the top five cities where Blacks and Latinos live. That Blacks and Latinos support the same candidates in some elections, but fail to do so in other contests, is useful as it helps clarify the factors that explain cross-ethnic voting among these two groups.

DATA AND METHODS

To conduct the content analysis of mayoral elections in these cities, I consider elections in the late 1990s through the spring 2015 mayoral elections because this picks up where the literature left off (Browning, Marshall, and Tabb 2003). For all elections in New York (1997, 2001, 2005, 2009, 2013), Los Angeles (1997, 2001, 2005, 2009, 2013), Houston (1997, 1999, 2001, 2003, 2005, 2007, 2009, 2011, 2013), and Chicago (1999, 2003, 2007, 2011, and 2015), I searched the *New York Times*, the *Los Angeles Times*, the *Houston Chronicle*, and the *Chicago Tribune* for newspaper articles regarding the election, 60 days before the general election.[9] I selected these newspapers because they represent the newspapers with the largest circulation in the selected cities (see Table 1.1). In order to quantify the co-ethnic elite endorsements, I searched the newspapers listed above 60 days prior to the mayoral election using the terms *mayor* and *election*. If parties held primaries or

TABLE 1.1 *Newspaper Circulation*

Newspaper	Circulation
New York Times	1,865,315
Los Angeles Times	653,868
Chicago Tribune	439,731
Houston Chronicle	360,251

runoff elections, I extended the search dates beyond the 60 days to include the full election period, until the city elected a new mayor. Then I coded endorsements for candidates with the words "endorse," "endorsed," "endorses," and "endorsement."[10] An endorsement is a formal, public announcement of support for a particular candidate. In this chapter, newspaper articles serve as the public space. I then created a data set with information about which organizations or leaders endorsed each candidate in each election.[11] If the race/ethnicity of the organization or endorser was not explicitly stated in the newspaper article, I did research to determine this information.[12] Sometimes this information was not available. When this information was not available, I left "race/ethnicity" blank in the data set. Endorsements without race/ethnicity information are noted in the total number of endorsements for each election in the summary that follows. For each election, I also note the race/ethnicity of the candidates and include that in the data set. To the extent that vote return data were available by racial/ethnic group, the endorsement data were then compared to the exit poll data. Exit poll data were available for many elections, but not all. Once I had a sense of the endorsements offered in an election, I turned my attention to the racial and ethnic salience of the election.

RACIAL AND ETHNIC SALIENCE IN RECENT LOCAL ELECTIONS

After coding for co-ethnic elite endorsements, I considered the newspaper articles together as a whole to determine the campaigns in which race/ethnicity was made salient (see Table 1.2).[13] For the purposes of this project, I measured racial and ethnic salience by quantifying the number of articles about the mayoral elections that mentioned the race/ethnicity of the candidate, the race ethnicity of the candidate's supporters, and the articles that discussed candidate positions on racial and ethnic issues.[14] This includes when the media highlights the potential for a particular

TABLE 1.2 *Relationship between Endorsements and Vote Choice by Racial/Ethnic Salience in Mayoral Elections*

Media Coverage of Race/Ethnicity	Presence of Racial and Ethnic Issues in the Election	
	No	Yes
Low	Low Impact Chicago 1999 ● Houston 2013 Los Angeles 1997 ● Los Angeles 2009 New York 2001	Moderate Impact Houston 1997 Los Angeles 2013 New York 2013
High	Moderate Impact Chicago 2003* ● New York 2009*	High Impact ● Chicago 2015* Houston 2001 Houston 2003 Los Angeles 2001* ● Los Angeles 2005 New York 1997 ● New York 2005

Bold = Co-ethnic Elite Cues Theory explains vote choice
* = Co-ethnic Elite Cues Theory does not explain vote choice
Elections when there were no exit poll data or no endorsement data (Chicago 2007, 2011; Houston 1999, 2005, 2007, 2009, 2011).

candidate to become the first Latino or Black mayor of the city. I then calculated the percent of articles that mention race/ethnicity for each election. In the 24 elections covered, the range is 0% racial/ethnic articles in Houston 2005 to 66% racial/ethnic articles in Houston 2001.[15] The mean percent of racial/ethnic articles is 31%, so I classify an election with less than 31% racial/ethnic coverage as low or below average on racial and ethnic salience. Those with more than 32% racial/ethnic coverage are classified as high or above average racial/ethnic salience (see Table 1.1A in the Appendix for this Chapter).[16] I also took note of candidates taking positions on racial or ethnic issues. For each election, racial or ethnic issues are either present or not. Based on this coding, the elections can be placed into one of four categories, which I present in Table 1.2. When the coverage of race and ethnicity are low and there are no racial or ethnic issues, I predict endorsements will matter less to voters. When coverage of race and ethnicity is low and there are racial and ethnic issues, then endorsements will have a moderate influence on vote choice. When the coverage of race and ethnicity is high and there are no racial or ethnic issues, I predict endorsements will matter to voters, but only moderately. Finally, when coverage of race and ethnicity is high and there are racial and ethnic issues, then endorsements will matter the most to voters. That is, the relationship between co-ethnic elite endorsements and vote choice will be stronger. This is consistent with the Co-ethnic Elite Cues Theory, which predicts endorsements from Blacks and Latinos will matter to Blacks and Latinos in local elections when Black and Latino voters are thinking about their racial and ethnic identities.

BEYOND BLACK AND WHITE: RACIAL AND ETHNIC IDENTITY IN RECENT LOCAL ELECTIONS

The Co-ethnic Elite Cues Theory outlined earlier assumes that most Blacks will vote for Black candidates, regardless of endorsements and racial salience, and that most Latinos will vote for Latino candidates, regardless of endorsements and racial salience. From election return data from Chicago, Houston, Los Angeles, and New York (see the Elections Appendix), there is a lot of evidence of co-ethnic voting among Blacks and Latinos. Black voters overwhelmingly support Black candidates in Houston 1997, 2001, and in New York 2009. Latino voters overwhelmingly support Latino candidates in Houston 2001, Los Angeles 2001, 2005, New York Democratic runoff 2001, and New York 2005. Previous research suggests that Black voters are more likely to vote for Black candidates (Philpot and Walton 2007, 1985) and Latinos are more likely to vote for Latino candidates (Barreto 2009).

But are Blacks more likely to support a White candidate or a Latino candidate for mayor, all else equal? The data in this chapter show that Black voters engaged in cross-ethnic voting for Latino candidates in three elections (New York Democratic runoff 2001; New York 2005; and Los Angeles 2005). In the 2001 election in Los Angeles, however, they supported a White candidate over a Latino. Similarly, in the absence of partisan cues, are Latinos more likely to support a White or a Black candidate for mayor? The data in this chapter show that in Houston 1997, Latino voters engaged in cross-ethnic voting for the Black candidate. Similarly, in New York 2009, Latino voters supported Thompson, a Black mayoral candidate, with 55% of the vote. However, in the Houston 2009 election, Latinos did not support the Black candidate.

PRELIMINARY DATA ANALYSIS OF ENDORSEMENTS

Exploring the racial and ethnic salience of these election campaigns, the race of the candidates, and the endorsements that are present in these elections will bring us one step closer to developing a cohesive explanation for the voting patterns among Blacks and Latinos in recent local elections. In this section, I present the data on the endorsements a candidate receives from Black and Latino organizations and leaders and the level of electoral support from Black and Latino voters, and I discuss levels of racial and ethnic saliency in the campaign. I expect co-ethnic elite endorsements to matter more when race and ethnicity are salient. I selected one election from the four categories in Table 1.2.[17] First, I discuss the New York 2001 election, which illustrates an election when the coverage of race and ethnicity is low and there are no racial or ethnic issues. Second, I discuss the Houston 1997 election, which illustrates an election when the coverage of race and ethnicity is low and racial and ethnic issues are mentioned. Finally, I discuss the New York 2005 election to illustrate what happens when coverage of race and ethnicity is high and there are racial and ethnic issues. While the theory works well in some cases, it does not work well in all cases. In the case of what happens when the coverage of race and ethnicity is high and there are no racial or ethnic issues, the theory does not work at all (New York 2009; Chicago 2003). In addition to this, there are two more instances when the theory does not work: Los Angeles 2001 and Chicago 2015. I discuss these two cases, along with the New York 2009 election, here as well. I conclude by offering some insights into why the theory does not work well in these cases.

LOW COVERAGE OF RACE AND ETHNICITY AND NO RACIAL/ETHNIC ISSUES

In New York in the 2001 general election, Michael Bloomberg, a White candidate, received three endorsements from Black leaders and organizations (the Black newspaper in New York City, the *Amsterdam News*; Councilwoman Priscilla A. Wooten; and the Guardians Association – a Black police officers' organization), while Mark Green, also a White candidate, received one endorsement from Black leaders and organizations (Council of Black Elected Democrats). Bloomberg received six endorsements from Latino leaders and organizations: the Bronx Dominican Coalition, former Ferrer campaign manager Dasdil Velez, the Federation of Hispanic Chambers of Commerce, the Hispanic Clergy

Association, the Spanish Newspapers *Hoy* and *El Diario/La Prensa*, and State Senator Olga Mendez. Green received one Latino endorsement from former mayoral candidate Fernando Ferrer, and one endorsement from the largely Black and Latino union (Service Employees International Union). A total of 40 endorsements was mentioned in the newspaper coverage of this election. In the election, there is evidence of cross-ethnic voting among Blacks, as Green received 75% of the Black vote (Bloomberg received only 25%). Bloomberg received 47% of the Latino vote, while Green received 49% of the Latino vote. In this case, the candidate with more Black endorsements did not receive the majority of Black votes. Similarly, the candidate with the most Latino leader and organization endorsements did not receive the majority of the Latino votes. Racial and ethnic salience were below average in this campaign – only 30% of the *New York Times* coverage focused on race and ethnicity, and the candidates did not take sides on any racial issues. Latino voters split their vote, which provides no evidence of cross-ethnic voting. Even though Bloomberg received six endorsements from Latino leaders and organizations, Green received only two Latino endorsements, if you include the Black–Latino Organization. However, given the low salience of race and ethnicity, I expected endorsements to influence vote choice only moderately here.

LOW COVERAGE OF RACE AND ETHNICITY IN THE PRESENCE OF RACIAL/ETHNIC ISSUES

In the Houston 1997 mayoral election, Robert Mosbacher, a White candidate, faced Lee Brown, a Black candidate, in the runoff election. During the general election, Blacks supported Brown at a high rate and Latinos supported a Latino candidate, Councilwoman Gracie Saenz, at a high rate. However, Saenz didn't garner enough support to move on to the runoff election. Mosbacher received no Black leader or organization endorsements and six Latino leader and organization endorsements, including endorsements from Saenz, the Houston Hispanic Chamber of Commerce's political action committee, the Comerciantes Latinos Unidos de Houston, Councilmember Orlando Sanchez, the Houston Hispanic Coalition, and the Mexican-American Sheriff's Organization. Brown received 11 Black leader and organization endorsements and three Latino leader and organization endorsements. His Black endorsements came from Councilmembers Anthony Hall and Ernest McGowen, Representative Sheila Jackson Lee, the Houston Black American Democrats, the Afro American Sheriff's Deputy League, the Houston

Black Firefighters' Association, the Gulf Coast AME Ministers' Alliance, the Ministers from the Church of God in Christ Texas, South Central Jurisdiction, the Afro-American Police Officers' League, the Harris County Council of Organizations (one of the oldest African American political organizations in Houston), and the Baptist Ministers' Alliance of Houston & Vicinity. His Latino endorsers included three state representatives: Jessica Farrar, Mario Gallegos, and Gerard Torres. In these election, 70 endorsements were mentioned in the newspapers. The *Houston Chronicle* coverage mentioned race and ethnicity in 31% of the articles written about the election, just below the average here, but there were some racial and ethnic issues; specifically, the city was voting on a referendum on the city's affirmative action policy.[18] The issue was whether 30% of contracts had to be awarded to minority-owned businesses.

In the election, Blacks supported the co-ethnic candidate, as Brown received 97% of the Black vote. There was also evidence of cross-ethnic voting among Latinos; he received 66% of the Latino vote. Mosbacher received 3% of the Black vote and 34% of the Latino vote. In this case, the Black candidate received the majority of the Black votes, as expected. The candidate with the most Latino endorsements did not receive the majority of the Latino vote, contrary to the expectation of my theory (though Latinos did engage in cross-ethnic voting). Race and ethnicity were not ignored in the election, but Brown reached out to all groups and ran a campaign that downplayed his race. Mosbacher did not try to highlight Brown's race. The newspapers did not draw much attention to the fact that Brown could be the first Black mayor of Houston. This is an example of a Black–Latino electoral coalition as Latinos and Blacks elected their preferred candidate.

HIGH COVERAGE OF RACE AND ETHNICITY IN THE PRESENCE OF RACIAL AND ETHNIC ISSUES

In the 2005 general election in New York City, Michael Bloomberg, a White candidate, received five endorsements from Black leaders and organizations, while Fernando Ferrer, a Latino candidate, received 10 endorsements from Black leaders and organizations. Bloomberg's Black endorsers included Pierre Sutton, the chairman of the Inner City Broadcasting Corporation; several Harlem ministers from the Mother AME Zion Church on West 137th; Reverend Calvin O. Butts III, pastor of the Abyssinian Baptist Church, the most politically influential church in

Harlem; hip-hop mogul Russell Simmons; and businessman Magic Johnson. Ferrer's Black endorsers included Reverend Al Sharpton; David Dinkins, former mayor of New York City; Reverend Clinton Miller of Brown Memorial Baptist Church in Fort Greene; Percy E. Sutton, former Manhattan borough president and an elder statesman of Harlem politics; 100 Blacks in Law Enforcement Who Care; State Senator Kevin Parker; New York State Senator David Paterson; American civil rights activist Jesse Jackson; the *Amsterdam News*; and Representative Charles B. Rangel. In addition to Black endorsements, Bloomberg received five endorsements from Latino leaders and organizations (Councilwoman Margarita Lopez; the mayor of San Juan, Puerto Rico, Jorge Santini Padilla; real estate broker, radio personality, and the son of the revered major league outfielder Roberto Clemente Jr.; the Latina Political Action Committee; and *Hoy*), while Ferrer received four endorsements from Latino leaders and organizations (the governor of Puerto Rico, Aníbal Acevedo Vilá; the National Latino Officers' Association; former Bronx Democratic Party chairman Roberto Ramirez; and *El Diario/La Prensa*). Ferrer also received one endorsement from a largely Black and Latino organization, the 1199 SEIU. The newspapers mentioned 63 endorsements in its campaign coverage. Almost 46% of the *New York Times* coverage of this election mentioned race and ethnicity, so racial and ethnic salience was above average or high in this campaign. The news media drew attention to the Ferrer campaign and the fact that he would be the first Latino mayor of New York if elected. In the election, Bloomberg received 46% of the Black vote and 34% of the Latino vote, while Ferrer received 53% of the Black vote, which provides evidence of cross-ethnic voting. He received 63% of the Latino vote, which is expected for a co-ethnic candidate. Given that Ferrer received so many more Black endorsements than Bloomberg, the candidate with more Black endorsements received the majority of the Black vote. This provides support for the Co-ethnic Elite Cues Theory.

EXCEPTIONS TO THE THEORY

High Coverage of Race and Ethnicity and No Racial or Ethnic Issues

The New York 2009 mayoral election featured Bill Thompson, the city comptroller, and the incumbent Michael Bloomberg. Thompson, an African American, received four Black endorsements, including one from President Barack Obama, one from former mayor David Dinkins,

46 *The Co-ethnic Elite Cues Theory*

one from Councilmember Letitia James, and one from former secretary of state Colin Powell. He received 76% of the Black vote, which is expected based on my theory. Bloomberg received three Black endorsements, from Cory Booker, the mayor of Newark; Reverend Calvin O. Butts III; and Reverend Floyd H. Flake, pastor of the Greater Allen A. M. E. Cathedral. Bloomberg captured 23% of the Black vote. The newspapers did not mention any Latino endorsements.[19] The newspapers noted 22 endorsements total in this election. Thompson received 55% of the Latino vote and Bloomberg received 43%. Finally, the coverage of the 2009 mayoral election was above average in terms of race and ethnicity (almost 43%), but there were no racial or ethnic issues. Neither candidate drew attention to race, because New York had already elected an African American mayor in 1993. The media did not highlight Thompson's race (he is Black). Thompson did receive the majority of the Black endorsements and votes, but that level of co-ethnic support is expected by the theory. With no data from the *New York Times* on Latino endorsements, we cannot draw any conclusions about the relationship between endorsements and candidate preference among Latinos in this election. Still, this represents a Black–Latino electoral coalition as a majority of Blacks and Latinos supported Thompson, but they were unsuccessful in electing him to office.

High Coverage of Race and Ethnicity in the Presence of Racial or Ethnic Issues

In the Los Angeles 2001 mayoral election, James Hahn, a White candidate, received four endorsements from Black leaders and organizations (from Magic Johnson; Representative Maxine Waters; Los Angeles County Supervisor Yvonne Brathwaite Burke; and Ethel Bradley, the wife of former Mayor Tom Bradley). Antonio Villaraigosa, a Latino candidate, also received four endorsements from Black leaders and organizations (from Bill Burke, Councilmember Mark Ridley-Thomas, Councilwoman Rita Walters, and AME Bishop John Bryant). Villaraigosa received two endorsements from Latino leaders and organizations (California's Lieutenant Governor Cruz Bustamante and Los Angeles County Supervisor Gloria Molina). Hahn received three endorsements from Latino leaders and organizations (Councilmen Alex Padilla and Nick Pacheco and State Senator Richard Polanco). In all, the *Los Angeles Times* mentioned 49 endorsements in this campaign. In the election, Here, Blacks engaged in cross-ethnic voting, as Hahn received 80%

of the Black vote, while Villaraigosa received 20% of the Black vote. Villaraigosa received 82% of the Latino vote to Hahn's 18%. Hahn and Villaraigosa shared the same number of Black endorsements, but Hahn clearly received a majority of the Black vote. Villaraigosa did receive the majority of the Latino vote, along with the majority of Latino endorsements, which is expected given that he is a Latino candidate (co-ethnic voting). Racial and ethnic salience was high or above average in this election because the news media focused on Villaraigosa's potential to be the first Latino mayor of Los Angeles in more than 100 years, which helped add to the 45% of news coverage in the *Los Angeles Times* that included racial and ethnic mentions. Further, Hahn ran a racial attack ad against Villaraigosa, linking him to a cocaine dealer.[20] The ad even featured a crack pipe. In this election, Black endorsements were split, but the Black vote was not split, as African Americans overwhelmingly supported Hahn. This election does not provide direct support for the Co-ethnic Elite Cues Theory, which predicted that endorsements would matter more to Black voters.

In the 2015 Chicago mayoral election, Emanuel faced four candidates in his bid for reelection: Chuy "Chico" Garcia, a Latino candidate; Willie Wilson and William "Dock" Wallis III, both Black candidates; and Robert Fioretti, a White candidate. Race and ethnicity was salient in this election, given that the *Chicago Tribune* made mention of race and ethnicity in 35% of the election coverage, which is above average. In addition, racial and ethnic issues were a part of the campaign as Garcia highlighted the high crime rates in Black and Latino neighborhoods[21] and the tickets issued from the red-light cameras that are hard on the poor in Black and Latino neighborhoods.[22] For the first time in city history, Garcia forced Emanuel into a runoff election. In the runoff, I expect Black endorsements to determine Black votes, given that race was salient in the election. Garcia sought Black endorsements early on, amassing several key endorsements, including those from the Reverend Jesse Jackson, Alderwoman Leslie Hairston, the Coalition of Black Women, former Illinois Senate president Emil Jones Jr., former mayoral candidate Willie Wilson, County Commissioner Bobbie Steele, and Chicago Teachers' Union president Karen Lewis. Garcia also highlighted something he called the "100 African-American Leaders," which was a list of supporters that included officials from unions and community organizers or activists. Emanuel received endorsements from the following African Americans: Pastor Albert Tyson, the reverend James Meeks, President Barack Obama, Alderwoman Michele Smith, and Magic Johnson (he has opened businesses in the city). The *Chicago Tribune* reported 28 endorsements during the campaign.²³ Despite receiving more Black endorsements, Garcia did not receive a majority of the Black vote, with 58% supporting Emanuel (cross-ethnic voting). Both candidates also received Latino endorsements, but as the Co-ethnic Elite Cues Theory predicts, Garcia won a majority of the Latino vote (Latinos engaged in co-ethnic voting as 68% of Latinos voted for Garcia). In summary, this election in Chicago demonstrates that even when race and ethnicity are salient, voters do not always rely on co-ethnic elite cues when casting their ballots.

AMENDING THE THEORY

The New York 2009, Los Angeles 2001, and Chicago 2015 elections do not support the Co-ethnic Elite Cues Theory. In two of these cases, one potential reason for this is incumbent candidates. In the New York 2009 and the Chicago 2015 elections, Bloomberg and Emmanuel had the benefit of already serving as mayor. Incumbency is usually an advantage to candidates (Hajnal 2001; Krebs 1998; Oliver and Ha 2007). The presence of incumbents also has implications for the level of competitiveness in any given contest. In the Los Angeles 2009; Houston 2005, 2007, 2011, and 2013 elections, the elections featured incumbents and were not very competitive. These contests did not yield much data in the way of endorsements data or exit poll data, so I could not analyze these elections. Of course, there are also elections where incumbents face tough challengers: Chicago 2015, Los Angeles 2005, New York 2005, but even in those cases, the challenger was only successful in one case, the Los Angeles 2005 election. The challengers lost in Chicago and New York.

The preliminary data presented here suggest a correlation between co-ethnic elite cues and voter behavior. Yet in previous analyses, endorsements are all treated equally. This helps keep the analysis simple, but that does not mean that all endorsements are created equal. That is, what does President Barack Obama's endorsement mean to voters? In Chicago 2015, Emanuel received a key endorsement from the most well-known Black leader at the time, the president of the United States and former senator from the state of Illinois, who also calls Chicago home, Barack Obama. It would be hard to dispute that this endorsement meant more to Blacks in the city than the endorsements of the local clergy. The Los Angeles 2001 race also highlights the weight of endorsements, as the endorsements from Maxine Waters and Magic Johnson seem to carry more weight than endorsements from city councilmembers (Councilmembers Mark Ridley-

Thomas and Rita Walters endorsed Villaraigosa in 2001, but Black voters did not support him). This is confirmed by the 2013 race in Los Angeles, when Greuel received endorsements from Waters and Johnson and won a majority of the Black votes, while Garcetti received endorsements from two city councilmembers: Jan Perry and Bernard Parks. Jan Perry had been in the election for mayor that year and received a majority of the Black votes, but that endorsement did not lead to a majority of the Black votes for Garcetti (see the Elections Appendix). The Co-ethnic Elite Cues Theory then needs to take account of incumbency and the caliber of the endorser. This allows for incumbents to enjoy the benefits of incumbency and note that when prominent community leaders and organization give endorsements, Black and Latino voters may give more weight to those endorsements when casting their ballots.

RACIAL AND ETHNIC SALIENCE IN CAMPAIGNS AND VOTE CHOICE: A SUMMARY

In Table 1.2, I provide a summary of all 25 elections. The pattern that emerges is that when racial and ethnic mentions were low, endorsements mattered less. This was true in the Chicago 1999 contest, the Houston 2009, 2011, and 2013 contests, the Los Angeles 1997, 2009 contests, and the New York 2001 election. When racial and ethnic mentions were low, but racial and ethnic issues were present, endorsements did a better job explaining vote choice. We saw this in the Houston 1997, Los Angeles 2013, and New York 2013 elections. When racial and ethnic mentions were high, but there were racial/ethnic issues, there is some support that endorsements mattered in the Houston 2003 election. However, the Chicago 2003 does not support the Co-ethnic Elite Cues Theory as African Americans did not support their co-ethnic candidate. The New York 2009 election provides mixed support at best, as African Americans did support the co-ethnic candidate, but there was not enough data to assess Latino support for a candidate based on endorsements. Finally, when racial and ethnic mentions were high and there were racial issues in the campaign, voters do rely on co-ethnic elite endorsements when they cast their votes. There is evidence of this in the Houston 2001, Los Angeles 2005, and New York 1997 and 2005 elections. However, in two elections where race and ethnicity were salient and racial and ethnic issues were mentioned, the endorsements did not help explain vote choice: Chicago 2015 and Los Angeles 2001. In both of these elections, Black endorsements did not influence Black vote choice.

ENDORSEMENTS: A REVIEW

These data also show that when elections are not competitive, fewer endorsements are offered during the campaign cycle. In several reelection campaigns where the incumbent was seen as a shoe-in, the sheer number of endorsers was low. In the Los Angeles 2009 and Houston 2005, 2007, 2011, and 2013 elections, the only endorsements reported were from the newspapers. This highlights two additional points about endorsements. One is that there is an incentive to endorse early because it means the newspapers will mention the endorsements again and again when the candidate receives another endorsement. Second, in these 25 contests, the local newspapers endorsed the winning candidate 21 times. These endorsements often show up just days before the election, so they do not lead to more endorsers, but these endorsements may be a calculation of viability. Previous research on newspaper endorsements is conclusive: they matter (Erickson 1976; Liu 2001, 2003).

PRELIMINARY CONCLUSIONS: ENDORSEMENTS AND CONTEXT MATTER

The data presented in this chapter are gathered from newspaper coverage of real-world mayoral elections in New York, Los Angeles, Houston, and Chicago, and these data allow me to investigate the Co-ethnic Elite Cues Theory in a variety of settings. The three factors that might explain variations in Black and Latino voting patterns in local elections are elites and their endorsements, the quality and demographic characteristics of the candidates, and the political context (racial/ethnic salience). Content analysis of the newspaper articles yields some preliminary conclusions that endorsements seem to matter to voters when race and ethnicity are salient. Of the 25 elections studied, 7 did not yield enough data (Chicago 2007, 2011; Houston 1999, 2005, 2007, 2011, and 2013) and 4 did not support the theory (Chicago 2003, 2015; Los Angeles 2001; and New York 2009), but the other 13 elections provide support for the Co-ethnic Elite Cues Theory (Chicago 1999; Houston 1997, 2001, 2003, 2009; Los Angeles 1997, 2005, 2009, 2013; and New York 1997, 2001, 2005, 2013). In these contests, when race and ethnicity were salient, endorsements helped explain vote choice. When race and ethnicity were less salient, endorsements were less important to voters.

The question remains: is it the case that leaders and candidates form coalitions and then bargain for endorsements so that voters know whom to support? Is it possible that certain candidates were already popular among voters, such that ambitious racial/ethnic leaders can capitalize on giving an endorsement to that candidate to remain in the favor of voters? The direction of the causal arrow is unclear using content analysis. In order to provide more conclusive evidence, I conduct an experiment to address these questions. The experiment also can provide insight into the cases where the theory did not work well. In those cases, we saw that incumbency and the caliber of the endorser seemed to matter. In the next chapter, I begin to explore what candidates can do to win over Black and Latino voters. I present data from a survey experiment that systematically tests how Black and Latino voting preferences vary based on elite cues and endorsements, candidates, and the racial/ethnic context of the election. In the experiment, there are no incumbent candidates and all the endorsements are from the same organization. In this way, I hope to address the limitations of the data presented in this chapter.

APPENDIX

TABLE 1.1A *Racial/Ethnic Newspaper Coverage and Racial/Ethnic Issues*

City	Election	% Racial/ Ethnic Articles	Racial/ Ethnic Issues	Issues
New York	1997	35.81%	Yes	Al Sharpton, Giuliani is not popular with Black and Latino voters– promises to build better relations in second term
New York	2001	30.71%	No	No racial issues in the runoff
New York	2005	45.95%	Yes	Police misconduct, Bloomberg tries to link Ferrer to Dinkins, the Apollo debate no show
New York	2009	42.25%	No	No racial issues
New York	2013	31.21%	Yes	Stop and Frisk, de Blasio's family (biracial six times), Bloomberg accuses de Blasio of running a racial campaign by featuring his family
Houston	1997	31.63%	Yes	First ethnic mayor, first Black mayor, affirmative action for contracts with new Arena
Houston	1999	38.78%	Yes	Affirmative action with arena deal
Houston	2001	66.67%	No	No racial issues

(continued)

TABLE 1.1A *(continued)*

City	Election	% Racial/ Ethnic Articles	Racial/ Ethnic Issues	Issues
Houston	2003	35.71%	Yes	Immigration and racial mailers
Houston	2005	0.00%	No	No racial issues
Houston	2007	6.25%	No	No racial issues
Houston	2009	28.24%	No	LGBT issues
Houston	2011	4.55%	No	LGBT issues
Houston	2013	29.63%	No	LGBT issues
Los Angeles	1997	28.09%	No	No racial issues
Los Angeles	2001	43.61%	Yes	Villaraigosa linked to crack cocaine ads
Los Angeles	2005	32.57%	Yes	Hahn fires Bernard Parks. Hahn implies that Villaraigosa is soft on gangs and brings up the crack cocaine ads
Los Angeles	2009	10.81%	No	No racial issues
Los Angeles	2013	26.24%	Yes	Ad about Greuel and Prop 187
Chicago	1999	29.63%	No	No racial issues
Chicago	2003	48.39%	No	No racial issues
Chicago	2007	32.86%	No	No racial issues
Chicago	2011	31.15%	No	No racial issues
Chicago	2015	35.24%	Yes	Crime in Black and Latino neighborhoods, red-light ticket cameras in Black and Latino neighborhoods

NOTES

1. This approach is rather cautious, as all endorsements are not created equal. That is, it will likely understate the value of some endorsements and overstate the value of others.
2. However, in two elections (New York 1997 and Los Angeles 2001), race was made salient in the campaign and co-ethnic leader endorsements did not influence vote choice in those elections.
3. www.pacificmarketresearch.com/ld/pdfs/latinodecisions_california_0807.pdf.
4. Los Angeles elected its first Latino mayor in 2005 (Villaraigosa), while New York elected its first Black mayor in 1993 and has yet to elect a Latino to that office.
5. This is not an exhaustive definition of an endorsement. Endorsements may take the form of pictures with the candidate or public appearances, but that is beyond the current scope of this project.
6. The AFL-CIO is, by its own admission, a liberal organization.

7. Puerto Ricans are citizens and may not face the same language hurdles given the status of Puerto Rico as a U.S. territory.
8. For the content analysis, racial salience is measured by the number of times the media mentions the race of the candidate in connection with that candidate's attempt to be the first Black or Latino mayor.
9. I used America's News, ProQuest, and LexisNexis to gather these newspaper articles.
10. I did not code for the words "support/s," "supported," "back/s," or "backed" because it could be argued that those were not real endorsements and I wanted to adopt a more conservative test of my hypothesis.
11. I recognize that all endorsements are not created equal, but for the sake of simplicity, I have adopted this more conservative assumption. In later iterations of this project, I hope to explore how and why some endorsements may be more effective than others.
12. Fortunately, many people cite their racial or ethnic background on their websites with statements about being the first African American or Hispanic to hold an office, or they say they are members of particular racial/ethnic groups.
13. There are about 2,400 articles total that discuss all the mayoral elections.
14. See Huber and Lupinski (2006), Mendelberg (2001), Reeves (1997), or Valentino et al. (2002).
15. This is likely because the campaign featured two minority candidates.
16. This is consistent with McIlwain and Caliendo (2011), who find that 25% of the media coverage is about race.
17. A discussion of all other elections can be found in the Elections Appendix.
18. A. Bernstein. "For Brown, ethnic medley with black chorus." *Houston Chronicle*. December 8, 1997, A1.
19. Fernando Ferrer did endorse Thompson, via New York One, the local television news channel, but it was not covered in the articles I read for this content analysis.
20. J. Rainey and B. Shuster. "Candidates wrap up an intense campaign." *Los Angeles Times*. June 5, 2001. A1.
21. K. Skiba and C. Dizikes. "Garcia raises money in Washington." *Chicago Tribune*. March 25, 2015.
22. B. Ruthhart." Tweak red light program or dump it, 75 percent say." *Chicago Tribune*. January 31, 2015.
23. This counts the "100 African-American Leaders" as one endorsement.

2

An Experimental Test of the Co-ethnic Elite Cues Theory

Elite Cues Move Blacks, but Latinos Are Not So Easily Swayed: Candidate Support and Evaluation among Blacks and Latinos

The results from the previous chapter indicate that endorsements have an effect on candidate preference in local elections, but are inconclusive with regard to the role of ethnic salience in campaigns. Moreover, the newspaper endorsements and exit poll data cannot be used to determine causality. As discussed previously, there is no way to know if candidates were already popular among voters and then received endorsements from co-ethnic leaders, or if co-ethnic leaders formed coalitions with candidates and then provided endorsements. One way to sort out this puzzle is through an experiment. The benefit of an experimental design is that it allows me to isolate the three factors relevant to the theory – the race of the candidate, the presence or absence of endorsements, and racial/ethnic salience – to determine if endorsements persuade Black and Latino voters to prefer one candidate to another.

In Chapter 1, we saw that recent mayoral elections in Houston, New York, Los Angeles, and Chicago yield no clear pattern of voting behavior for Blacks and Latinos from one election to the next. Black and Latino voters support the same candidates in some mayoral elections, but in others, their preferences diverge. I also presented the Co-ethnic Elite Cues Theory, which is designed to account for the development of Black–Latino voting blocs. I argue that in the absence of partisan cues, when race becomes salient in an election, candidate endorsements by co-ethnic leaders will prompt minority group members to engage in cross-ethnic voting. I expect that whenever a Black or Latino candidate is running, Black and Latino voters will provide high levels of support for candidates belonging to their racial or ethnic group, regardless of leader endorsements (co-ethnic voting). When Blacks and Latinos do not have the option to [*or more powerful*] support a co-ethnic candidate, I expect the candidate that receives more Black endorsements to receive more Black voter support and the candidate that receives more Latino endorsements to receive more Latino voter support. The campaign context is also an important factor in my theory, such that when racial or ethnic issues are particularly salient in the campaign, then co-ethnic elite cues (endorsements) should be especially influential. If race is not salient in an election, co-ethnic endorsements should have less of an effect.

In a preliminary test of the Co-ethnic Elite Cues Theory in Chapter 1, I presented content-analysis data about the relationship between co-ethnic leader endorsements and vote choice in recent elections in New York, Houston, Chicago, and Los Angeles. Using newspaper endorsements and exit poll data, I showed that when race or ethnicity is made salient in a campaign, there is a relationship between the number and direction of co-ethnic leader endorsements and candidate preference among Black and Latino voters.[1] That is, the candidate with the most endorsements from Black and Latino leaders and organizations also received a majority of votes from those voting blocs. It was when race and ethnicity was not salient in a campaign that the relationship between co-ethnic leader cues and candidate preference mattered less.[2] For example, the 2001 Los Angeles mayoral election pitted Kenneth Hahn, a White candidate, against Antonio Villaraigosa, a Latino candidate. Race was a salient feature in this campaign, as the media often discussed Villaraigosa's status as the first viable Latino candidate to run for mayor in Los Angeles for a century and ads ran that linked Villaraigosa to crime.[3] During this election, Black elites publicly endorsed Hahn and Villaraigosa with Hahn receiving four endorsements. Villaraigosa also received four endorsements from Black community leaders (see Chapter 1). In that election, Black voters supported Hahn, giving him 80% of the African American vote.[4] But, by the time the two candidates faced off again in 2005, race was also salient in that campaign after Hahn did not reappoint Bernard Parks, an African American, to another term as police chief. Black leaders were not happy about this decision. In turn, African American leaders gave Villaraigosa six endorsements to Hahn's two. In this election, 58% of Black voters voted for Villaraigosa over his opponent, which represents a shift in support of almost 40 percentage points, relative to the 2001 campaign.[5]

Further exploration of recent mayoral elections that did not feature a Latino candidate showed that for Latino voters, the relationship between co-ethnic elite endorsements and Latino votes is not as clear as the pattern for Black voters. In the Houston 1997 election, racial mentions were low, but there was a racial issue (affirmative action), and the candidate who received the most endorsements from Latino leaders and organizations, Mosbacher, did not receive a majority of the Latino vote. Latinos supported the Black candidate, Lee Brown. In the New York 2009 election, there was not much information about endorsements, but again, Latinos offered their support to the Black candidate, Bill Thompson. The New York elections do provide one piece of additional information: Michael Bloomberg has been a candidate in the past three mayoral elections in New York. Since 2001, Bloomberg's percentage of the Latino vote has been 47% in 2001, 34% in 2005, and 43% in 2009. In the 2005 election, there was a Latino candidate, which offers some explanation for the percent of the vote in that election. The percentage of Latinos who voted for the other candidates that ran against Bloomberg varied. Green received 49% of the Latino vote, Ferrer received 63% of the Latino vote, and Thompson received 55% of the Latino vote. So the difference between the Latino votes for Bloomberg and the more liberal candidate in each election is 2% in 2001, 29% in 2005, and 12% in 2009. All of this leads to the question: under what conditions will Latino voters prefer a more liberal candidate to a conservative candidate? I believe the data from the survey experiment can help us answer this question, but before I get into the details of the experiment, I will briefly review each of the three main factors.

LOCAL ELECTIONS: THE CANDIDATES MATTER

Local elections serve as the initial venue for racial and ethnic minorities to gain access to political representation and incorporation (Browning, Marshall, and Tabb 1984; Dahl 1962; and Wolfinger 1965). According to Dahl, co-ethnic surnames served as cues to make it easy for co-ethnics to vote for the candidate from their in-group (1962). The theory of racial voting suggests that Blacks and Latinos will vote for in-group candidates barring a serious reason to do otherwise (Bullock and Campbell 1984; Hero 1992). More recent scholarship has confirmed that this is the case for Blacks (Philpot and Walton 2007) and Latinos (Barreto 2007). Barreto's study of co-ethnic voting in local elections in Denver, Houston, Los Angeles, New York, and San Francisco provides some of the strongest evidence that Latinos act as a group and vote for co-ethnic candidates. He finds this is true regardless of party and ideology. Using ecological inference, Barreto finds that districts with large Latino populations overwhelmingly voted for the Latino candidate in each election a Latino candidate was on the ballot (Barreto 2007, 432–34). Additionally, his data show that districts with large Black populations voted for the Black candidate when there was one on the ballot (ibid., 433). Yet, in some elections, Blacks and Latinos may not have the option to vote for a candidate from their in-group.[6] Hajnal and Trounstine find that all racial and ethnic groups exhibit high levels of group voting; even when they compare nonpartisan elections to partisan elections, there is "little drop in the levels of cohesion" (2014, 80). Research on campaigns and campaign effects confirms the importance of partisanship, even in nonpartisan elections (Krebs 1998; Oliver and Ha 2007; Schaffner, Streb, and Wright 2001; Squire and Smith 1988). Yet, partisan cues are not the only cues available to voters. The race of the candidate may also provide a useful cue for voters (Conover and Feldman 1989; McDermott 1998). Previous research shows that minority candidates and women are often perceived as more liberal than White male candidates (McDermott 1998). Essentially, voters rely on stereotypes about candidates when they do not have more concrete information.

This leads to an important question: what happens when there is not an in-group candidate? One goal of this chapter is to determine if the race of the candidates matters to Blacks and Latinos, particularly when neither candidate is a member of their racial group. Recent research on Latinos has found that they often feel closer to Whites than Blacks (Kaufmann 2003a; McClain et al. 2006). Blacks, on the other hand, state that they feel close to Latinos. This suggests that Black and Latino voters may simply respond to the race of the candidate when casting votes. The race of the candidate is not the only racial or ethnic cue in these elections. As we saw in the mayoral election in Houston in 1997, sometimes organizations that offer endorsements carry a racial and ethnic cue as well. Krebs (1998) and Lieske (1989) find evidence that endorsements (from local organizations and newspapers) help explain vote choice in local elections. In the next section, I explore this relationship further by considering the potential for Black and Latino endorsements to persuade Black and Latino voters to prefer a candidate who does not belong to their own racial or ethnic group.

CO-ETHNIC ELITE CUES AND CANDIDATE PREFERENCES

The second goal of this chapter is to determine the extent to which elite cues or endorsements from co-ethnic leaders matter to Black and Latino voters. Previous research demonstrates that cues from a variety of sources can be an effective tool for voters to use when they lack other information. These include opinion leaders (Druckman 2001; Zaller 1992), organizations (Arceneaux and Kolodny 2009), news stations (Turner 2007), and interest groups (Lupia 1994). However, these studies have not focused on co-ethnic elite endorsements. Co-ethnic elite endorsements from Black and Latino politicians, Black and Latino organizations, Black and Spanish news sources, and racial and ethnic interest groups have the potential to be quite influential to Black and Latino voters.

Implicit in this study is that Blacks trust Black leaders because of their shared identity. Campbell and colleagues hypothesized about the relationship between Black endorsements and the Black vote in the 1952 presidential election. Their data show that when a majority of Black leaders supported Stevenson, Blacks voters did as well. Four years later, when the Black leadership was not unified behind a single candidate, the Black vote was split (Campbell et al. 1960, 316). Further, Kuklinksi and Hurley find that among Blacks, the race of the source cue trumps the ideology of the cue-giver with respect to Black support for affirmative action policies (1994, 737). Irrespective of the ideology of the Black leader, when he endorses the notion that Blacks should stop making excuses, Blacks agree with this statement. Yet, when the statement is attributed to no one, Black support for the statement is extremely low. Kuklinski and Hurley conclude that Blacks believe that "black leaders will always look out for my interests better than white leaders" (ibid., 749). Among Latinos, there is some research on endorsements and Latino candidate preferences that indicates that Latinos may also rely on these cues (Barreto et al. 2008). This chapter builds on these findings and extends them to mayoral candidate preferences among Blacks and Latinos. I maintain that the effect of co-ethnic elite endorsements is conditional on racial salience and the race of the candidate. Next I turn to a more in-depth discussion of identity and politics.

GROUP IDENTITY AND THE POLITICAL ARENA

In addition to partisan identity, there is evidence to suggest an important relationship between social, racial, and ethnic group identities and political preferences. Tajfel and Turner find that group identities matter, even when groups are randomly assigned and new (1979). Conover distinguishes between objective group membership, group identification, and group consciousness. These distinctions have implications for Blacks and

Latinos because some may view themselves as group members in name only, while others have high levels of group consciousness and a commitment to working toward group goals (1988). Subsequent research on African Americans shows that there is a strong political commitment to the group (Dawson 1994). White finds that, among Blacks, explicit messages about race help activate feelings of in-group identity (2007). This has not been the case among Latinos (Masuoka 2006; Sanchez and Masuoka 2010). While Blacks demonstrate high levels of linked fate – the belief that what happens to one member of the racial group effects other members of the group, lasting feelings of linked fate among Latinos have not been observed (Dawson 1994; Sanchez and Masuoka 2010).

Several factors might explain low levels of linked fate among Latinos. First, Latinos may still prefer their national identity to a pan-ethnic identity (Beltran 2010; Masuoka 2008). Masuoka finds that among those who self-identify as Latinos, there is a greater commitment to Latino political issues than those who self-identify with their national group (2008). Second, the group is heterogeneous and researchers have shown that varying experiences with immigration, assimilation, and discrimination help shape these identity choices (Beltran 2010; Masuoka 2008; Sanchez and Masuoka 2010; Segura and Rodrigues 2006). The research on Latino identity suggests that the ideal co-ethnic source cue for Latinos may be a cue from an elite associated with national identity groups or it may be a cue from elites speaking from a pan-ethnic Latino identity. This does not mean that Latinos do not work together or experience a shared identity. As mentioned earlier, Barreto provides strong evidence that this is the case when a Latino candidate runs for mayor (2007). Without a co-ethnic candidate on the ballot, campaign issues may create a context where identity becomes important. This was the case in the 2008 Democratic primary after Bill Richardson dropped out of the election (Barreto et al. 2008). In their careful analysis of those elections, Barreto and colleagues find that Latino endorsements help explain Latino support for Hillary Clinton in the 2008 Democratic primary (2008). Finally, the context will still matter here: if Latinos are thinking about Latino issues, it may be more likely that the co-ethnic elite endorsements will be persuasive.

THE CAMPAIGN CONTEXT MATTERS

The final goal of this chapter is to determine if racial/ethnic salience matters in the context of local elections. The previous sections have examined several factors (candidate characteristics, identity politics, and co-ethnic elite endorsements) that might explain Black and Latino vote choice in local elections. Yet, missing from these explanations are contextual factors that distinguish one election from another. I posit that heightened racial/ethnic salience in a campaign may increase the importance of racial and ethnic identities for Black and Latino subjects, rendering co-ethnic elite cues more effective. Issue positions are an important aspect of elections, but here the focus is specifically on racial and ethnic issues because voters often know how they feel about racial issues (Converse 1964; Downs 1957; and Oliver and Ha 2007). Previous research shows that race or ethnicity may become salient in a campaign through issues that relate to race and ethnicity (Barreto 2009; Campbell et al. 1960; Gilens 1999; Kaufmann 2004; Mendelberg 2001; Reeves 1997; White 2007). Kaufmann shows that when the political context focuses on racial/ethnic issues, voters rely on their racial/ethnic identities when casting their votes (2004). Yet, minority candidates are often advised not to focus on race, so as not to alienate White voters (Hero 1989, 1992; Perry 1991). Federico Peña's 1983 and 1987 mayoral campaigns in Denver serve as a good example of how a minority candidate can run a campaign without focusing on racial issues while still garnering support from minority voters (Hero, 1989, 1992). Racial/ethnic salience is perhaps the most important factor in understanding Black and Latino vote choice in local elections. Simply put, the endorsements and the race of the candidates alone are not likely to influence vote choice because Blacks and Latinos may not be thinking about their racial/ethnic identities until issues are mentioned in the campaign.

HYPOTHESES

Given that Blacks are politically homogenous, Black voters are more likely to rely on co-ethnic elite endorsements. Latinos, on the other hand, are much more politically heterogeneous and may not respond in a comparable manner to the co-ethnic elite endorsements.

> H_1: Co-ethnic elite endorsements will be more persuasive among Blacks than Latinos because of the political homogeneity of Blacks and the political heterogeneity of Latinos.

The campaign context is very important here. I argue that when Blacks and Latinos are thinking about their racial and ethnic identities, co-ethnic elite endorsements will work better. Simply put, the endorsements and the race of the candidates alone are not as likely to influence vote choice because Blacks and Latinos may not be thinking about their racial and ethnic identities until racial and ethnic issues are mentioned in the campaign. The presence of racial and ethnic issues should *enhance* the effects of endorsements. This is because racial and ethnic salience makes minorities' racial and ethnic identity salient in their vote considerations. On this basis, I make the following hypotheses:

H_2: Co-ethnic elite endorsements will be more persuasive among Blacks and Latinos when race/ethnicity is salient.

H_3: Co-ethnic elite endorsements will be more persuasive among Blacks and Latinos when the candidate is a minority.

H_4: Co-ethnic elite endorsements will be more persuasive among Blacks and Latinos when the endorsed candidate is a minority and race/ethnicity is salient.

METHODS AND PROCEDURES

In order to the test these hypotheses, I develop a 2 × 2 × 2 experimental design. The benefit of this experimental design is that it permits the isolation of causal mechanisms, which is not possible using real-world data (Kinder and Palfrey 1993). Indeed, given the high profile of many mayoral elections, it is likely that under more real-world circumstances, voters might possess more crystallized opinions about the candidates. That is, the experimental design allows me to move beyond opinions about particular candidates and isolate the mechanisms at work: to what extent the racial or ethnic salience (issues) in the campaign, the race of the candidate, or the presence of an endorsement influence candidate preferences among Black and Latino voters. By using a generic organization for the endorsement and focusing on only one issue, the experiment is a conservative test of the relationship between endorsements and preferences. The design is biased against finding a result.

EXPERIMENTAL DESIGN

In the experiment, I manipulate the race/ethnicity of the more liberal candidate, the extent to which the campaign focused on racial/ethnic issues, and whether an African American or Latino political group endorsed the more liberal candidate.[7] In order to determine if the race of the candidate influences candidate preferences among Black subjects, the more liberal candidate is depicted as White in half of the experimental cells and as Latino in the other half. For Latino subjects, the liberal candidate is White in half of the experimental cells and Black in the other half.

In order to determine if co-ethnic elite endorsement influences candidate preference, I manipulate the endorsement conditions. For Black subjects, half of the treatments provide no endorsement from African American groups, while the other treatment shows the more liberal candidate as the unambiguous choice of Black political elites. For the Latino sample, half of the treatments have no endorsement, while in the other half of the treatments, a Latino group provides an endorsement. McDermott (2006) finds that endorsements from the AFL-CIO encourage liberals to vote for the endorsed Democratic candidate, while labor endorsements for Republican candidates do not influence voters. As such, the endorsements provided here are meant to convey that the leaders had the respondents' best interests at heart (Kuklinski and Hurley 1994).

Finally, in order to test the effect of racial/ethnic salience, half of the treatments depict the campaign as focusing on a nonracial/ethnic issue, whereas the other half focuses on explicitly racial/ethnic policies. For the Black sample, the issue is affirmative action, while the issue in the Latino sample is English-only laws for public services.

In order to deliver the treatment, I designed eight mostly identical newspaper articles, complete with photographs of the candidates, which differed only along the three factors identified earlier (the race of the candidate, the presence of a co-ethnic elite endorsement, and racial/ethnic salience). In every article, the more conservative candidate is depicted in the accompanying photograph as a middle-aged White American. In four of the articles, the more liberal candidate is depicted as a White middle-aged man. In the other four articles, the more liberal candidate is depicted as a middle-aged Latino man (for Black respondents) or a middle-aged Black man (for Latino respondents). In four articles, endorsements are given to the more liberal candidate from either the "Local Association of Black Leaders" or the "Local Association of Latino Leaders." These generic organizations are meant to signal co-ethnic leader support for the endorsed candidate.

All of the articles focus on an environmental company seeking to renew its trash-burning contract. The conservative candidates always support the contract renewal because the city needs more time to develop a recycling program. The liberal candidates always oppose the contract renewal and support an immediate recycling program. The story ends with a fact about the percentage of voters who felt the environment was important in the election. For the treatment in which race/ethnicity is not salient, the articles focus solely on the environmental company. For the treatment in which race/ethnicity is salient, the articles still focus on the environmental company and the contract renewal, except in these versions, the story also says that the company "received the contract, despite several bids from minority companies and a promise from the city to use the newly enacted affirmative action laws" or "received the contract, despite several concerns about the company's English-only policy and a promise from the city to end business with such companies." In these treatments, the liberal candidates still oppose the contract for the same reasons listed in the environment-only articles. The versions of the story that highlight the racial/ethnic issues also end with a fact about the percentage of voters who felt affirmative action/English-only was important in the election (see Appendices 3A and 3B).

DATA COLLECTION

Following other race and politics experiments, these data come from a community sample of Black and Latino adults collected in the summer of 2008 and spring of 2009 (see, for example, Hutchings et al. 2004 and Valentino, Hutchings, and White 2002). For the Black sample, the author and Black research assistants attended community events in the greater Detroit metro area. These events were not political in nature.[8] Respondents were approached and asked to complete a short political survey in exchange for $5 cash. The surveys were completed in a paper-and-pencil format. Respondents read the fictional news article (see Appendices A and B) and then answered a short questionnaire assessing their support for the candidates for mayor. The response rate among Blacks was one in eight; roughly 13% of those approached to take the survey completed the survey. For the Latino sample, the author employed a similar strategy with Latino research assistants in the greater Detroit metro area and Southern California where roughly half of the surveys were collected using the paper-and-pencil format. In order to complete the data collection, however, the author also contacted Latino organizations to recruit respondents to the online version.[9] The organizations were not told they were being contacted because they were Latino organizations.[10] These respondents were emailed a $5 gift card. Comparisons between the online and paper surveys indicate there are no differences between the two samples (see Appendices 3A and 3B). The response rate for the paper surveys among Latinos was about 10%. The online surveys indicate that of the people who started the survey, 1 out of 20 did not complete it.

INFORMATION ABOUT THE SAMPLE

The respondents were randomly assigned to one of the treatments for their race/ethnicity, such that differences I observe in candidate preferences are attributed to the treatment (Valentino et al. 2002). Respondents in both samples are much more educated,[11] and younger than the American National Election Study (ANES) 2008 for Blacks and the Nation National Survey for Latinos. In the Black sample, no respondents selected strong Republican, compared to the 85% of ANES Blacks who said Democrat and the 47% who said strong Democrat. The Latino sample here is slightly more Democratic than the Latino National Survey. For the sake of comparison, we can look at some descriptive data from the Latino National Survey, which had more than 8,000 respondents. In that national sample, the ages ranged from 18 to 97. Only 50% identified themselves as Democrats, while 17% said they were Republicans and 12% said they were independents. The rest said they did not know or supported some other party (21%). In terms of place of birth, only 29% of the sample was born in the United States and 66% said they were born in some other country. Of the 66% born outside of the United States, 70% were born in Mexico. Additionally, 35% preferred to use the term *Hispanic* to identify themselves, 33% said either *Latino* or *Hispanic* was fine, and only 13% preferred the term *Latino*. Finally, 62% asked that the survey be administered in Spanish (see Tables 2.1 and 2.2).

The purpose of this experiment is to determine levels of candidate support based on endorsements, the race/ethnicity of the candidate, and the racial/ethnic salience in a campaign. As such, I am interested in voters. Higher levels of education are associated with increased participation among Blacks and Latinos (Leighley and Vedlitz 1999; Verba, Schlozman, and Brady 1996). Among Latinos, those born in the United States and those who speak English are more likely to vote (Cho 1999). While the samples used here are more educated, they provide useful insights into Black and Latino voting behavior.

PUTTING IT TO THE TEST AMONG BLACK VOTERS: LATINO CANDIDATES, ENDORSEMENTS, AND RACIAL SALIENCE

Candidate preference among Blacks was measured with the following question: "If the election were held today, which candidate would you vote for?" Response options for the treatments that featured two White Candidates were "Jeremy Broadman," "Henry Brewer," or "Undecided."

TABLE 2.1 *Black Sample Demographics*

	Black Sample	Blacks in the 2008 ANES
Sample Size	266	569
Partisanship	24% Strong Democrat	70% Democrat
	38% Weak Democrat	23% Independent
	10% Democrat	3% Republican
	23% Independent	
	5% Republican	
Mean Income	$40,001 to $50,000	$15,000 to $20,000
Education	29% Some College	20% Some College
	29% Completed College	24% Completed College
	19% Advanced Degree	10% Advanced Degree
Ideology	28% Extremely Liberal	8% Extremely Liberal
	19% Liberal	25% Liberal
	27% Moderate or Middle of the Road	41% Moderate or Middle of the Road
Age Range	19–65	18–90 or older
Women	57%	57%
Immigration	13% Immigration should be increased a lot	
–Increased		
–Stay the same	18% Immigration should be increased a little	
–Decreased		
	32% Immigration should remain the same	
	18% Immigration should be decreased	
Data Collection Locations	Detroit Metro Area	

In the treatments that featured a White and a Latino Candidate, response options were "Jeremy Broadman," "Anthony Gonzalez," or "Undecided." Responses were coded into a dichotomous variable where "1" indicates that the respondent selected the more liberal candidate and "0" indicates that the respondent selected the more conservative candidate or "Undecided." Roughly 40% of the subjects said they would vote for the more liberal candidate.[12] In order to test my hypotheses among Blacks, I used logistic regression analysis to estimate support for candidate 2 by treatment group as compared to the baseline. In the baseline treatment, subjects read an article where there was no endorsement and two White candidates, and race was not salient. The functional form of the model is as follows:

TABLE 2.2 *Latino Sample Demographics*

	Latino Sample	Latino National Survey
Sample Size	192	8,634
Partisanship	16% Strong Democrat	35% Democrats
	11% Weak Democrat	17% Independents
	38% Democrat	11% Republicans and did
	4% Republican	21% Don't Know or some
	1% Strong Republican	other party
Mean Income	$50,001 to $60,000	$35,000 to $44,999
Education	36% Some College	19% Some College
	31% Completed College	9% Completed College
	24% Advanced Degrees	6.2% Advanced Degrees
Ideology	15% Extremely Liberal	13% Liberal
	35% Liberal	17% Middle of the Road
	19% Moderate or Middle of the Road	21% Conservative
Age Range	18–67	18–97
Women	66%	55%
Born in the US	70%	28% Mainland, 5% Puerto Rico
Only Speak English in the Home	50%	62% asked that the survey be administered in Spanish
National Origin	Mexican	
	Dominican	
	Puerto Rican	
	Cuban	
	South American	
	Other	
Immigration –Increased –Stay the same –Decreased	23% Immigration should be increased a lot	
	26% Immigration should be increased a little	
	26% Immigration should remain the same	
	10% Immigration should be decreased	
Data Collection Locations	Detroit Metro Area (84)	
	Northern CA (34)	
	Southern CA (47)	
	New York City (8)	
	Other (19)	

All surveys from the Detroit Metro Area were completed using the paper-and-pencil format. Nine surveys from Southern CA were completed using the paper-and-pencil format.

Putting It to the Test among Black Voters

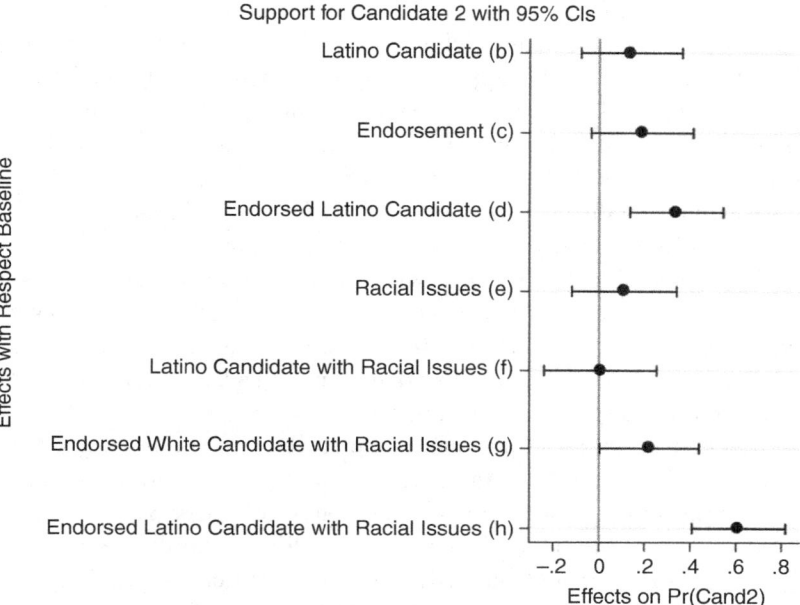

FIGURE 2.1 Support for Candidate 2 among Blacks, by Treatment
Marginal effects estimated from Table 2.1 in the Appendix for this chapter

$$\text{Candidate Preference among Blacks} =$$
$$B_1(\textit{Latino Candidate Treatment}) + B_2(\textit{Endorsement Treatment}) +$$
$$B_3(\textit{Endorsed Latino Candidate Treatment}) + B_4(\textit{Racial Issues Treatment}) +$$
$$B_5(\textit{Latino Candidate with Racial Issues Treatment}) +$$
$$B_6(\textit{Endorsement with Racial Issues Treatment}) +$$
$$B_7(\textit{Endorsed Latino Candidate with Racial Issues Treatment}) + \textit{Constant}$$
(2.1)

All the regression tables can be found in the Appendix for this chapter. Given the use of logistic regression, it is easier to interpret the predicted probabilities for levels of support for candidate 2 by treatment. I present these figures next. The results in Figure 2.1 show differences in levels of support for candidate 2 by the treatment groups, though these results are largely conditional on the context of the campaign. My hypotheses for the Black sample focus on B_2(*Endorsement Treatment*), B_3(*Endorsed Latino Candidate Treatment*), B_6(*Endorsement with Racial Issues Treatment*), and B_7(*Endorsed Latino Candidate with Racial Issues Treatment*), and predict that these estimates will be positive and large relative to the baseline. First, there is little support for hypothesis one, that co-ethnic elite endorsements will be more persuasive among Blacks than Latinos, because of the political homogeneity of Blacks and the political heterogeneity of Latinos. The predicted probability of support for candidate 2 is not distinguishable from zero for B_2(*Endorsement Treatment*), which suggests that endorsements alone are not enough.

The other three treatments with an endorsement are all positive and large relative to the baseline. The results in Figure 2.1 show that when the liberal Latino candidate receives a Black endorsement B_3(*Endorsed Latino Candidate Treatment*), Blacks are 34 percentage points more likely to indicate support for the candidate ($p < 0.01$). Here we see that when a minority candidate receives an endorsement, Blacks prefer him to the baseline candidate. This provides support for hypothesis three that ethnic endorsements will be more persuasive when the candidate is a minority. When a White liberal candidate receives a Black endorsement and the article mentions the city's new affirmative action law, B_6(*Endorsement with Race Salient Treatment*) Blacks also prefer him to the baseline liberal White candidate (22 percentage points, $p < 0.05$). This provides some support for hypothesis two, that endorsements are more persuasive when race is salient. Additionally, the endorsed Latino candidate receives more support than the baseline liberal White candidate when race is salient B_7(*Endorsed Latino Candidate with Racail Issues Treatment*) (61 percentage points, $p < 0.001$), which provides support for hypothesis four, that co-ethnic elite endorsements will be more persuasive when the endorsed candidate is a minority and race is salient.[13] These results are consistent with Campbell and colleagues, who found a similar relationship in the 1952 presidential election (1960), and Kuklinski and Hurley (1994), who showed that Blacks even preferred a policy that was against their self-interest when a Black leader endorsed that issue position.

Returning to the 2001 Los Angeles mayoral election can help us place these experimental results in a larger context. In the real-world election, James Hahn was perceived as sympathetic to Black issues because of his father's strong relationship with the Black community.[14] The results from the experiment presented here suggest that Villaraigosa needed more Black endorsements in 2001 in order to win Black votes. The experiment shows similar levels of support for the endorsed Latino candidate and the endorsed White candidate when race is salient, which suggests that a

White candidate needs Black leader support *and* racial salience in order to win over Black voters. A Latino candidate simply needs Black endorsements to gain Black voter support. Yet, when Black leaders endorse the Latino candidate and racial issues are mentioned, the level of Black voter support for the Latino candidate is quite high. In the experiment, the more liberal candidates do not explicitly take any issue positions, but simply mentioning the issues along with an endorsement is enough to make a difference to the respondents. These results are consistent with Kaufmann's argument that when racial issues become a part of the campaign, voters are more likely to think about their own racial identity when casting votes (2004). Thus, vote choice among Blacks in local elections is conditional on the context of the campaign, which is why Blacks are more willing to support the Latino candidate with an endorsement when the issue of affirmative action is a part of the campaign.

MORE THAN VOTES: THE POTENTIAL FOR COALITIONS. PERCEIVED CANDIDATE SYMPATHY AMONG BLACKS

The results above show that, together, the race of the candidate, endorsements, and making race salient in a campaign (as in the Endorsed Latino Candidate with Racial Issues treatment) influence candidate preference among Blacks, but that is only one way to evaluate the validity of my theory. Candidate preference is very important, as it represents the closest measure to voting in this study. But it is also important to know how these three factors shape the way Black voters perceive the candidate's sympathy towards Blacks and their ability to represent their interests in politics. This is may help us better understand how the racial context of a campaign, candidate race, and elite endorsements can foster the development of cross-ethnic electoral coalitions. I maintain that the interaction of these factors is important in part because they signal to Black voters that a candidate will address group-specific concerns, even if they are not members of their racial group.

Perceived candidate sympathy was measured with the following question: "Which candidate cares about people like you?" As in the previous analysis, response options for the treatments that featured two White Candidates were "Jeremy Broadman," "Henry Brewer," or "Undecided." In the treatments that featured a White and a Latino candidate, response options were "Jeremy Broadman," "Anthony Gonzalez," or "Undecided." Responses were recoded into a dichotomous variable where "1" indicates the respondent selected "Henry Brewer" or "Anthony Gonzalez," and "0" indicates the respondent selected "Jeremy Broadman" or "Undecided." Roughly 30% of the subjects said either Brewer or Gonzalez cared about people like them.[15] The results from the previous analysis suggest that when candidates are endorsed and the candidate is Latino, Black subjects are more likely to prefer the Latino candidate, compared to situations where there are no endorsements and both candidates are White. The functional model for this analysis is as follows:

$$\text{Perceived Candidate Sympathy among Latinos} = \\ B_1(\text{Latino Candidate Treatment}) + B_2(\text{Endorsement Treatment}) + \\ B_3(\text{Endorsed Latino Candidate Treatment}) + B_4(\text{Racial Issues Treatment}) + \\ B_5(\text{Latino Candidate with Racial Issues Treatment}) + \\ B_6(\text{Endorsement with Racial Issues Treatment}) + \\ B_7(\text{Endorsed Latino Candidate with Racial Issues Treatment}) + \text{Constant}$$

(2.2)

In Figure 2.2, I examine the relationship between the treatment effects and perceived candidate sympathy. These results are quite similar to the previous results. The respondents did not prefer the endorsed White candidate B_2(*Endorsement Treatment*), any more than the baseline White candidate. Again, this is not expected based on hypothesis one, that co-ethnic elite endorsements will be persuasive to Blacks because of the political homogeneity of the group. We do see that respondents were more likely indicate that candidate 2 was sympathetic to Blacks when they read about an endorsed Latino candidate, B_3(*Endorsed Latino Candidate Treatment*). Here the predicted probability of perceiving candidate 2 is sympathetic to Blacks is 32 percentage points higher ($p < 0.05$). The respondents are more persuaded by the Endorsed Latino Candidate with Race Salient treatment B_7(*Endorsed Latino Candidate with Racial Issues Treatment*). The predicted probability of perceiving candidate 2 as sympathetic to Blacks is quite large − 61 percentage points ($p < 0.001$).[16] This provides strong support for hypothesis four, that co-ethnic elite endorsements will be persuasive when the candidate is a minority and race is salient. Finally, these results provide support for hypothesis two, that co-ethnic elite endorsements will be persuasive to Blacks when race is salient. The belief that candidate 2 is sympathetic to Blacks is also high on the Endorsed White Candidate with Race Salient treatment B_6 (*Endorsement with Racial Issues Treatment*). It appears that the combination of elite

Putting It to the Test among Latino Voters

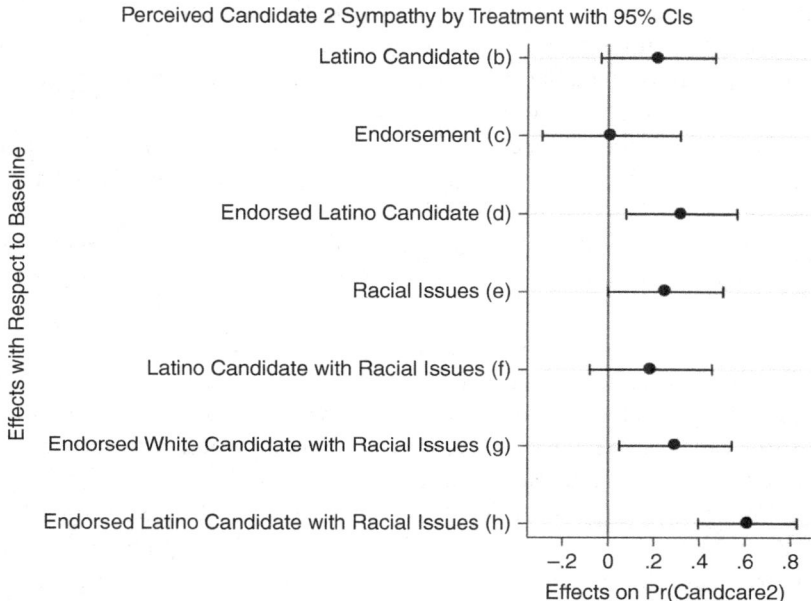

FIGURE 2.2 Perceived Sympathy by Candidate 2 among Blacks, by Treatment
Marginal effects estimated from Table 2.1 in the Appendix for this chapter

endorsements and racial salience is enough to prompt Blacks to view the liberal candidate as sympathetic to their needs, even when he is depicted as White. Overall, the results demonstrate that simply endorsing a candidate is not enough. The White candidate needs the endorsement and Blacks must be thinking about racial issues. Latino candidates can get by with just an endorsement, but they do better when the issues are also mentioned. These results indicate that endorsements are an important part of signaling to Blacks that a candidate will work on their behalf.

PUTTING IT TO THE TEST AMONG LATINO VOTERS: BLACK CANDIDATES, ENDORSEMENTS, AND ETHNIC SALIENCE

These results provide new insights into co-ethnic elite endorsements among Blacks when race is salient in a campaign. As expected, Black endorsements are persuasive to Blacks when the articles highlight racial issues. When the candidate is Latino, though, the endorsement is enough to move Black voters. The other goal of this chapter is to explore these relationships among Latinos. Latinos indicate strong levels of co-ethnic voting (Barreto 2007; Hajnal and Trounstine 2014), indicate that they do not feel close to Blacks (Kaufmann 2003; McClain et al. 2006), and have many identity choices (Beltran 2010; Masuoka 2008). While scholars have called on Latino leaders to help foster better cross-racial alliances (Kaufmann 2003), it is not clear that Latinos will find these calls persuasive. Yet, the research on Latino voting behavior and endorsements suggests that they can be persuasive under the right conditions (Barreto et al. 2008).

In order to explore this relationship among Latinos and to test my hypotheses, I replicate the previous analysis. The main dependent variable of candidate preference among Latinos was measured using the question: "If the election were held today, which candidate would you vote for?" I coded this in the exact same manner as in the previous analyses, where a "0" indicates a preference for "Broadman" or "Undecided" and a "1" indicates a preference for "Brewer" or "Jackson." Roughly 52% of the subjects said they would vote for either Brewer or Jackson.[17] In the baseline article, subjects read an article where there was no endorsement and two White candidates, and ethnicity was not salient. I then used logistic regression analysis that included the experimental treatments to assess the levels of support for candidate 2 compared to the baseline treatment. The functional form of the model is as follows:

$$\text{Candidate Preference among Latinos} =$$
$$B_1(\textit{Black Candidate Treatment}) + B_2(\textit{Endorsement Treatment}) +$$
$$B_3(\textit{Endorsed Black Candidate Treatment}) + B_4(\textit{Ethnic Issues Treatment}) +$$
$$B_5(\textit{Black Candidate with Ethnic Issues Treatment}) +$$
$$B_6(\textit{Endorsement with Ethnic Issues Treatment}) +$$
$$B_7(\textit{Endorsed Black Candidate with Ethnic Issues Treatment}) + \text{Constant}$$

(2.3)

Overall, the results in Figure 2.3 indicate that co-ethnic elite endorsements, the race of the candidate, and highlighting ethnic issues are not persuasive to Latinos when it comes to selecting a candidate. Latinos in this sample did not express different levels of support for candidate 2, even when more than one factor was present in the treatment. The predicted probabilities are small and not significant; though some of them move in

Putting It to the Test among Latino Voters

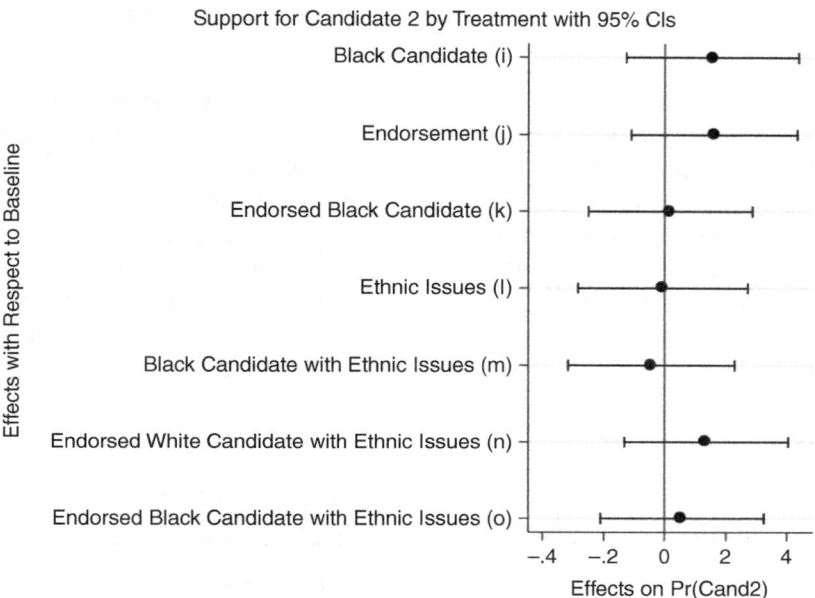

FIGURE 2.3 Support for Candidate 2 among Latinos, by Treatment
Marginal effects estimated from Table 2.2 in the Appendix for this chapter

the correct direction, they are not different from the baseline treatment. Moreover, Latinos in this sample do not respond to the experimental treatments the way Blacks did. This is true, even when the articles highlight racial/ethnic issues. With regard to hypothesis one, that co-ethnic elite endorsements will be more persuasive among Blacks than Latinos because of the political homogeneity of Blacks and the political heterogeneity of Latinos, we see that the endorsement alone treatment does not move Latino voters. In fact, overall, the endorsements were not persuasive at all, even when the candidate is a minority or when the treatments highlight ethnic issues. These null results do not provide support for any of the hypotheses. The null results suggest that the political heterogeneity among Latinos is very real. While Latino candidates have the potential to overcome this hurdle, cross-ethnic candidate support requires more than just a co-ethnic elite endorsement, even when ethnic issues are brought up. These null results highlight the possibility that the term *Latino* is not the most effective term because it might not be the identity choice for those in the sample (Beltran 2010; Masuoka 2008).

VOTING IS NOT ENOUGH: CANDIDATE PERCEPTIONS AMONG LATINOS

We know that Blacks are willing to engage in cross-ethnic voting at higher levels than Latinos and perceive out-group candidates as sympathetic to Blacks when certain factors are present. In this section, I explore how co-ethnic elite endorsements, the race of the candidate, and racial/ethnic salience shape the way Latino voters perceive a candidate's sympathy toward Latinos. This will help us to explore the ways in which the racial/ethnic context of the campaign, candidate race, and elite endorsements can foster cross-ethnic electoral coalitions. The presence of these factors is important in part because they send a cue to Latinos that a candidate will address group-specific issues and concerns, even when those candidates are not Latino. The functional model is as follows:

$$\text{Perceived Candidate Sympathy among Latinos} = \\ B_1(Black\ Candidate\ Treatment) + B_2(Endorsement\ Treatment) + \\ B_3(Endorsed\ Black\ Candidate\ Treatment) + B_4(Ethnic\ Issues\ Treatment) + \\ B_5(Black\ Candidate\ with\ Ethnic\ Issues\ Treatment) + \\ B_6(Endorsement\ with\ Ethnic\ Issues\ Treatment) + \\ B_7(Endorsed\ Black\ Candidate\ with\ Ethnic\ Issues\ Treatment) + Constant$$

(2.4)

To explore this relationship, I used the following question: "Which candidate cares about people like you?" to create dichotomous dependent variable such that a "0" means the subject indicated "Broadman" or "Undecided" and a "1" means the subjects indicated "Brewer" or "Jackson." Roughly 37% of the subjects said either Brewer or Jackson cared about people like them.[18] Turning to Figure 2.4, we see that, unlike the previous analysis, co-ethnic elite endorsements are persuasive to Latinos under certain conditions. Respondents believe that some candidates are more sympathetic to their needs than others. We still find that endorsements alone are not enough to make Latinos perceive the White candidate as sympathetic to Latinos, as the coefficient on $B_2(Endorsement\ Treatment)$ is not different from zero (hypothesis two). When subjects read the Endorsed Black Candidate with Ethnicity salient treatment $B_7(Endorsed\ Black\ Candidate\ with\ Ethnic\ Issues\ Treatment)$, they were 46 percentage points more likely to indicate that he cares about people like them (p < 0.01). When Latinos read the Endorsed Black

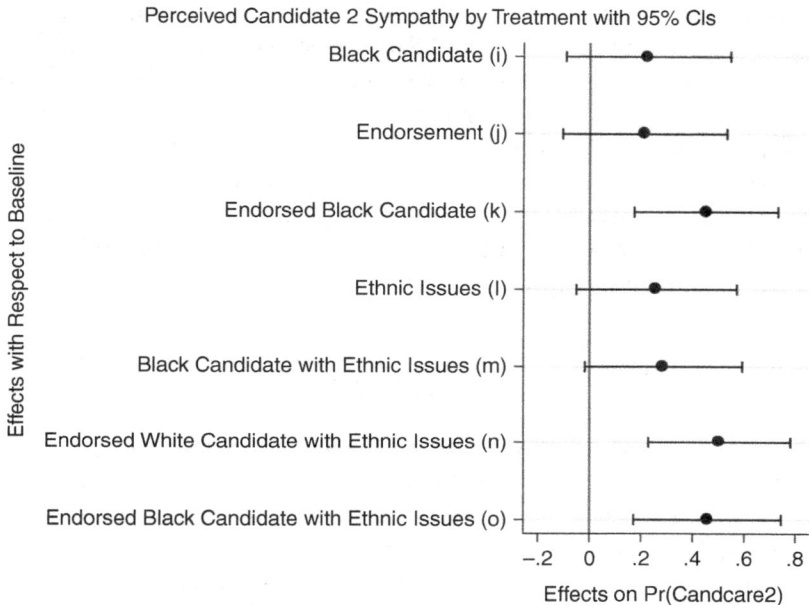

FIGURE 2.4 Perceived Sympathy by Candidate 2 among Latinos, by Treatment
Marginal effects estimated from Table 2.2 in the Appendix for this chapter

Candidate treatment B_3(*Endorsed Black Candidate Treatment*), they were 45 percentage points more likely to indicate that the candidate cares about people like them ($p < 0.01$). This provides some support for hypothesis three, that co-ethnic endorsements will be more persuasive when the candidate is a minority. Yet, we see the greatest support for candidate 2 when Latinos read the Endorsed White Candidate with Ethnicity Salient treatment B_6(*Endorsement with Ethnic Issues Treatment*). The likelihood of indicating that candidate 2 is sympathetic is 50 percentage points ($p < 0.001$). These results offer some support for hypothesis two, that co-ethnic elite endorsements will be more persuasive when ethnicity is salient, and for hypothesis four, that co-ethnic elite endorsements will be more persuasive when the endorsed candidate is a minority and ethnicity is salient. That Latinos perceive the endorsed White candidate in a race-salient campaign positively is consistent with previous literature that shows that Latinos feel closer to Whites (Kaufmann 2003a; McClain et al. 2006).

These results are also consistent with the Mayoral Elections Data Set, as it shows that Latinos readily support White candidates (Hajnal and Trounstine 2014). Overall, the co-ethnic elite endorsements are *less* persuasive to Latinos in this sample. While we did not see any differences by treatment with respect to candidate preferences in the previous analysis, there are some conditions in which co-ethnic elite endorsements *can* persuade Latinos. This is different from the Black respondents in my sample. Latinos are not willing to vote for a particular candidate even with an endorsement, but they do seem to recognize that some candidates have the potential to represent their interests better than others. Latinos in this sample may be open to the right out-group candidate, but they are not going to vote for him just yet.

THE CO-ETHNIC ELITE CUES THEORY: LESSONS FROM LOS ANGELES 2013[19]

The experimental results just cited provide some support for the Co-ethnic Elite Cues Theory, especially among African Americans, but there are some limitations to the experiment. In particular, while high on internal validity, there may be real questions about the viability of the theory in the real world. In this section, I test the theory using a real-world election. Testing the Co-ethnic Elite Cues Theory in the real world means that there is less control over the factors of interest (the race and ethnicity of the candidate, the presence of co-ethnic elite endorsements, and the racial and ethnic salience of the campaign). Unlike in the experiment, these three factors are out of my control. The goal of this section is to link racial and ethnic groups to vote choice via endorsements in a real-world election. Based on the evidence from the experiments, co-ethnic elite endorsements have the potential to send the message to co-ethnics that a particular candidate has the groups' interests at heart. To the extent that voters identify with the group, the endorsement serves as a powerful piece of information about which candidate to select, even when I control for the other factors that may also explain vote choice. However, given the previous experimental results, I argue that the co-ethnic elite endorsements will matter most when race and ethnicity are highlighted in the campaign.

CO-ETHNIC ELITE ENDORSEMENTS AND SALIENCE IN LOS ANGELES

In order to test the Co-ethnic Elite Cues Theory in a real-world election, I rely on exit poll data from the mayoral runoff election between Eric Garcetti and Wendy Greuel in Los Angeles in 2013 (Guerra and Gilbert

2013). The election is a good test case for the theory because mayoral elections in Los Angeles are nonpartisan, there was not an incumbent candidate, and for the most part, the candidates held similar policy positions. There was one exception: the issue of union pensions (Enten 2013; Medina 2013a, 2013b). Although Greuel and Garcetti had "roughly the same position on pensions," Gruel was backed by the unions, while Garcetti was not (Enten 2013; Maddaus 2013). In the experiment, racial and ethnic issues heightened racial and ethnic salience in a campaign, but in this mayoral election, the candidates did not take sides on any specific racial and ethnic issues, though one candidate was accused of supporting Proposition 187, which is considered an anti-immigration law. However, race and ethnicity were still salient in this campaign, in part due to media coverage of the candidates themselves. While reporting on the election, the media may take note of the race and ethnicity of the candidates, especially when the candidate has the potential to be the first African American, female, Jewish, or Latino mayor. By calling attention to the race and ethnicity of the candidates, the media helped make race and ethnicity salient in the campaign (Grofman, Handley, and Niemi 1994, 107; Reeves 1997, 21). In addition to this coverage, linking a candidate to Proposition 187 helped make race and ethnicity salient in the 2013 Los Angeles mayoral election. The media noted that Eric Garcetti had the potential to be the "first Jew appointed to the top city post" (Medina 2013b). But Eric Garcetti's ethnic/racial identity becomes much more complicated as he describes himself as White, Jewish, and Latino. His multiethnic identity allows us to explore the role of this type of candidate attribute in this setting. Garcetti won the election on May 21, 2013, beating Greuel by roughly 10 percentage points.

CO-ETHNIC ELITE CUES: REPLICATION IN THE REAL WORLD

Based on the Co-ethic Elite Cues Theory and given the discussion of racial and ethnic identity of the candidates in the campaign, I expect that Black voters are more likely to rely on co-ethnic elite endorsements. Among Latinos, the test is not as clear-cut. The media highlighted Garcetti's Jewish identity, but Latinos may have viewed Garcetti as a co-ethnic candidate, even though he lacked a co-ethnic surname (Barreto 2007). Garcetti's ambiguous ethnic identity allows us to explore the relationship between co-ethnic elite endorsements and candidate preferences among Latinos a little more deeply. If Latinos viewed him as Jewish, they may have relied on co-ethnic elite endorsements when casting their votes. The

Co-ethnic Elite Cues Theory predicts that Latino voters will rely on co-ethnic elite endorsements if there is no evidence of co-ethnic voting. Finally, the data allow a test of the relationship between co-ethnic elite endorsements and cross-ethnic voting for Greuel.

Previous studies of voting in Los Angeles rely on issue positions to help explain candidate choice. I only focus on the issue of union pensions as the media portrayed the candidates as having different positions on this issue, even though this was not the case. Still, given that the union issue was not racial, I believe that for Black and Latino voters, co-ethnic elite endorsements will do a better job explaining vote choice than union membership.

THE 2013 LOS ANGELES MAYORAL ELECTION EXIT POLL DATA

These data were collected by Fernando Guerra and Brianne Gilbert of the Thomas and Dorothy Leavey Center for the Study of Los Angeles at Loyola Marymount University in Los Angeles, California.[20] In collaboration with the principal investigators, the polls included specific questions about endorsements in the mayoral election. Guerra and Gilbert contacted each candidate and asked the candidates to name their top Black, Latino, and White endorsers. Those names were then added to the survey with the following question: "Which individual(s) endorsed the mayoral candidate for whom you voted today?" Eric Garcetti included Councilwoman Jan Perry as his top Black endorser and actress Salma Hayek as his top Latina endorser. Additionally, the Spanish newspaper (*La Opinion*) endorsed Garcetti. Wendy Greuel included County Supervisor Gloria Molina as her top Latina endorser and Magic Johnson as her top Black endorser. An analysis of the data in Los Angeles indicates that between 2% and 19% of voters in Los Angeles knew about at least one of the endorsements. While this list of endorsers is not exhaustive, it does represent who the candidates believed were their top Black and Latino endorsers. In addition to these questions, respondents were asked basic demographic information and their opinions on local issues. Again, because of the similarities between the candidates on most of the issues, the only perceived contentious issue was regarding unions, and respondents were asked: "What is your household's experience in labor unions?" Response options were: "I or someone in my household is a member" or "No one in my household belongs to a union."

The survey included responses from 1,159 Angelinos. Of those, 54% were women. The respondents were racially and ethnically diverse as well.

The sample was about 28% Latino, 46% White, 17% Black, and 5% Asian.[21] More than half of the respondents described themselves as liberal (very liberal and somewhat liberal), while a little less than a quarter of the respondents described themselves as conservative (very conservative and somewhat conservative). The rest said they were moderate. The sample is also highly educated with more than 80% indicating they had completed some college or more. The mean household income was $40,000–$59,999 per year. Roughly 10% of the respondents said they were Jewish, compared to 32% who identified as Catholic and 25% who identified as Protestant. The sample is also highly Democratic in terms of partisan identity, with 70% of respondents saying they identified as Democrats. Only 15% of respondents identified with the Republican Party. Finally, 68% of the respondents said that no one in their household was a member of a union.

LATINO VOTERS AND CO-ETHNIC CANDIDATE SUPPORT (CO-ETHNIC VOTING)

Before I delve deeper into the relationship between co-ethnic elite endorsements and vote choice in Los Angeles, I first replicate a basic analysis of vote choice for Garcetti (see, for example, Abrajano, Nagler, and Alvarez 2005) in order to determine which factors help explain vote choice in this election. In the following analyses, I present the marginal effects of support for Garcetti (all the regression tables can be found in the Appendix for this chapter). I coded vote choice such that "1" indicates a preference for Garcetti and "0" indicates a preference for Greuel. In this first model, I include race/ethnicity variables, basic demographic measures including age, income, ideology, gender, party identification, household union membership, and whether respondents live in the San Fernando Valley.[22] The goal of this first analysis is to test whether Latinos or Jewish voters perceived Garcetti as a co-ethnic candidate. Figure 2.5 shows that there is evidence of co-ethnic voting among Latinos. Latinos are 11 percentage points more likely to support Garcetti ($p < 0.05$). This provides support for the Co-ethnic Elite Cues Theory. Despite the media highlighting Garcetti's Jewish identity, there is no evidence that Jewish voters were more likely to vote for Garcetti. Blacks, as a group, were 27 percentage points less likely to support Garcetti ($p < 0.001$) in the election, and this is true even when we control for union membership. Finally, given the media's assessment that Greuel was pro-union (even though both candidates held similar stances on the union pension issue), the data

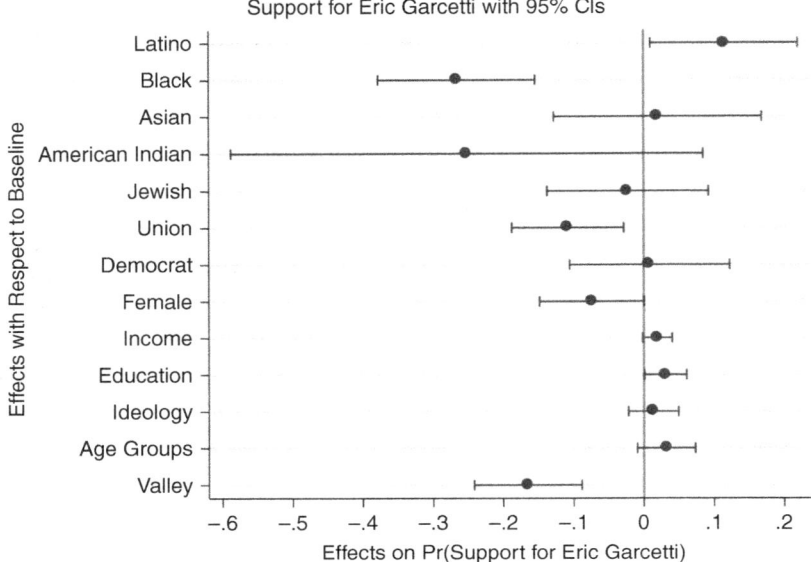

FIGURE 2.5 Support for Garcetti (Marginal Effects)
Marginal effects estimated from Table 2.3 in the Appendix for this chapter

show that union households were 11 percentage points (p < 0.01) less likely to support Garcetti. The next step is assessing the relationship between co-ethnic elite endorsements and vote choice among Blacks and Latinos.[23]

CO-ETHNIC ELITE ENDORSEMENTS EXPLAIN BLACK VOTE CHOICE

In order to test the Co-ethnic Elite Cues Theory among Blacks, Garcetti and Greuel said their top Black endorsers were Jan Perry (city councilmember and mayoral candidate in 2013) and Magic Johnson (former Los Angeles Laker and entrepreneur), respectively. For each candidate, I estimate a model of support among African Americans, including controls, and their knowledge of the Black endorsement. In Figure 2.6, I estimate support for Wendy Greuel among Black voters, including the Magic Johnson endorsement and union membership. The data show that only the endorsement explains vote choice, as the Magic Johnson endorsement increased support for Greuel by 50 percentage points (p < 0.001).

Co-ethnic Elite Endorsements Explain Black Vote Choice

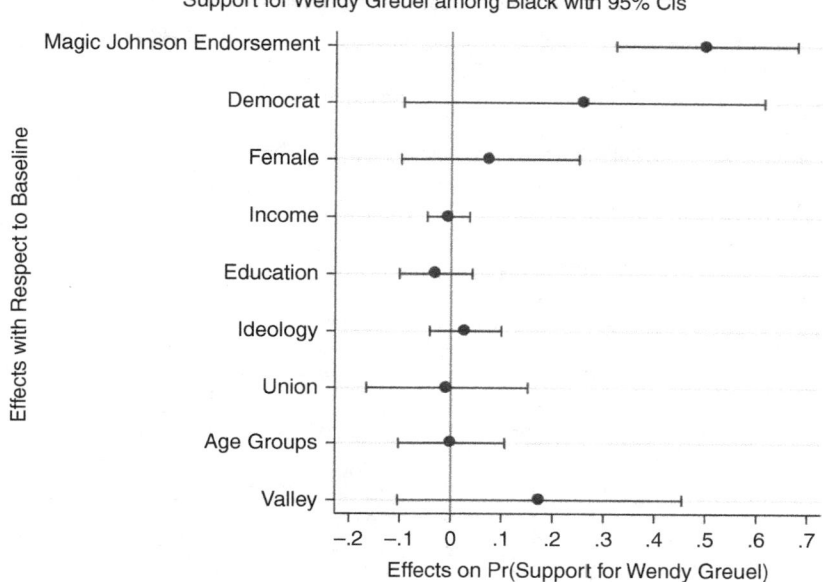

FIGURE 2.6 Support for Greuel among Blacks (Marginal Effects)
Marginal effects estimated from Table 2.4 in the Appendix for this chapter

Next, in Figure 2.7, I estimate a similar model for Garcetti using the Jan Perry endorsement. Even when I include household union membership and Jan Perry's endorsement, the relationship is only strong between the endorsement and vote choice. The Jan Perry endorsement increased support for Garcetti by 41 percentage points ($p < 0.001$).

Taken together, these results provide strong support for the Co-ethnic Elite Cues Theory. These results replicate the experimental treatments (Endorsed White Candidate with Racial Issues Treatment (g) and Endorsed Latino Candidate with Racial Issues Treatment (h)). In the context of a racially salient campaign, when Blacks were faced with a White candidate (Greuel) with an endorsement from a co-ethnic elite (Magic Johnson), the co-ethnic elite endorsement was persuasive and Black voters engaged in cross-ethnic voting. This was also the case when Blacks were faced with a Latino candidate (Garcetti) with an endorsement from a co-ethnic elite (Jan Perry). This was true, even when I controlled for demographics and issues.

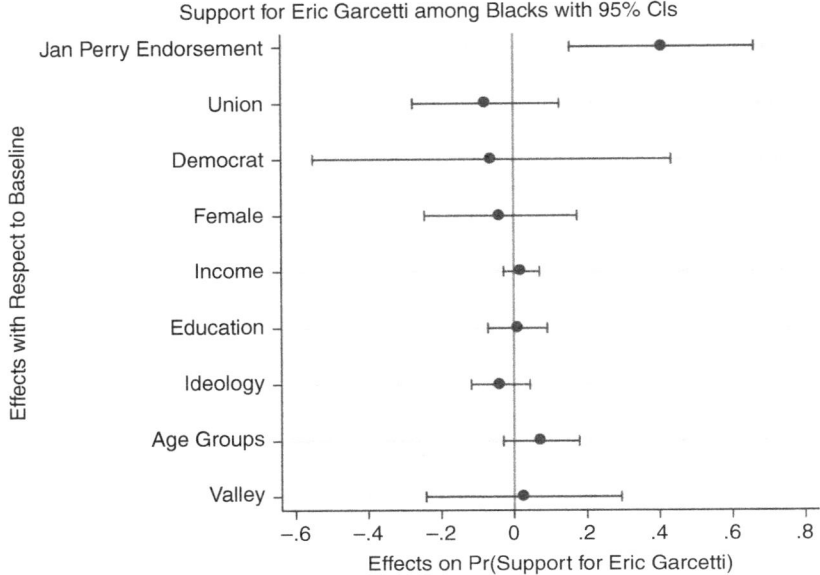

FIGURE 2.7 Support for Garcetti among Blacks (Marginal Effects)
Marginal effects estimated from Table 2.7 in the Appendix for this chapter

CO-ETHNIC ELITE ENDORSEMENTS AND LATINO VOTERS: IT'S COMPLICATED

The data from the experiment and Los Angeles show the relationship between co-ethnic elite endorsements and vote choice is quite strong among African Americans. While the data from Los Angeles provide support for the Co-ethnic Elite Cues Theory among Latinos, the experimental data presented earlier in this chapter are less conclusive with regards to Latinos. Testing the Co-ethnic Elite Cues Theory among Latinos who engaged in co-ethnic voting to support Garcetti is a little more complicated than the experiments. We can still test the theory with Greuel, who was not a co-ethnic candidate, which allows us to test the relationship between co-ethnic elite endorsements and vote choice among Latinos in Los Angeles. Further, we can still assess when Latinos might use co-ethnic elite endorsements and how persuasive they are even when Latinos support a co-ethnic candidate.

First, Greuel indicated her endorsement from Gloria Molina (a former Los Angeles County supervisor, she also served on the city council and in

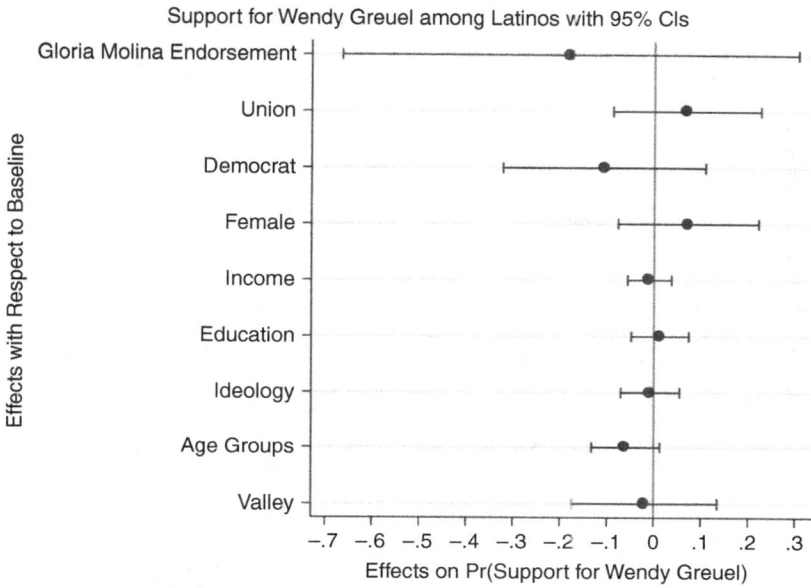

FIGURE 2.8 Support for Greuel among Latinos (Marginal Effects) Marginal effects estimated from Table 2.6 in the Appendix for this chapter

the state legislature) was her top Latina endorsement. In Figure 2.8, I estimate support for Gruel, which shows that Gloria Molina's endorsement is negative and not significant. Among Latinos, the endorsement did not help Latinos vote for Greuel. Latinos in Los Angeles did not rely on a co-ethnic elite endorsement when voting for Greuel. This result is consistent with the first experimental result among Latinos, as they did not indicate a candidate preference, even with a co-ethnic elite endorsement and when ethnic issues were present.

To test the theory further (with a co-ethnic candidate), I turn to support for Garcetti among Latinos. Garcetti listed Salma Hayek as his top Latina endorser. However, the local Spanish newspaper, *La Opinion*, also endorsed him, so there are two Latino endorsements to consider for Garcetti. In Figure 2.9, I estimate support for Garcetti and the *La Opinion* endorsement among Latinos. The *La Opinion* endorsement increased support for Garcetti by 42 percentage points (p < 0.10). However, this is not the case with the Salma Hayek endorsement. Here, the relationship is weak, indicating that this particular endorsement did not help Latino voters make a candidate choice in this election. In Figure 2.10,

84 An Experimental Test of the Co-ethnic Elite Cues Theory

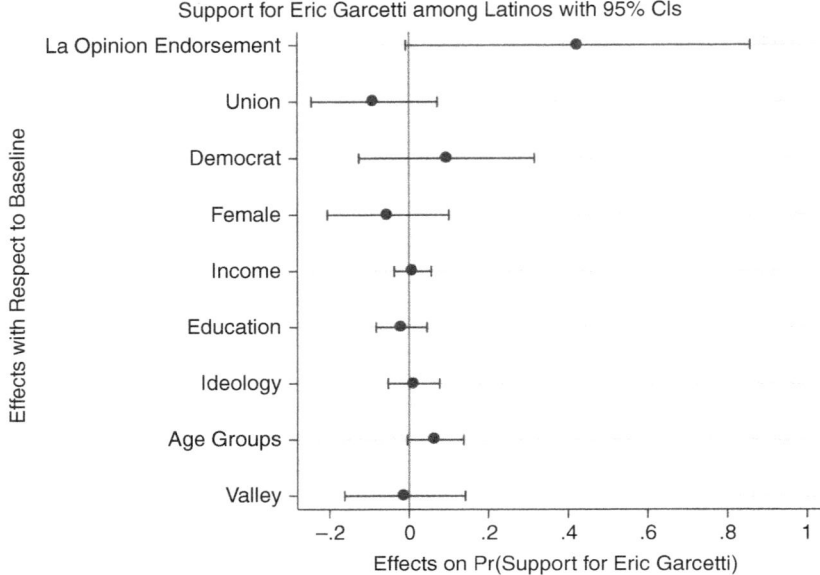

FIGURE 2.9 Support for Garcetti among Latinos *(La Opinion)* (Marginal Effects)
Marginal effects estimated from Table 2.7 in the Appendix for this chapter

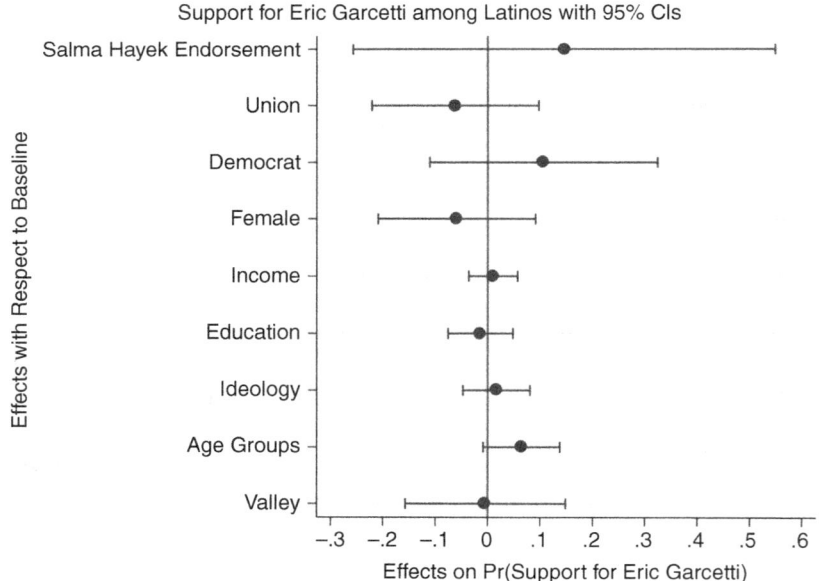

FIGURE 2.10 Support for Garcetti among Latinos (Salma Hayek) (Marginal Effects)
Marginal effects estimated from Table 2.7 in the Appendix for this chapter

I present the marginal effects of support for Garcetti among Latinos with the Salma Hayek endorsement, which shows that the Salma Hayek endorsement does not explain support for Garcetti. For Garcetti, though, this does provide support for the Co-ethnic Elite Cues Theory, as we expect Latinos to support the Latino candidate (which they did here), but it also shows that even when there is a co-ethnic candidate, some endorsements help voters, while others are less persuasive.

CO-ETHNIC ELITE ENDORSEMENTS WORK WELL AMONG BLACKS, BUT LATINOS ARE NOT CONVINCED

In the first half of this chapter, I presented experimental data designed to test the Co-ethnic Elite Cues Theory. The theory predicts a relationship between the presence of endorsements, the race of the candidate, and racial/ethnic salience in the campaign and candidate preferences among Blacks and Latinos. Then, in order to test the theory outside of the lab, I incorporated exit poll data to show that there is a strong relationship between co-ethnic elite endorsements and vote choice among Black voters in Los Angeles. However, the data show that for Latinos, this relationship is not as strong. In particular, the relationship was strong only between the endorsement from the Spanish newspapers and vote choice. The relationship was weak between endorsements from Latino political leaders and celebrities. The data did provide some support for the Co-ethnic Elite Cues Theory, as there was evidence of co-ethnic candidate support among Latinos.

The Co-ethnic Elite Cues Theory provides evidence about *when* co-ethnic elite endorsements move Blacks and Latinos toward out-group candidates and when they do not. For African Americans, I demonstrated that alone, endorsements from Black leaders, the race of the candidate and racial salience did not seem to move Black subjects to prefer a candidate over the baseline candidate. Endorsements work better in conjunction with the other two factors. Blacks did distinguish between Latino candidates with endorsements (when racial and ethnic issues were present and when they were not). In real-world elections, we see evidence of this in New York in 2005 when a majority of Blacks supported Fernando Ferrer for mayor (he had many Black endorsements and even called on Blacks to support his Elite Black–Latino Coalition). Los Angeles 2005 may also shed some light on the experimental data. Villaraigosa did receive a majority of Black endorsements in that campaign, and a majority of Blacks voted for him. Blacks in this sample also expressed support for a

White candidate with an endorsement when race was salient. This situation is similar to Los Angeles in 2001, when Blacks overwhelmingly supported Hahn in the mayoral election. This suggests that Black voters may be more likely to prefer Latino candidates to White candidates when Black leaders and organizations give endorsements. But, if White candidates can gain Black leader support and express an issue preference that is in line with Black preferences, then they might enjoy the support of Black voters.

The data from the Latino sample demonstrated that the relationship between elite endorsements, candidate characteristics, ethnic issues and candidate preference among Latinos is weaker. Latinos were not more likely to indicate a preference for any of the candidates compared to the baseline candidate. While previous research shows that Latinos are more likely to turn out in local elections when there is a Latino candidate, it may be that these experimental treatments, which did not feature a Latino candidate, did not mobilize them. Alternatively, when it came to thinking about perceived candidate sympathy, the evidence shows that Latinos were more likely to think Black candidates with endorsements from Latino organizations cared about them (this was true when ethnicity was salient and when it was not salient) compared to the baseline treatment. Similarly, Latinos in this experimental sample believed that, when racial and ethnic issues were present, the White candidate with an endorsement cared about them.

The results from Los Angeles provide an external validity check on the experimental data. Just as in the experiments, the relationship between co-ethnic elite endorsements and cross-ethnic voting among Blacks was strong when race was salient. The Los Angeles data also show that this relationship was weaker among Latinos, as neither endorsements from the candidates' top endorser helped explain vote choice. The data from Los Angeles confirm other studies of newspaper endorsements, as the endorsement from *La Opinion* helped explain vote choice among Latinos (Erickson 1976).

While this chapter cannot address Elite Black–Latino Coalitions directly (as there was no direct question about levels of support for such a coalition), it can provide some insight into the real-world elections and the voting patterns of Black and Latinos in local elections. The experimental data presented here suggest that Blacks and Latinos may rely on co-ethnic elite endorsements in local elections, but they do not matter in every election. Instead, we might expect them to matter to African Americans when race becomes part of the campaign, which we saw using the Los Angeles 2013 mayoral election. Among Latinos, the hurdle is much higher: Black candidates should seek out Latino endorsements, but there is little they can do to make sure that ethnicity does not become salient in the campaign, a factor that led to more support for White candidates. Taken together, data suggest that the most likely Elite Black–Latino Coalition will come in the form of a Latino candidate who has support from Black leaders.

NEXT STEPS

In Chapter 3, I build on the results found here and present data from a nationally representative survey experiment among Blacks, Latinos, and Whites in order to provide more generalizability for the Co-ethnic Elite Cues Theory. In the next experiment, in addition to the endorsements, I include an explicit call to support an Elite Black–Latino Coalition and I find that Blacks and Latinos are largely supportive of out-group minority candidates under those conditions. These new data also offer a more complete picture of the role of race and ethnicity in local elections and allow me to test White voter responses to Black and Latino candidates and calls to support Elite Black–Latino Coalitions.

APPENDIX

TABLE 2.1A *Logistic Regression Analysis of Support for Candidate 2 among Blacks, by Treatment*

	Candidate Selection (Baseline = 2 White Candidates (a))	Candidate Sympathy (Baseline = 2 White Candidates (a))
Intercept	−1.50** (0.45)	−2.19*** (0.60)
Latino Candidate Treatment (b)	0.72 (0.57)	1.21 (0.72)
Endorsement Treatment (c)	0.95 (0.58)	0.08 (0.86)
Endorsed Latino Candidate Treatment (d)	1.72** (0.56)	1.79* (0.71)
Racial Issues Treatment (e)	0.56 (0.59)	1.39 (0.72)

(continued)

TABLE 2.1A (continued)

	Candidate Selection (Baseline = 2 White Candidates (a))	Candidate Sympathy (Baseline = 2 White Candidates (a))
Latino Candidate with Racial Issues Treatment (f)	0.04 (0.64)	1.04 (0.76)
Endorsed White Candidate with Racial Issues Treatment (g)	1.12* (0.57)	1.65* (0.57)
Endorsed Latino Candidate with Racial Issues Treatment (h)	3.11*** (0.63)	3.41*** (0.73)
Log likelihood	−154.16	−129.08
N	266	240

Notes: * p < 0.05; ** p < 0.01; *** p < 0.001 for a two-tailed test.

This analysis uses logistic regression to estimate candidate selection and beliefs that the candidate cares about people like them among Black respondents.

No Endorsement, White vs. White, No Racial Issues (a) (33), No Endorsement, White vs. Latino, No Racial Issues (b) (35), Endorsement, White vs. White, No Racial Issues (c) (30), Endorsement, White vs. Latino, No Racial Issues (d) (36), Endorsement, No Endorsement, White vs. White, Racial Issues (e) (32). No Endorsement, White vs. Latino, Racial Issues (f) (32), Endorsement, White vs. White, Racial Issues (g) (32), Endorsement, White vs. Latino, Racial Issues (h) (36)

TABLE 2.2A *Logistic Regression Analysis of Support for Candidate 2 among Latinos, by Treatment*

	Candidate Selection (Baseline = 2 White Candidates (a))	Candidate Sympathy (Baseline = 2 White Candidates (a))
Intercept	−0.15 (0.39)	−1.99 (0.61)
Black Candidate Treatment (i)	0.63 (0.59)	1.07 (0.78)
Endorsement Treatment (j)	0.66 (0.57)	1.01 (0.78)
Endorsed Black Candidate Treatment (k)	0.07 (0.56)	2.14** (0.73)
Ethnic Issues Treatment (l)	−0.03 (0.59)	1.23 (0.76)

(continued)

TABLE 2.2A *(continued)*

	Candidate Selection (Baseline = 2 White Candidates (a))	Candidate Sympathy (Baseline = 2 White Candidates (a))
Black Candidate with Ethnic Issues Treatment (m)	−0.18 (0.57)	1.36 (0.75)
Endorsed White Candidate with Ethnic Issues Treatment (n)	0.55 (0.56)	2.39** (0.73)
Endorsed Black Candidate with Ethnic Issues Treatment (o)	0.23 (0.56)	2.17** (0.75)
Log likelihood	−130.68	−113.17
N	192	186

Notes: * $p < 0.05$; ** $p < 0.01$; *** $p < 0.001$ for a two-tailed test.

This analysis uses logistic regression to estimate candidate selection and the belief that the candidate cares about people like them among Latino respondents.

No Endorsement, White vs. White, No Ethnic Issues (a) (26), No Endorsement, White vs. Black, No Ethnic Issues (i) (21), Endorsement, White vs. White, No Ethnic Issues (j) (24), Endorsement, White vs. Black, No Ethnic Issues (k) (26), No Endorsement, White vs. White, Ethnic Issues (l) (22), No Endorsement, White vs. Black, Ethnic Issues (m) (24), Endorsement, White vs. White, Ethnic Issues (n) (25), Endorsement, White vs. Black, Ethnic Issues (o) (25)

TABLE 2.3A *Logistic Regression Analysis of Support for Garcetti*

Variables	Garcetti Estimate (S.E.)
Constant	−0.52 (0.57)
Political Party	0.04 (0.26)
Ideology	0.06 (0.08)
Demographics	
Latino	0.52* (0.25)
Black	−1.21*** (0.27)
Asian	0.09 (0.34)

(continued)

TABLE 2.3A *(continued)*

Variables	Garcetti Estimate (S.E.)
American Indian	−1.14
	(0.79)
Jewish	−0.10
	(0.27)
Female	−0.34+
	(0.17)
Age	0.15
	(0.10)
Education	0.14*
	(0.07)
Income	0.09+
	(0.05)
San Fernando Valley	−0.75***
	(0.18)
Issues	
Union	−0.49**
	(0.19)
Log likelihood	−122.59
N	685

Notes: + p < 0.10; * p < 0.05; ** p < 0.01; *** p < 0.001 for a two-tailed test.

Racial group variables are relative to Whites. Black is a dichotomous variable where 1 = Black, 0 = Not Black. Latino is a dichotomous variable where 1 = Latino, 0 = Not Latino. Asian is a dichotomous variable where 1 = Asian, 0 = Not Asian. American Indian is a dichotomous variable where 1 = American Indian, 0 = Not American Indian. Jewish is a dichotomous variable where 1 = Jewish, 0 = Not Jewish. Party is a dichotomous variable where 1 = Democrat, 0 = Republican. Ideology is a categorical variable, where lower values indicate a liberal response and higher values indicate a conservative response (Very Liberal, Somewhat Liberal, Moderate, Somewhat Conservative, and Very Conservative). Age is a categorical variable, where ages are grouped as follows: 18–29, 30–44, 45–64, and 65 and over. Female is a dichotomous variable where 1 = Female, 0 = Not Female. Education is a categorical variable, where lower values indicate a less education and higher values indicate more education (Less than high school, High school graduate, Some college/technical school, College degree(s), Some graduate school, and Graduate degree(s)). Income is a categorical variable, where lower values indicate less income and higher values indicate more income (Less than $20,000, $20,000 to $39,999, $40,000 to $59,999, $60,000 to $79,999, $80,000 to $99,999, $100,000 to $149,999, $150,000 to $250,000, and More than $250,000). Valley is a dichotomous variable where 1 = Live in the San Fernando Valley, 0 = Do Not Live in the San Fernando Valley. Union is a dichotomous variable where 1 = I or someone in my household is in a union, 0 = No one in my household belongs to a union.

TABLE 2.4A *Logistic Regression Analysis of Candidate Support (Greuel) among Black voters*

Variables	Greuel Estimate (S.E.)
Constant	−1.80
	(1.82)
Political Party	1.58
	(1.15)
Ideology	0.18
	(0.22)
Demographics	
Female	0.47
	(0.56)
Age	0.01
	(0.32)
Education	−0.18
	(0.23)
Income	−0.03
	(0.13)
San Fernando Valley	1.06
	(0.89)
Issues	
Union	−0.04
	(0.50)
Endorsements	
Magic Johnson	3.05***
	(0.81)
Log likelihood	−56.17
N	119

Notes: + p < 0.10; * p < 0.05; ** p < 0.01; *** p < 0.001 for a two-tailed test.

Party is a dichotomous variable where 1 = Democrat, 0 = Republican. Ideology is a categorical variable, where lower values indicate a liberal response and higher values indicate a conservative response (Very Liberal, Somewhat Liberal, Moderate, Somewhat Conservative, and Very Conservative). Age is a categorical variable, where ages are grouped as follows: 18–29, 30–44, 45–64, and 65 and over. Female is a dichotomous variable where 1 = Female, 0 = Not Female. Education is a categorical variable, where lower values indicate a less education and higher values indicate more education (Less than high school, High school graduate, Some college/technical school, College degree(s), Some graduate school, and Graduate degree(s)). Income is a categorical variable, where lower values indicate less income and higher values indicate more income (Less than $20,000, $20,000 to $39,999, $40,000 to $59,999, $60,000 to $79,999, $80,000 to $99,999, $100,000 to $149,999, $150,000 to $250,000, and More than $250,000). Valley is a dichotomous variable where 1 = Live in the San Fernando Valley, 0 = Do Not Live in the San Fernando Valley. Union is a dichotomous variable where 1 = I or someone in my household is in a union, 0 = No one in my household belongs to a union.

TABLE 2.5A *Logistic Regression Analysis of Candidate Support (Garcetti) among Black voters*

Variables	Garcetti Estimate (S.E)
Constant	−1.84
	(1.93)
Political Party	−0.32
	(1.32)
Ideology	−0.20
	(0.22)
Demographics	
Female	−0.19
	(0.57)
Age	0.39
	(0.28)
Education	0.06
	(0.22)
Income	0.12
	(0.13)
San Fernando Valley	0.14
	(0.73)
Issues	−0.40
Union	(0.55)
Endorsements	
Jan Perry	2.16**
	(0.82)
Log likelihood	−66.50
N	119

Notes: + p < 0.10; * p < 0.05; ** p < 0.01; *** p < 0.001 for a two-tailed test.

Party is a dichotomous variable where 1 = Democrat, 0 = Republican. Ideology is a categorical variable, where lower values indicate a liberal response and higher values indicate a conservative response (Very Liberal, Somewhat Liberal, Moderate, Somewhat Conservative, and Very Conservative). Age is a categorical variable, where ages are grouped as follows: 18–29, 30–44, 45–64, and 65 and over. Female is a dichotomous variable where 1 = Female, 0 = Not Female. Education is a categorical variable, where lower values indicate a less education and higher values indicate more education (Less than high school, High school graduate, Some college/technical school, College degree(s), Some graduate school, and Graduate degree(s)). Income is a categorical variable, where lower values indicate less income and higher values indicate more income (Less than $20,000, $20,000 to $39,999, $40,000 to $59,999, $60,000 to $79,999, $80,000 to $99,999, $100,000 to $149,999, $150,000 to $250,000, and More than $250,000). Valley is a dichotomous variable where 1 = Live in the San Fernando Valley, 0 = Do Not Live in the San Fernando Valley. Union is a dichotomous variable where 1 = I or someone in my household is in a union, 0 = No one in my household belongs to a union.

TABLE 2.6A *Logistic Regression Analysis of Candidate Support (Greuel) among Latino voters*

Variables	Greuel Estimate (S.E.)
Constant	0.31
	(0.96)
Political Party	−0.48
	(0.50)
Ideology	−0.03
	(0.14)
Demographics	
Female	0.33
	(0.35)
Age	−0.28
	(0.17)
Education	0.06
	(0.14)
Income	−0.04
	(0.11)
San Fernando Valley	−0.08
	(0.36)
Issues	
Union	0.31
	(0.37)
Endorsements	−0.81
Gloria Molina	(1.13)
Log likelihood	−115.89
N	182

Notes: + $p < 0.10$; * $p < 0.05$; ** $p < 0.01$; *** $p < 0.001$ for a two-tailed test.

Party is a dichotomous variable where 1 = Democrat, 0 = Republican. Ideology is a categorical variable, where lower values indicate a liberal response and higher values indicate a conservative response (Very Liberal, Somewhat Liberal, Moderate, Somewhat Conservative, and Very Conservative). Age is a categorical variable, where ages are grouped as follows: 18–29, 30–44, 45–64, and 65 and over. Female is a dichotomous variable where 1 = Female, 0 = Not Female. Education is a categorical variable, where lower values indicate a less education and higher values indicate more education (Less than high school, High school graduate, Some college/technical school, College degree(s), Some graduate school, and Graduate degree(s)). Income is a categorical variable, where lower values indicate less income and higher values indicate more income (Less than $20,000, $20,000 to $39,999, $40,000 to $59,999, $60,000 to $79,999, $80,000 to $99,999, $100,000 to $149,999, $150,000 to $250,000, and More than $250,000). Valley is a dichotomous variable where 1 = Live in the San Fernando Valley, 0 = Do Not Live in the San Fernando Valley. Union is a dichotomous variable where 1 = I or someone in my household is in a union, 0 = No one in my household belongs to a union.

TABLE 2.7A *Logistic Regression Analysis of Candidate Support (Garcetti) among Latino Voters*

Variables	Garcetti Estimate (S.E.)	Garcetti Estimate (S.E.)
Constant	−0.42 (1.01)	−0.50 (0.96)
Political		
Party	0.44 (0.52)	0.48 (0.51)
Ideology	0.06 (0.15)	0.08 (0.15)
Demographics		
Female	−0.24 (0.37)	−0.27 (0.35)
Age	0.31+ (0.17)	0.30+ (0.17)
Education	−0.09 (0.15)	−0.07 (0.14)
Income	0.05 (0.11)	0.05 (0.11)
San Fernando Valley	−0.05 (0.36)	−0.02 (0.35)
Issues		
Union	−0.40 (0.38)	−0.30 (0.37)
Endorsements		
La Opinion	1.97+ (1.07)	
Salma Hayek		0.66 (0.93)
Log likelihood	−113.09	−116.09
N	182	182

Notes: + p < 0.10; * p < 0.05; ** p < 0.01; *** p < 0.001 for a two-tailed test.

Party is a dichotomous variable where 1 = Democrat, 0 = Republican. Ideology is a categorical variable, where lower values indicate a liberal response and higher values indicate a conservative response (Very Liberal, Somewhat Liberal, Moderate, Somewhat Conservative, and Very Conservative). Age is a categorical variable, where ages are grouped as follows: 18–29, 30–44, 45–64, and 65 and over. Female is a dichotomous variable where 1 = Female, 0 = Not Female. Education is a categorical variable, where lower values indicate a less education and higher values indicate more education (Less than high school, High school graduate, Some college/technical school, College degree(s), Some graduate school, and Graduate degree(s)). Income is a categorical variable, where lower values indicate less income and higher values indicate more income (Less than $20,000, $20,000 to $39,999, $40,000 to $59,999, $60,000 to $79,999, $80,000 to $99,999, $100,000 to $149,999, $150,000 to $250,000, and More than $250,000). Valley is a dichotomous variable where 1 = Live in the San Fernando Valley, 0 = Do Not Live in the San Fernando Valley. Union is a dichotomous variable where 1 = I or someone in my household is in a union, 0 = No one in my household belongs to a union.

APPENDIX 2A: FICTIONAL NEWS STORIES (BLACK SAMPLE)

Candidates Take Stance on Environment, [Brewer/Gonzalez Endorsed by Association of Local Black Leaders]

Jonathon Childs – Staff

As the nonpartisan mayoral election approaches, the candidates have stepped up their game and are preparing for the last leg of their respective campaigns. Last night, the major candidates used a locally televised debate to outline their platforms and display their personalities to the voters.

Last night's debate showed a different side of local politics, as the candidates focused on elevating themselves rather than undermining their opponents. With the current mayor leaving after an eight-year term, many people have called for a successor who will shake things up. Jeremy Broadman and [**Henry Brewer/Anthony Gonzalez**] answered tough questions from area voters, on topics ranging from education to zoning.

Marty Gray, a former schoolteacher, wanted to know how the candidates planned to address the recent funding cuts to after school programs. "What are students going to do now that the programs are being cut? What are the options for working parents?" Both Broadman and [**Brewer/Gonzalez**] said they were willing to work with area organizations such as the YMCA and Boys and Girls Club to address the situation until permanent funds could be secured. However, neither candidate was clear about the possible sources for these funds.

Most importantly, the candidates finally took sides on the issue of whether or not the city will renew its contract with Enviro-Tech [**despite several bids from smaller companies, the city decided to go with the country's largest trash-burning company/which received the contract, despite several bids from minority companies and a promise from the city to use the newly enacted Affirmative Action laws.**] Broadman, 46, supports the contract renewal: "The city needs more time to fully develop and implement a recycling plan." [**Brewer/Gonzalez**], 47, does not want to renew the contract: "We can start recycling immediately and send the non-recyclable trash to landfills. The burning has to stop!" [**Brewer/Gonzalez mentioned during the debate that his position was supported by the Local Association of Black Leaders, who have also endorsed his candidacy.**]

In a recent poll, 63% of voters felt [that the environment/that Affirmative Action] had become an important issue in this election.

Over the past few weeks, both sides tried to convince the candidates to take a stand on this issue. It looks as if the voters will have their say on Election Day regarding the issue of trash burning in the city.

Photos of the fictional candidates can be viewed at andreabenjaminphd. com/onlineappendix/.

APPENDIX 2B: FICTIONAL NEWS STORIES (LATINO SAMPLE)

Candidates Take Stance on Environment, [Brewer/Jackson Endorsed by Association of Local Latino Leaders]

Jonathon Childs – Staff

As the nonpartisan mayoral election approaches, the candidates have stepped up their game and are preparing for the last leg of their respective campaigns. Last night, the major candidates used a locally televised debate to outline their platforms and display their personalities to the voters.

Last night's debate showed a different side of local politics, as the candidates focused on elevating themselves rather than undermining their opponents. With the current mayor leaving after an eight-year term, many people have called for a successor who will shake things up. Jeremy Broadman and [**Henry Brewer/Andre Jackson**] answered tough questions from area voters, on topics ranging from education to zoning.

Marty Gray, a former schoolteacher, wanted to know how the candidates planned to address the recent funding cuts to after school programs. "What are students going to do now that the programs are being cut? What are the options for working parents?" Both Broadman and [**Brewer/Jackson**] said they were willing to work with area organizations such as the YMCA and Boys and Girls Club to address the situation until permanent funds could be secured. However, neither candidate was clear about the possible sources for these funds.

Most importantly, the candidates finally took sides on the issue of whether or not the city will renew its contract with Enviro-Tech, [**despite several bids from smaller companies, the city decided to go with the country's largest trash-burning company/despite several concerns about the company's English-only policy and a promise from the city to end business with such companies.**] Broadman, 46, supports the contract renewal: "The city needs more time to fully develop and implement a recycling plan." [**Brewer/Jackson**], 47, does not want to renew the contract: "We can start recycling immediately and send the non-recyclable trash to landfills. The burning has to stop!" Brewer/Jackson mentioned during the debate that his position was supported by the Local Association of Latino Leaders, who have also endorsed his candidacy.

In a recent poll, 63% of voters felt [**that the environment/that English-only policies**] had become an important issue in this election. Over the past few weeks, both sides tried to convince the candidates to take a stand on this issue. It looks as if the voters will have their say on Election Day regarding the issue of trash burning in the city.

Photos of the fictional candidates can be viewed at andreabenjaminphd.com/onlineappendix/.

NOTES

1. This approach is rather cautious, as all endorsements are not created equal. That is, it will likely understate the value of some endorsements and overstate the value of others.
2. However, in two elections (New York 1997; Los Angeles 2001), race was made salient in the campaign and co-ethnic leader endorsements did not influence vote choice in those elections.
3. Note that Hahn also tried to link Villaraigosa to drug dealers. See R. Orlov. "Fight to the finish; candidates criss-cross city; two years of campaigning gets down to the final hours." June 3, 2001. *The Daily News of Los Angeles*, N1.
4. Note that many Blacks liked and respected Hahn's father, who was also a prominent politician in Los Angeles with long-standing ties to the Black community.
5. 1993–2001. Sonenshein and Pinkus 2005, The Center for the Study of Los Angeles.
6. I researched the race of the candidates in all the elections used in the larger Hajnal and Trounstine data set: Austin, Baltimore, Boston, Chicago, Columbus, Dallas, Denver, Detroit, El Paso, Houston, Indianapolis, Jacksonville, Los Angeles, Memphis, Milwaukee, Nashville, New York, Philadelphia, Phoenix, San Antonio, San Diego, San Francisco, San Jose, Seattle, and Washington (2014, 69). I also examined the race of the candidates in the 96 mayoral and runoff elections ranging from 1989 to 2009, plus I added New York and Los Angeles in 2009 and 2013 and Houston in 2005, 2007, 2009, 2011, and 2013 (105 elections total). There were 65 elections when Blacks had the opportunity to vote for a Black candidate. There were 24 elections when Latinos had the opportunity to vote for a Latino candidate.
7. This allows me to keep the basic information about the candidate the same across all the treatments and to change only the race of the candidate, the presence of an endorsement, and the racial/ethnic salience. Previous research shows that people often assume the Black candidate is more liberal, so this helps me to account for that (McDermott 1998).
8. One event was Juneteenth in Ann Arbor, MI. The other event was Arts, Beats, and Eats in Pontiac, MI. Again, these events were simply places where large numbers of African Americans were available to take the survey.
9. Using Qualtrics, an online survey program.
10. The text for the email recruitment is as follows: "Are you interested in politics? How would you like to make $5 for simply giving your opinion? Simply complete this short political survey and you can receive a $5 gift card

to Amazon. Amazon carries music, books, shoes, clothing, etc." The link to the survey was then embedded in the email.
11. Higher education is associated with greater electoral participation (Verba, Schlozman, and Brady 1996).
12. Very few (20) respondents in any treatment cell selected Jeremy Broadman, so I combined undecided and Jeremy Broadman for ease of analysis. However, I did run the analysis comparing support for candidate 2 to support for candidate 1. The results are not very helpful because in three cases, no Black respondents selected candidate 1, which meant those subjects were dropped from the analyses.
13. In a test to see if the effects are different from one another, I find that the estimate for the endorsed Latino candidate when race is salient treatment (B_7) is different from the endorsed Latino candidate treatment (B_3) ($p < 0.001$; two-tailed test) and the endorsed White candidate when race is salient treatment (B_6) ($p < 0.001$; two-tailed test). However, the difference between the endorsed Latino candidate treatment (B_3) and the endorsed White candidate when race is salient treatment (B_6) is not statistically significantly different.
14. "Kenneth Hahn's legacy serves his son well in mayor's race." *Los Angeles Times*. April 3, 2001.
15. Again, not enough respondents in any treatment cell selected "Jeremy Broadman," so I combined "Undecided" and "Jeremy Broadman" for ease of analysis.
16. The results in cell (h) are also statistically significant relative to cells (d) and (g) ($p < 0.01$; two-tailed test).
17. Only 15 respondents said they would vote for Jeremy Broadman.
18. Only seven respondents selected Jeremy Broadman.
19. These data are part of a coauthored project with Boris Ricks.
20. While all polling places in the city of Los Angeles were eligible for selection, only 25 polling places were selected and the racially stratified homogenous precinct methodology was applied to the Mayoral General Election Exit Poll (five polling places of each racial/ethnic category: White, Black/African American, Latino, Asian, and mixed precincts), because of the size of Los Angeles and consideration for a manageable research. At each selected polling place, CSLA researchers implemented a 2–2 skip pattern. Survey distributors were advised to ask every other person who exited the polling place to participate in the survey, regardless of whether they agreed to participate. Surveys were administered during polling hours, from 7 A.M. to 8 P.M., to same-day voters at the selected polling locations (Guerra and Gilbert 2013).
21. According to the Census, Los Angeles was 48% Latino, 28% White, non-Latino, 9% Black, and 11% Asian American (http://quickfacts.census.gov/qfd/states/06/0644000.html).
22. The San Fernando Valley is more conservative, is Whiter than the rest of the city, and has tried to secede from the rest of the city in the past.
23. We did not ask the candidates to indicate a top Jewish endorser.

3

The Co-ethnic Elite Cues Theory and Elite Black–Latino Coalitions

Dispelling the Myth: Blacks and Latinos Support Elite Black–Latino Coalitions

"Black and Latino coalitions may appear to work on a political level, with mayoral candidate Fernando Ferrer enjoying the backing of many of the city's black leaders. But those alliances are harder to build on the streets."
– "Blacks & Mexicans scrap in S.I." *New York Daily News*[1]

INTRODUCTION

As cities like Chicago, Houston, Los Angeles, and New York grow more diverse, the question of the viability of electoral coalitions becomes increasingly important. As we saw in the Introduction, candidates must appeal to voters from more than one racial/ethnic group in order to win elections. Unlike state and national elections, many local elections are nonpartisan. This means that relying on the party cue next to a candidate's name is not an option for voters in local elections. The data from recent local elections in Chicago, Los Angeles, New York, and Houston suggest that voters rely on other cues: the race of the candidate and the racial composition of the candidate's supporters (see local election results in the Elections Appendix). The general pattern that emerges from recent elections is simple: Blacks and Latinos typically vote for in-group candidates – candidates from their own racial/ethnic groups – at high rates. This was the case in Houston in 1997 and 2001 and in New York in 2009 for a majority of African-American voters. A majority of Latino voters also demonstrated strong in-group candidate support in Houston in 2001, New York in 2001 in the Democratic runoff and 2005, and in Los Angeles in 2001, 2005, and 2013.

The real-world elections also demonstrate that Blacks and Latinos engage in cross-ethnic voting (support out-group candidates). Sometimes, a majority of Blacks vote for Latino candidates (Los Angeles 2005; New York 2001 in the Democratic runoff and 2005) and a majority of Latinos votes for Black candidates (Houston 1997; New York 2009). One alternative explanation for why Blacks and Latinos may support out-group candidates is that the out-group candidates share their issue position (Bullock and Campbell 1984; Downs 1957). One weakness of election data is that we do not know *why* Blacks and Latinos voted for out-group candidates. That Blacks and Latinos voted for the same candidate does not prove that votes were cast in support of an Elite Black–Latino Coalition. In the New York 2005 mayoral election, co-ethnic elites called on Blacks and Latinos to support the Latino candidate in an explicit Elite Black–Latino Coalition. Blacks and Latinos heard the call and voted accordingly, but the Latino candidate, Ferrer, did not win the election. However, in the Chicago 2015 election, the Latino candidate called on Blacks to support an explicit Elite Black–Latino Coalition, but he was unsuccessful at gaining a majority of the Black vote. The first goal of this chapter is to determine if Blacks and Latinos are simply voting for the same candidate because of issue positions, or if they are supportive of out-group minority candidates in the context of an Elite Black–Latino Coalition.

The pattern among White voters in these local elections is less clear. When faced with one minority candidate, a majority of White voters often select the White candidate (Los Angeles 2001; New York 2001, 2005, and 2009; and Houston 1997). It may be that White voters simply prefer the White candidate on the basis of issues (Bullock and Campbell 1984). But White voters do not always vote for White candidates. In Los Angeles in 2005, a majority of White voters did vote for the Latino candidate, along with Blacks and Latinos. Adding an additional layer to the puzzle is the fact that, if there is a candidate supported by a majority of Blacks and a majority of Latinos, Whites often do not support that candidate (Houston 1997; New York 2001, 2005, and 2009). This is particularly true when that candidate is a minority, as in Houston 1997 and New York 2005 and 2009 – the minority candidate garnered only 30% of White votes in each of these contests. The second goal of this chapter is to determine how White voters respond to Black and Latino candidates and, perhaps more importantly, how they respond to those candidates in the context of an Elite Black–Latino Coalition. In the Introduction, we saw that Whites and Latinos often support the same winning candidates, that Blacks and Latinos often support the same losing candidates, and that Whites and Blacks hardly ever support the same candidates (Hajnal and Trounstine 2014). This chapter asks what is the most effective tool for candidates: to go it alone, receive endorsements, or form explicit coalitions?

ELITE BLACK–LATINO COALITIONS: THE ROUTE TO INCORPORATION

The literature regarding the success of liberal coalitions suggests that Whites and minorities can work together to gain entry into local government when certain conditions are met (Browning, Marshall, and Tabb 1984; Sonenshein 1993). These conditions include shared ideology, interests, population, and leaders willing to work together to build the coalition. In these studies, liberal White voters were very important since the data were collected at a time when most localities were not majority-minority. Today, cities like Chicago, Los Angeles, Houston, and New York are majority-minority cities. In this context, it is a plausible assumption that Blacks and Latinos may decide to build their own coalitions, given their shared experiences with discrimination, a shared wealth gap compared to Whites, and segregation (Segura and Rodrigues 2006). The winner-take-all nature of mayoral elections, coupled with the fact that racial/ethnic groups may not be able to go it alone, means that coalitions are one, but not the only route that groups may take to elect their preferred candidate to office.

THREAT AND PREFERENCES: WHITE VOTERS AND THE FEAR OF MINORITY POLITICS

Even though cities like Los Angeles, New York, and Houston have grown more diverse, White voters are still very important because of their high levels of voter turnout compared to Blacks and Latinos (Burns et al. 2001; Rosenstone and Hansen 1993). This means that even the most confident candidate cannot discount White voters in his or her quest to win an election. Hajnal and Trounstine find that overall voter turnout is low in many local elections, but that White voters are less likely to turn out as the size of the minority populations increase (2005). Further, after they simulate 10 mayoral elections, they find that *if* Latinos had turned out at higher rates, the losing candidate would have won the election (New York 2001; Houston 2001; and San Diego

2004). Increased minority populations are also associated with a decrease in turnout among Whites in the South (Key 1949; Leighley 2001; and Leighley and Vedlitz 1999). Kaufmann found that when race becomes salient in local elections, White voters, especially moderate Whites, are more likely to vote for White candidates (2004). It could be the case, however, that White voters simply prefer a particular candidate because of his or her issue stance (Bullock and Campbell 1984; Campbell et al. 1960). Finally, as the real-world elections show, when Blacks and Latinos form a coalition, as they did in the 2005 New York mayoral election, Whites tend to vote for the non-minority candidate. While this one election is instructive, it is not clear how White voters will perceive a call for an explicit Elite Black–Latino Coalition. This chapter also considers the relationship between the context of local elections and White voter response.

CO-ETHNIC ELITE CUES AND CANDIDATE SUPPORT

Campbell and colleagues said that endorsements were the "transmissions of standards" for identity groups (1960, 313). The authors showed that when Black leaders were nearly unanimous in their support for the Democratic ticket in 1952, Blacks responded with nearly unanimous support at the polls. When the Black leadership divided tits support four years later, the Black votes were also divided (Campbell et al. 1960). Lau and Redlawsk note that endorsements allow voters to rely on trusted individuals to help them make tough decisions (2001). Rappaport, Stone, and Abramowitz showed that endorsements from women's groups are less persuasive to women, but that endorsements from teachers' and labor unions move union members to vote for a particular candidate (1991). McDermott also found that union endorsements persuaded liberal voters to prefer Democratic candidates, but when unions endorsed Republican candidates, conservatives did not prefer the endorsed candidate (2006). Taken together, this suggests that endorsements from co-ethnic elites may help Black and Latino voters decide to vote for candidates from the out-group. In Chapter 2, I provided evidence to support this claim, based on the Co-ethnic Elite Cues Theory, which suggests that *in the absence of partisan cues and in-group candidates, when race/ethnicity becomes salient in an election, candidate endorsements by co-ethnic leaders would prompt minority group members to vote for a particular candidate, even if the candidate is from another ethnic group.* Experimental data presented in Chapter 2 show that when racial and ethnic issues are a part of the campaign, Blacks are willing to vote for a Latino candidate. This is especially true when the Latino candidate receives a Black endorsement. Latino voters also perceive Black candidates with Latino endorsements as sympathetic, but when ethnicity becomes salient, they are also more likely to perceive a White candidate with a Latino endorsement as sympathetic. Building on the results from Chapter 2, this chapter seeks to assess levels of cross-ethnic voting when co-ethnic elite endorsements are present in the context of a call to support an Elite Black–Latino Coalition.

In this chapter, the context of the Elite Black–Latino Coalition is meant to heighten racial and ethnic salience. Racial and ethnic salience can enter the campaign context in a number of ways: when the news covers the campaign and mentions candidates' race or ethnicity, when candidates themselves mention race or ethnicity, or when candidates take positions on issues that are racial or ethnic in nature. In this chapter, then, there are some treatment conditions in which the candidates themselves are making race and ethnicity salient by asking voters to support them in the context of the Elite Black–Latino Coalition. This serves two purposes: it allows me to present evidence that race and ethnicity can become salient in multiple ways. In Chapter 2, issues were mentioned in some of the experimental treatments. In this chapter, the treatment mentions the race and ethnicity of supporters. This context also allows me to assess levels of support for candidates in the context of Elite Black–Latino Coalitions among Blacks, Latinos, and Whites.

HYPOTHESES

H_1: Blacks and Latinos will be more supportive of out-group minority candidates that have co-ethnic elite endorsements.

H_2: Blacks and Latinos will be more supportive of out-group minority candidates in the context of an Elite Black–Latino Coalition.

H_3: White voters will be less supportive of minority candidates; this will be especially true when the minority candidate has been endorsed by Blacks or Latinos in the context of an Elite Black–Latino Coalition.

DATA AND METHODS

In the summer of 2012, I fielded a nationally representative survey experiment to assess the levels of mayoral candidate support among

Blacks and Latinos for Elite Black–Latino Coalitions and the White response to these coalitions.[2] The results from the experiments in Chapter 2 provided one test of the Co-ethnic Elite Cues Theory, but I wanted the opportunity to test the theory using a nationally representative sample. Additionally, Whites were not included in the survey experiments in Chapter 2, so this experimental sample includes Whites. The experimental design featured seven treatments with mostly identical newspaper stories about a local mayoral election (see Table 3.1 for an overview and this chapter's Appendix for full treatments). The treatments included photographs of the candidates. Each article described how the fictional candidates planned to handle unemployment in the city. In each article, Jack Brown (a White candidate) plans to create new jobs through tax incentives that will draw businesses to the area. Candidate 2 (which varies by treatment) plans to create jobs by making it easier for community members to open businesses in the area. In one condition, candidate 2 is Jim Davis and he is White. Whites, Blacks, and Latinos read this treatment. In three conditions, candidate 2 is Juan Garcia and he is Latino. Only Whites and Blacks read these treatments. In three conditions, candidate 2 is James Washington and he is Black. Only Whites and Latinos read these treatments. In the treatment with two White candidates, only the issues are discussed. In the subsequent treatments, I manipulate the race of the candidate (Black or Latino), add an endorsement for the Black or Latino candidate (from Latino leaders or Black leaders, respectively), and finally, I add a call to voters to support the candidate in an Elite Black–Latino Coalition. White subjects were randomly assigned to one of the seven treatments. Blacks and Latinos were randomly assigned to one of four treatments. The data from the real-world elections provide plenty of evidence that Blacks will support a Black candidate and Latinos will support a Latino candidate, so I exposed only Black and Latino subjects to out-group minority candidates as candidate 2.

After reading one of the fictional newspaper articles, subjects were asked about their willingness to support Brown or Davis/Garcia/Washington. The randomization worked across all treatments, for all racial/ethnic groups. One of the benefits of using the Knowledge Networks data is that they ask the demographic information outside of the context of the survey experiment. This is particularly important here as it allows me to consider the role of racial and ethnic identity without asking the respondents their racial and ethnic identities. In all, there were 784 respondents, which include 369 Whites, 212 Blacks, and 203 Latinos.

TABLE 3.1 *Experimental Treatments*

1. Universal Baseline: Two White Candidates
   Headline: Nonpartisan election coming down to the wire
   Photos of both candidates
   Body: Candidate stances on issues
   Read by Blacks, Latinos, and Whites

Out-Group Baseline	No Coalition	Coalition
2. White Candidate (1) vs. Latino Candidate (2)	3. White Candidate (1) vs. Latino Candidate (2)	4. White Candidate (1) vs. Latino Candidate (2)
Headline: Nonpartisan election coming down to the wire	Headline: Nonpartisan election coming down to the wire, Black leaders endorse Garcia	Headline: Nonpartisan election coming down to the wire, Black leaders endorse C2, note Black–Latino coalition
Photos of both candidates	Photos of both candidates	Photos of both candidates
Body: Candidate stances on issues	Body: Several Black leaders recently endorsed Garcia, citing the high numbers of unemployed Blacks and Latinos in the city.	Body: Several Black leaders recently endorsed Garcia, citing the high numbers of unemployed Blacks and Latinos in the city. They called on Blacks and Latinos to come together in this election and support the Black–Latino coalition in the city.
Read by: Blacks and Whites	Read by: Blacks and Whites	Read by: Blacks and Whites
5. White Candidate (1) vs. Black Candidate (2)	6. White Candidate (1) vs. Black Candidate (2)	7. White Candidate (1) vs. Black Candidate (2)
Headline: Nonpartisan election coming down to the wire	Headline: Nonpartisan election coming down to the wire, Latino leaders endorse Washington	Headline: Nonpartisan election coming down to the wire, Latino leaders endorse Washington, note Black–Latino coalition
Photos of both candidates	Photos of both candidates	Photos of both candidates
Body: Candidate stances on some issues	Body: Several Latino leaders recently endorsed Washington, citing the high numbers of unemployed Blacks and Latinos in the city.	Body: Several Latino leaders recently endorsed Washington, citing the high numbers of unemployed Blacks and Latinos in the city. They called on Blacks and Latinos to come together in this election and support the Black–Latino coalition in the city.
Read by: Latinos and Whites	Read by: Latinos and Whites	Read by: Latinos and Whites

The average level of education for all three groups was a high school diploma. Fifty-one percent of the subjects were women. The average age of the White subjects was 50. The average age for Blacks and Latinos was a little lower, at 47 and 41, respectively. In terms of average income, Whites had an average household income of $50,000–$59,000 per year. Blacks and Latinos both had an average household income of $35,000–$39,000 per year. Fifty-three percent of Whites in the sample are Republicans, 70% of the Latinos are Democrats, while 96% of the Blacks are Democrats.

TESTING THE VIABILITY OF ELITE BLACK–LATINO COALITIONS

In order to test my hypotheses, candidate preference was measured with the following question: "If the election were held today, which candidate would you vote for?" Response options for the treatments that featured two White candidates were "Jack Brown," "Jim Davis," or "Undecided." In the treatments that featured a White and a Latino candidate, response options were "Jack Brown," "Juan Garcia," or "Undecided." In the treatments that featured a White and a Black candidate, response options were "Jack Brown," "James Washington," or "Undecided." Responses were coded into a dichotomous variable where "1" indicates the respondent selected "Jim Davis," "Juan Garcia," or "James Washington," and a "0" indicates the respondent selected "Jack Brown" or "Undecided." A little more than 30% of the subjects selected a candidate, which means that most subjects abstained from this fictional election, which is consistent with recent levels of voter turnout in local elections. I use logistic regression analysis to estimate support for the minority candidate (Garcia or Washington, compared to support for Davis, the White candidate with the same issue positions as Garcia and Washington) by the various treatments among the three racial and ethnic groups.

Initially, I estimated these models with the endorsement and endorsement/coalitions treatments separate; however, while both treatments were significant from the baseline, they were not significant from one another, so I combined these two treatments for the analyses. Given this, I combine hypotheses one and two: $H_{1\,Combined}$: Blacks and Latinos will be more supportive of out-group minority candidates with co-ethnic elite endorsements in the context of an Elite Black–Latino Coalition.

Support for Black Candidates & Elite Black–Latino Coalition

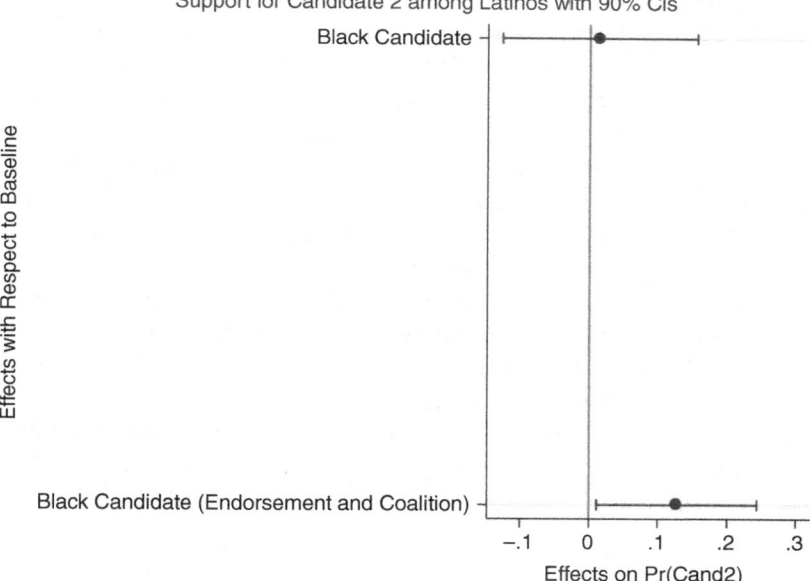

FIGURE 3.1 Support for Candidate 2 among Latinos
Marginal effects estimated from Table 3.1A in the Appendix for this chapter

LATINO SUPPORT FOR BLACK CANDIDATES AND AN ELITE BLACK–LATINO COALITION

To begin, I assess the level of support for Jim Washington among Latino Respondents. In Figure 3.1, I present the predicted probabilities for support for candidate 2, based on the logistic regression results, which can be found in the Appendix of this chapter. I consider the relationship between support for Washington among Latinos and the experimental conditions. The baseline here is the White vs. White treatment, and all comparisons are made against this treatment. When Latinos read about Washington, without any other information, they do not see a difference between him and Davis (one percentage point, not significant). Simply having a Black candidate does not lead Latinos in this sample to support the Black candidate (cross-ethnic voting). There is no difference in preference for candidate 2 between the baseline condition (Davis) and the condition in which candidate 2 is Black (Washington). When Latinos read about Washington with an endorsement from local Latino leaders/with an endorsement from local Latino leaders in the context of an Elite Black–Latino Coalition, Latino voters were 13 percentage points more likely to prefer him to Davis (p < 0.10). This lends some support to hypotheses one and two combined, that Blacks and Latinos will be more supportive of out-group minority candidates with co-ethnic elite endorsements and in the context of a coalition. This is different from the results we saw in Chapter 2. In that experiment, endorsements from Latinos leaders did not move Latino voters to prefer Black candidates. Here, we see that the endorsements do move respondents.

In sum, Latinos will not simply vote for any Black candidate. In the presence of a co-ethnic elite endorsement and in the context of an Elite Black–Latino Coalition, however, Latinos are more likely to prefer a Black candidate. These results suggest that if Black candidates want support from Latino voters, they will have to do more than simply be Black candidates: they must seek out Latino endorsements and publicize their involvement in an Elite Black–Latino Coalition.

BLACK SUPPORT FOR LATINO CANDIDATES AND AN ELITE BLACK–LATINO COALITION

Now I turn to Black support for Latino candidates and Elite Black–Latino Coalitions. I compare support for Garcia and Davis among Black subjects, and I present these results in Figure 3.2 (for the logistic regression results, please see the Appendix for this chapter). Here I am interested in levels of support for Garcia by the treatment conditions. Similar to the results among Latinos, there is no difference between support for Garcia and support for Davis. When Blacks read about Garcia on his own, they are not more likely to prefer him to Davis (14 percentage points, not significant). There is no evidence of cross-ethnic voting here. When Blacks read about Garcia with an endorsement/in the context of an Elite Black–Latino Coalition, they are 22 percentage points more likely to prefer him to Davis (p < 0.01). These results provide support for hypotheses one and two combined, that Blacks and Latinos will be more supportive of out-group minority candidates with co-ethnic elite endorsements/in the context of an Elite Black–Latino Coalition.

Blacks, like Latinos in this sample, are reluctant to support the out-group candidate on his own, but when that candidate is endorsed by a co-ethnic/that candidate is part of an Elite Black–Latino Coalition, Blacks are much more likely to support the Latino candidate. To the

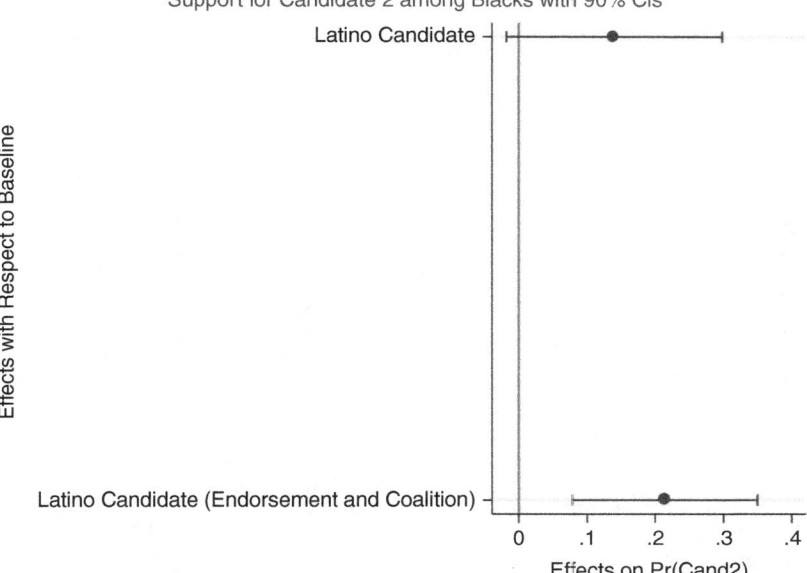

FIGURE 3.2 Support for Candidate 2 among Blacks
Marginal effects estimated from Table 3.2A in the Appendix for this chapter

extent that Latino candidates need support from Black voters, they will also have to do more than simply be Latino candidates: they should seek out Black endorsements and publicize their involvement in an Elite Black–Latino Coalition. There is no evidence of cross-ethnic voting without co-ethnic endorsements or coalitions among Blacks and Latinos in this study.

WHITES, MINORITY CANDIDATES, AND ELITE BLACK–LATINO COALITIONS

These results show that Blacks and Latinos are amenable to vote for outgroup minority candidates when an in-group member endorses the outgroup candidate and in the context of an Elite Black–Latino Coalition. Now we turn to the White voters in this sample. Whites were randomly assigned to all the treatments. First, I consider their support for Washington, the Black candidate. Then, I present results on White support for Garcia, the Latino candidate. In Figure 3.3, I estimate support for

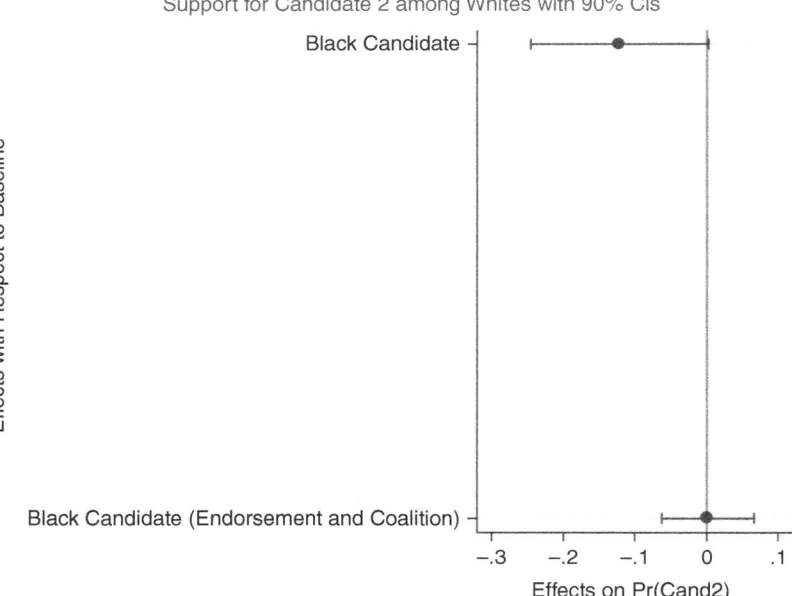

FIGURE 3.3 Support for Candidate 2 among Whites
Marginal effects estimated from Table 3.3A in the Appendix for this chapter

Washington among Whites. As you can see, Whites are less likely to prefer Washington. This might be because the election depicted in the experiment indicates that there is not an incumbent in the election. Hajnal finds that Whites are more likely to support Black mayors when they are incumbents (2001). When Whites read about Washington alone, they were 12 percentage points less likely to prefer Washington (p < 0.10). This provides some evidence for the first part of hypothesis three, that White voters will be less supportive of minority candidates. But, when a minority candidate is working with another minority group, as evidenced by an endorsement from the out-group and in the context of an Elite Black–Latino Coalition, there is no difference in support for Washington, which does not provide support for the second part of hypothesis three, that this will be especially true when the minority candidate has been endorsed by the out-group and in the context of an Elite Black–Latino Coalition. Thus it is not the Black candidate's involvement in an Elite Black–Latino Coalition/his receiving Latino endorsements that renders him less appealing to White voters. In this sample, a Black candidate

Whites, Minority Candidates, & Elite Black–Latino Coalitions

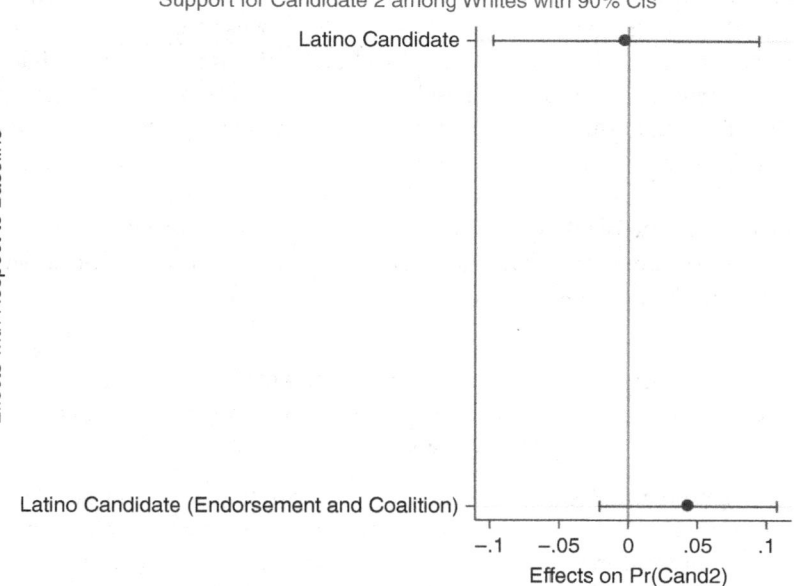

FIGURE 3.4 Support for Candidate 2 among Whites
Marginal effects estimated from Table 3.4A in the Appendix for this chapter

with Latino endorsements/in an Elite Black–Latino Coalition is equally appealing to White voters. In this sample, though, a Black candidate without Latino ties is less likely to get White votes.

In Figure 3.4, I consider White preferences for the Latino candidate, Garcia. The analysis shows that there is no difference in preference for Garcia over the non-Latino candidates by any of the treatments – none that is significant. These results suggest that voters are engaged in issue voting (Bullock and Campbell 1984). That is, they are not concerned with race or ethnicity as much as they are concerned with the issue positions of the candidates. That Whites see no difference between Garcia and the White candidate may indicate that when it comes to a Latino candidate, it is about issues, not ethnicity. These findings are contrary to previous experimental findings that Whites are less likely to support Latino candidates (McConnaughy et al. 2010). These results provide no support for hypothesis three, that White voters will be less supportive of minority candidates; this will be especially true when the minority candidate has been endorsed by Blacks or Latinos and in the context of a Black–Latino coalition. However, the results for the Black candidate (without a Latino

112 Co-ethnic Elite Cues and Elite Black–Latino Coalitions

endorsement and without an Elite Black–Latino Coalition) suggest it is still about race, not just issues. That Whites in this sample were less likely to vote for a candidate when he is Black, even when the candidate had the same issue position as the baseline candidate, is troubling. When presented with Latino candidates, White voters seem unconcerned about ethnicity, but with a Black candidate alone, race concerns them. Yet, when Latinos support the Black candidate (as signaled through endorsements/an Elite Black–Latino Coalition), Whites did not punish the Black candidate. It may be because the Latino endorsements and coalition send a signal to Whites that Blacks are less group-oriented.

CO-ETHNIC ENDORSEMENTS AND ELITE BLACK–LATINO COALITIONS MOVE LATINO AND BLACK VOTERS, WITHOUT ALIENATING WHITE VOTERS

This chapter had several aims: the first was to show that Blacks and Latinos are willing to support out-group minority candidates with co-ethnic elite endorsements and the second was to determine levels of cross-ethnic voting in the context of Elite Black–Latino Coalitions. Blacks and Latinos were more supportive of the out-group minority candidate in the endorsement and coalition treatments, so I combined them for the analyses. The data presented here indicate that Blacks and Latinos do not automatically vote for out-group minority candidates, but that they will vote for out-group minority candidates when there is a co-ethnic elite endorsement/when that candidate calls on them to support an Elite Black–Latino Coalition. One important finding in this chapter is that Blacks *and* Latinos indicate a higher level of support for Garcia and Washington, compared to Davis, when these candidates receive endorsements from co-ethnic leaders/in the context of an Elite Black–Latino Coalition. This is similar to the results we saw in Chapter 2 among Blacks. The results among Latinos are different from Chapter 2, where we observed that Latinos did not distinguish between the candidates even when there was a co-ethnic elite endorsement in the experimental data and in Los Angeles, where only the Spanish newspaper endorsement increased support for Garcetti. Here, Latinos expressed greater support for Candidate Washington when local Latino leaders endorsed him/in the context of the Elite Black–Latino Coalition.

These results suggest that Black and Latino candidates may do well to simply seek out endorsements from out-group community leaders and organizations. Here, the real-world election results are also instructive:

only two elections featured an explicit call to support an Elite Black–Latino Coalition (New York 2005 and Chicago 2015). The Latino candidate was successful in gaining Black and Latino support in the New York 2005 context, but this was not the case in the Chicago 2015 election. Blacks did not rise up to support that candidate, even as he made explicit appeals to Black voters about the coalition. Yet, many real-world elections feature Black candidates with Latino endorsements and Latino candidates with Black endorsements. Given the lack of explicit Black–Latino coalitions in the real world, candidates do not gain more support from forming an explicit coalition, so it seems they are doing all they need to do to gain support from voters from the out-group.

The third aim of this chapter was to assess how White voters respond to minority candidates in a variety of contexts. The data presented here provide no support for hypothesis three, that White voters will be less supportive of minority candidates; this will be especially true when the minority candidate has been endorsed by the out-group and in the context of an Elite Black–Latino Coalition. Whites did not punish the Black candidate when he had Latino endorsements/in the context of an Elite Black–Latino Coalition. Similarly, they did not punish the Latino candidate in any treatment. In many ways, this is good news. It was long feared that Black and Latino candidates had to appease White voters or fear losing elections. That is, Whites expressed similar levels of support for the liberal White candidate and the Latino candidate regardless of the treatment. Only the Black candidate alone received less support. It is still the case that White voters often make up a majority of voters in many cities. The data presented here indicate that Black and Latino candidates need not worry too much about scaring off White voters. With the exception of the case when a Black candidate does not have Latino support, Whites in this sample appear to focus more on the issues than on the race and ethnicity of the candidates. This suggests that Black candidates would do well to seek out Latino endorsements, as it seems that with them, Whites are less likely to punish the Black candidate (see Tables 3.3A and 3.4A in the Appendix for this chapter).

CONCLUSIONS

Consistent with the Co-ethnic Elite Cues Theory, this chapter shows that Latinos and Blacks do rely on co-ethnic elite cues when deciding to engage in cross-ethnic voting. These co-ethnic elite endorsements are persuasive in the context of calls to support an Elite Black–Latino Coalition with co-ethnic elite endorsements. There are, however, several limitations to this study. First, there is no coalition-only treatment, as co-ethnic elite endorsements are also present in these treatments. This makes it hard to determine if Blacks and Latinos were responding to the endorsements or to the call to support the coalition, so I combined these two treatments for my analysis. Note, though, that it is hard to imagine an Elite Black–Latino Coalition that did not feature endorsements. These results are consistent with the 2005 New York mayoral race, in which Fernando Ferrer received several key endorsements from Black leaders across the city and called on Blacks and Latinos to support his Elite Black–Latino Coalition. A majority of Blacks and Latinos voted for Ferrer in that election (see the Elections Appendix). Still, more research is needed to fully disentangle these differences.

White voters did not seem to distinguish candidates by their race or ethnicity. With the exception of the Black candidate without Latino endorsements or coalitions, Whites were not more likely to vote for a White candidate than a minority candidate with the same issue positions. Among Whites, the real-world elections are also instructive. Whites were willing to support the Latino candidate in Los Angeles in 2005 along with Blacks and Latinos (see the Elections Appendix). The experimental data suggest that Latino candidates may have the freedom to work with Blacks without alienating White voters. If there is a new liberal coalition, Latino candidates have the potential to be the face of such a coalition. Given that Black voters are more likely to vote for a Latino candidate with Black endorsements and that White voters do not punish that Latino candidate, Latino candidates may appeal to the greatest number of voters. With the right leadership, there seems to be room for Blacks to support Latino candidates and still reach White voters (Sonenshein 1993).

NEXT STEPS

While this chapter has established a clearer picture of the effects of co-ethnic elite endorsements and minority coalitions on support for outgroup minority candidates among Blacks, Latinos, and Whites, there is still one aspect we have not addressed. Thus far, this book has not provided any information on the ways in which co-ethnic elite endorsements may influence racial attitudes among Blacks, Latinos, and Whites. In the next chapter, I use the data from the study in this chapter to explore this relationship.

APPENDIX

TABLE 3.1A *Logistic Regression Analysis of Support for Candidate 2 among Latinos*

	2 White Candidates= Baseline	Marginal Effects Likelihood of Preferring Candidate 2
Intercept	−2.66*** (0.60)	
Black Candidate Treatment	0.14 (0.79)	0.01 (0.09)
Black Candidate with Latino Endorsement and Black Candidate with Latino Endorsement and Coalition Treatments Combined	1.18+ (0.65)	0.13+ (0.07)
Log Likelihood	−74.59	
N	203	203

Notes: +p < 0.10; * p < 0.05; ** p < 0.01; *** p < 0.001 for a two-tailed test, except for constant.

This analysis uses logistic regression to estimate the relationship between candidate preferences by experimental treatment. All comparisons are to the baseline, which featured two White candidates. The results show that Latinos are more likely to express a preference for a Black candidate, but only when that candidate receives a Latino endorsement or in the context of an Elite Black–Latino Coalition. Marginal effects are the likelihood of preferring candidate 2, given the treatment, compared to the baseline).

TABLE 3.2A *Logistic Regression Analysis of Support for Candidate 2 among Blacks*

	2 White Candidates= Baseline	Marginal Effects Likelihood of Preferring Candidate 2
Intercept	−2.24*** (0.47)	
Latino Candidate Treatment	0.85 (0.59)	0.14 (0.10)
Latino Candidate with Black Endorsement and Latino Candidate with Black	1.30** (0.51)	0.22** (0.08)

(continued)

TABLE 3.2A *(continued)*

	2 White Candidates= Baseline	Marginal Effects Likelihood of Preferring Candidate 2
Endorsement and Coalition Treatments Combined		
Log Likelihood	−106.89	
N	212	212

Notes: +p < 0.10; *p < 0.05; **p < 0.01; ***p < 0.001 for a two-tailed test, except for constant.

This analysis uses logistic regression to estimate the relationship between candidate preferences by experimental treatment. All comparisons are to the baseline, which featured 2 White candidates. These results show that Blacks are more likely to prefer a Latino candidate when he has received a Black endorsement and in the context of an Elite Black–Latino Coalition. Marginal effects are the likelihood of preferring candidate 2, given the treatment, compared to the baseline.

TABLE 3.3A *Logistic Regression Analysis of Support for Candidate 2 among Whites*

	Non-Black Candidates= Baseline	Marginal Effects Likelihood of Preferring Candidate 2
Intercept	−1.72***	
	(0.19)	
Black Candidate Treatment	−1.01+	−0.12+
	(0.63)	(0.07)
Black Candidate with Latino Endorsement and Black Candidate with Latino Endorsement and Coalition Treatments Combined	0.02 (0.32)	0.01 (0.04)
Log Likelihood	−148.27	
N	369	369

Notes: +p < 0.10; *p < 0.05; **p < 0.01; ***p < 0.001 for a two-tailed test, except for constant.

This analysis uses logistic regression to estimate the relationship between candidate preferences by experimental treatment. Marginal effects are the likelihood of preferring candidate 2, given the treatment, compared to the baseline.

TABLE 3.4A *Logistic Regression Analysis of Support for Candidate 2 among Whites*

	Non-Latino Candidates= Baseline	Marginal Effects Likelihood of Preferring Candidate 2
Intercept	−1.92***	
	(0.21)	
Latino Candidate Treatment	−0.02	0.01
	(0.48)	(0.06)
Latino Candidate with Black Endorsement and Latino Candidate with Black Endorsement and Coalition Treatments Combined	0.36 (0.32)	0.06 (0.05)
Log Likelihood	−149.37	
N	369	

Notes: +p < 0.10; *p < 0.05; **p < 0.01; ***p < 0.001 for a two-tailed test, except for constant.

This analysis uses logistic regression to estimate the relationship between candidate preferences by experimental treatment. Marginal effects are the likelihood of preferring candidate 2, given the treatment, compared to the baseline.

TREATMENTS

Universal Baseline (Read by Blacks, Latinos, and Whites)

Nonpartisan Election Coming Down to the Wire
Staff Desk

Despite unemployment rising above 10%, there is one job few people in the city seem to want: mayor. Still, if elections are all about the economy, it would seem both candidates are up for a challenge. Local unemployment has been higher than the state and national average over the past three years. Mayoral candidates Jack Brown, 44, and Jim Davis, 42, are battling in a tight runoff election to replace term-limited Mayor Susan Perry. The men come to the race having each served on the city council for the past four years.

In many ways, the candidates' policies are in sync on transportation, crime, and housing. While Brown and Davis both emphasized plans to create jobs, they disagree on how to accomplish this goal.

Brown says he'll create jobs by offering incentives to new businesses that bring jobs in the area. "If we can entice companies to come here, we can provide them with the workers they need."

Davis says he plans to create jobs by changing the city's loan program for small businesses. "We should offer more incentives for the members of this community to create jobs in this community."

Still, serious discussion about tax incentives, small businesses, and jobs is a worthy debate that highlights the range of economic issues facing the city.

Photos of the fictional candidates can be viewed at andreabenjaminphd.com/onlineappendix/.

Latino Candidate Treatment (Read by Whites and Blacks)

Nonpartisan Election Coming Down to the Wire
Staff Desk

Despite unemployment rising above 10%, there is one job few people in the city seem to want: mayor. Still, if elections are all about the economy, it would seem both candidates are up for a challenge. Local unemployment has been higher than the state and national average over the past three years. Mayoral candidates Jack Brown, 44, and Juan Garcia, 42, are battling in a tight runoff election to replace term-limited Mayor Susan Perry. The men come to the race having each served on the city council for the past four years.

In many ways, the candidates' policies are in sync on transportation, crime, and housing. While Brown and Garcia both emphasized plans to create jobs, they disagree on how to accomplish this goal.

Brown says he'll create jobs by offering incentives to new businesses that bring jobs in the area. "If we can entice companies to come here, we can provide them with the workers they need."

Garcia says he plans to create jobs by changing the city's loan program for small businesses. "We should offer more incentives for the members of this community to create jobs in this community."

Still, serious discussion about tax incentives, small businesses, and jobs is a worthy debate that highlights the range of economic issues facing the city.

Photos of the fictional candidates can be viewed at andreabenjaminphd.com/onlineappendix/.

Latino Candidate with Black Endorsement Treatment (Read by Blacks and Whites)

Nonpartisan Election Coming Down to the Wire, Black Leaders Endorse Garcia
Staff Desk

Despite unemployment rising above 10%, there is one job few people in the city seem to want: mayor. Still, if elections are all about the economy, it would seem both candidates are up for a challenge. Local unemployment has been higher than the state and national average over the past three years. Mayoral candidates Jack Brown, 44, and Juan Garcia, 42, are battling in a tight runoff election to replace term-limited Mayor Susan Perry. The men come to the race having each served on the city council for the past four years.

In many ways, the candidates' policies are in sync on transportation, crime, and housing. While Brown and Garcia both emphasized plans to create jobs, they disagree on how to accomplish this goal.

Brown says he'll create jobs by offering incentives to new businesses that bring jobs in the area. "If we can entice companies to come here, we can provide them with the workers they need."

Garcia says he plans to create jobs by changing the city's loan program for small businesses. "We should offer more incentives for the members of this community to create jobs in this community."

Several Black leaders recently endorsed Garcia, citing the high numbers of unemployed Blacks and Latinos in the city.

Still, serious discussion about tax incentives, small businesses, and jobs is a worthy debate that highlights the range of economic issues facing the city.

Photos of the fictional candidates can be viewed at andreabenjaminphd.com/onlineappendix/.

Latino Candidate with Black Endorsement in a Black–Latino Coalition Treatment (Read by Blacks and Whites)

Nonpartisan Election Coming Down to the Wire, Black Leaders Endorse Garcia, Note Local Black–Latino Coalition

Staff Desk

Despite unemployment rising above 10%, there is one job few people in the city seem to want: mayor. Still, if elections are all about the economy, it would seem both candidates are up for a challenge. Local unemployment has been higher than the state and national average over the past three years. Mayoral candidates Jack Brown, 44, and Juan Garcia, 42, are battling in a tight runoff election to replace term-limited Mayor Susan Perry. The men come to the race having each served on the city council for the past four years.

In many ways, the candidates' policies are in sync on transportation, crime, and housing. While Brown and Garcia both emphasized plans to create jobs, they disagree on how to accomplish this goal.

Brown says he'll create jobs by offering incentives to new businesses that bring jobs in the area. "If we can entice companies to come here, we can provide them with the workers they need."

Garcia says he plans to create jobs by changing the city's loan program for small businesses. "We should offer more incentives for the members of this community to create jobs in this community."

Several Black leaders recently endorsed Garcia, citing the high numbers of unemployed Blacks and Latinos in the city. They called on Blacks and Latinos to come together in this election and support the Black–Latino coalition in the city.

Photos of the fictional candidates can be viewed at andreabenjaminphd.com/book.

Black Candidate Treatment (Read by Latinos and Whites)

Nonpartisan Election Coming Down to the Wire
Staff Desk

Despite unemployment rising above 10%, there is one job few people in the city seem to want: mayor. Still, if elections are all about the economy, it would seem both candidates are up for a challenge. Local unemployment has been higher than the state and national average over the past three years. Mayoral candidates Jack Brown, 44, and James Washington, 42, are battling in a tight runoff election to replace term-limited Mayor Susan Perry. The men come to the race having each served on the city council for the past four years.

In many ways, the candidates' policies are in sync on transportation, crime, and housing. While Brown and Washington both emphasized plans to create jobs, they disagree on how to accomplish this goal.

Brown says he'll create jobs by offering incentives to new businesses that bring jobs in the area. "If we can entice companies to come here, we can provide them with the workers they need."

Washington says he plans to create jobs by changing the city's loan program for small businesses. "We should offer more incentives for the members of this community to create jobs in this community."

Still, serious discussion about tax incentives, small businesses, and jobs is a worthy debate that highlights the range of economic issues facing the city.

Photos of the fictional candidates can be viewed at andreabenjaminphd.com/onlineappendix/.

Black Candidate with Latino Endorsement Treatment
(Read by Latinos and Whites)

Nonpartisan Election Coming Down to the Wire, Latino Leaders Endorse Washington
Staff Desk

Despite unemployment rising above 10%, there is one job few people in the city seem to want: mayor. Still, if elections are all about the economy, it would seem both candidates are up for a challenge. Local unemployment has been higher than the state and national average over the past three years. Mayoral candidates Jack Brown, 44, and James Washington, 42, are battling in a tight runoff election to replace term-limited Mayor Susan Perry. The men come to the race having each served on the city council for the past four years.

In many ways, the candidates' policies are in sync on transportation, crime, and housing. While Brown and Washington both emphasized plans to create jobs, they disagree on how to accomplish this goal.

Brown says he'll create jobs by offering incentives to new businesses that bring jobs in the area. "If we can entice companies to come here, we can provide them with the workers they need."

Washington says he plans to create jobs by changing the city's loan program for small businesses. "We should offer more incentives for the members of this community to create jobs in this community."

Several Latino leaders recently endorsed Washington, citing the high numbers of unemployed Blacks and Latinos in the city.

Still, serious discussion about tax incentives, small businesses, and jobs is a worthy debate that highlights the range of economic issues facing the city.

Photos of the fictional candidates can be viewed at andreabenjaminphd.com/onlineappendix/.

Black Candidate with Latino Endorsement in a Black–Latino Coalition
Treatment (Read by Latinos and Whites)

Nonpartisan Election Coming Down to the Wire, Latino Leaders Endorse Washington, Note Local Black–Latino Coalition
Staff Desk

Despite unemployment rising above 10%, there is one job few people in the city seem to want: mayor. Still, if elections are all about the economy, it would seem both candidates are up for a challenge. Local unemployment has been higher than the state and national average over the past three years. Mayoral candidates Jack Brown, 44, and James Washington, 42, are battling in a tight runoff election to replace term-limited Mayor Susan Perry. The men come to the race having each served on the city council for the past four years.

In many ways, the candidates' policies are in sync on transportation, crime, and housing. While Brown and Washington both emphasized plans to create jobs, they disagree on how to accomplish this goal.

Brown says he'll create jobs by offering incentives to new businesses that bring jobs in the area. "If we can entice companies to come here, we can provide them with the workers they need."

Washington says he plans to create jobs by changing the city's loan program for small businesses. "We should offer more incentives for the members of this community to create jobs in this community."

Several Latino leaders recently endorsed Washington, citing the high numbers of unemployed Blacks and Latinos in the city. They called on Blacks and Latinos to come together in this election and support the Black–Latino coalition in the city.

Photos of the fictional candidates can be viewed at andreabenjaminphd.com/onlineappendix/.

NOTES

1. "Blacks & Mexicans scrap in S.I." *New York Daily News*, November 6, 2005.
2. This survey experiment was conducted in August 2012 by GfK (formerly Knowledge Networks), which recruits participants using an address-based probability sampling frame. In exchange for responding to various surveys, participants receive free Internet access and a computer if they need them. This results in high-quality national probability samples and even includes households that may not have had Internet access or a computer initially.

4

The Co-ethnic Elite Cues Theory and Racial Attitudes

Priming Attitudes about Racial and Ethnic Groups: Can Elite Cues Help Foster More Positive Feelings among Blacks, Latinos, and Whites?

If endorsements can help Blacks and Latinos prefer an out-group minority candidate, as we saw in the previous chapters, they also have the potential to help Blacks and Latinos think more positively about the out-group. That is, in addition to the electoral context and candidates, co-ethnic elite cues may send the signal to voters that members of the out-group are not so bad. The Co-ethnic Elite Cues Theory may also be applied to racial attitudes and provide new insights into the study of racial attitudes. We can use the Co-ethnic Elite Cues Theory to test the extent to which Blacks' and Latinos' feelings about the minority out-group rely on racial/ethnic stereotypes or on co-ethnic elite cues.

Cues from various sources influence public opinion on policies (Cohen 2003; Kam 2005; Nicholson 2011). Nicholson finds this is less true depending on the policy and on stereotypes about the groups benefiting from the policy (2011). That is, the relationship between elite cues and racial attitudes may be weaker when citizens can rely on group stereotypes as voters are taking their cues from stereotypes rather than from elites (ibid.). However, co-ethnics did not give the elite cues in Nicholson's study. Hurley and Kuklinski (1994) found that Blacks are more likely to support a policy position when a Black leader, regardless of the leader's political affiliation, endorses that position. It is likely that Blacks will indicate more positive feelings toward Latinos if they read about a Black endorsement of a Latino candidate. Among Latinos, we know very little about whether racial attitudes about Blacks influence support for Black candidates. Yet researchers have shown that when Latinos prefer a pan-ethnic identity, they feel closer to Blacks (Kaufmann 2003a). While Black racial attitudes toward Latinos are fairly positive, Latinos' negative feelings about Blacks wane as they spend more time in the United States (McClain et al. 2006). Because of this, I expect that co-ethnic elite cues may help Black express even more positive attitudes toward Latinos and help Latinos express more positive feelings about Blacks.

The goal of this chapter is to determine if Black and Latino respondents indicate more positive feelings toward members of the minority out-group in the context of co-ethnic elite endorsements in a race salient campaign. That is, do co-ethnic elite endorsements work as a heuristic to signal that members of the out-group are not so bad? The data from the previous chapters show that under certain conditions, co-ethnic elite endorsements can move Blacks and Latinos to prefer out-group minority candidates. Do co-ethnic elite cues change feelings as well? This leads to two hypotheses:

H_1: Blacks and Latinos will express more positive feelings toward each other when a co-ethnic elite endorses a minority out-group candidate.

H_2: Blacks and Latinos will express more positive feelings toward each other when the out-group candidate is a part of an Elite Black–Latino Coalition.

It is possible that Blacks and Latinos, contrary to my hypotheses, have firm racial attitudes about each other, and that, therefore, co-ethnic elite endorsements and biracial alliances are not enough to shift racial attitudes. This chapter will address this question.

RACIAL ATTITUDES AND MINORITY CANDIDATE SUPPORT AMONG WHITES

This chapter also explores how the campaign context (here, the explicit call to support a Black or Latino candidate in an Elite Black–Latino Coalition) influences racial attitudes among Whites. The previous research has been clear about Whites' racial attitudes toward Blacks (Kinder and Sanders 1996; Mendelberg 2001; Reeves 1997; Valentino, Hutchings, and White 2002). However, this chapter is interested in the extent to which exposure to Blacks and Latinos *working together* makes Whites express more or less positive feelings toward Blacks *and* Latinos. The data in the previous chapter showed that Whites did not punish the Black candidate when he was endorsed by a Latino organization and in an Elite Black–Latino Coalition. Similarly, they did not punish the Latino candidate when he was endorsed by a Black organization and in an Elite Black–Latino Coalition. Much of the literature on racial threat has focused on getting the context just right, as scholars have used the size and scope of minority populations at various levels (county, city, state) to explain voting behavior and the way Whites feel about minorities more generally (Oliver and Mendelberg 2000; Taylor 1998). While none of these scholars have considered that the size of the population may not matter as much as the perception that minorities are working together to make political gains, I use an experiment to explore this possibility. Here, I expect exposure to Black candidates to lead to more negative feelings towards Blacks. In terms of Latinos, the literature has focused on White attitudes towards immigrants, not Latinos in general (Brader, Valentino, and Suhey 2008). My treatments do not explicitly refer to Latinos as immigrants, but given the negative feelings Whites have demonstrated about immigrants, I expect exposure to Latino candidates will lead to more negative feelings toward Latinos.

H_3: Whites will be more likely to express negative feelings toward Blacks/Latinos when exposed to a context in which Blacks and Latinos endorse minority candidates.

H_4: Whites will be more likely to express negative feelings toward Blacks/Latinos when exposed to a context in which Blacks and Latinos have formed an Elite Black–Latino Coalition.

DATA AND METHODS

This chapter uses the same data from the study in Chapter 3. The study was conducted in the summer of 2012. I randomly assigned Blacks, Latinos, and Whites to read newspaper articles about fictional mayoral candidates discussing unemployment in the city (see Table 3.1).[1] In every article, candidate 1 is Jack Brown, a White man; he plans to create new jobs through tax incentives that will draw businesses to the area. In one treatment, candidate 2 is Jim Davis (a rival White candidate), and he plans to create jobs by making it easier for community members to open businesses in the area. In three conditions, candidate 2 is Juan Garcia, a Latino candidate. In three conditions, candidate 2 is James Washington, a Black candidate. In the treatment with two White candidates, the issues are discussed. In the subsequent treatments, the issues are discussed, and I manipulate the race of the candidate (Black or Latino), add an endorsement for the Black or Latino candidate (from Latino leaders or Black leaders, respectively), and add a call to support the candidate in an Elite Black–Latino Coalition. White subjects were randomly assigned to one of the seven treatments. Blacks were randomly assigned to one of four treatments – the two White candidates treatment or the treatments that featured Juan Garcia. Latinos were also randomly assigned to one of four treatments – the two White candidates treatment or the treatments that featured James Washington. I only exposed Black and Latino subjects to out-group minority candidates as candidate 2.

PRIMING: ARE ELITES THE KEY TO BETTER INTERGROUP FEELINGS?

In this survey experiment, respondents were randomly assigned to treatments, followed by questions about candidate preferences, and then they were asked about racial attitudes toward Blacks and Latinos. This allows me to test the claim that endorsements from a co-ethnic and endorsements from a co-ethnic in the context of an Elite Black–Latino Coalition would prime Latinos and Blacks to express more positive feelings about members of the minority out-group. If Blacks and Latinos do not like one another, as previous research has found, then we should find the most negative feelings toward the minority out-group in the treatments featuring no endorsement and no call to support an Elite Black–Latino Coalition, as respondents assigned to those treatments will react based on the racial prime alone (Mendelberg 2001). In the following analyses, I am not interested in candidate preferences; instead, I am interested in the extent to which endorsements from co-ethnics and Elite Black–Latino Coalitions provide a heuristic to Blacks and Latinos that primes them to express more positive feelings about Latinos and Blacks (respectively) than they would absent these cues.

CO-ETHNIC ELITE ENDORSEMENTS AND PRIMING AMONG LATINOS

In Chapter 3, I presented data that Latinos do not prefer Black candidates alone, only expressing greater levels of support for a Black candidate over a White candidate with identical issue positions when there was a co-ethnic elite endorsement or in the context of an Elite Black–Latino Coalition. This may be due to negative racial attitudes toward Blacks, but the results demonstrate that elite cues may help Latinos overlook racial feelings and support a Black candidate. Perhaps even more importantly, it may be that co-ethnic elite endorsements and calls to support an Elite Black–Latino Coalition prime Latinos to feel more positively toward Blacks. In order to test these claims, I estimate several regression models to assess feelings toward the out-group based on the experimental treatments. The dependent variables are Black competition, Black discrimination, and Black closeness. The Black competition variable comprises a series of questions that asks Latino respondents about a sense of competition with Blacks over jobs, politics, and housing. I code "0" as a competitive with Blacks and "1" as not competitive with Blacks. Similarly, the Black discrimination variable comprises a series of questions determining the extent to which Latino respondents think Blacks face discrimination in jobs and housing; I code "0" as the case in which respondents state that Blacks do not face discrimination and "1" as the case in which respondents state that Blacks do face discrimination. Finally, Black closeness is measured by asking how close Latinos feel to Blacks; "0" indicates not close at all and "1" indicates very close to Blacks. If my hypotheses are correct, then Latinos who read the article with the Latino endorsement or the Elite Black–Latino Coalition will express more positive feelings toward Blacks than those who read the baseline treatment. In the previous chapter, I used the treatment that featured two White candidates as the baseline. In this chapter, I rely on the treatments that feature the White vs. Black candidate or the White vs. Latino candidate without any other information as the baseline measure of how Latinos, Blacks, and Whites in this sample feel toward Blacks and Latinos. Comparisons in these analyses will be relative to those treatments.

In Table 4.1, I present the results of the regression models, showing variation in Latino's racial attitudes about Blacks based on treatment. As you can see, there is no evidence of priming in the case of Black competition. Regardless of the treatment, Latinos were no more or less likely to indicate a sense of competition with Blacks in jobs, politics, or housing, compared to the reference treatment. All the values are closer to one, indicating that Latinos do not feel competition with Blacks across all treatments. Turning to Black discrimination, Latinos were no more or less likely to think Blacks face discrimination in jobs and housing. Finally, we look at Black closeness and we see that Latinos did not say they felt closer to Blacks, even when there was a co-ethnic elite endorsement or in the context of a Black–Latino coalition.

Figure 4.1 illustrates the results, which shows that there are no priming effects about attitudes toward Blacks among Latinos, when compared to the reference treatment that featured a Black candidate. The figures show that on par, Latinos don't feel very competitive with Blacks, but when it comes to believing that Blacks face discrimination or feelings of closeness to Blacks, those numbers are relatively low. These results provide no

TABLE 4.1 *Regression Analysis of Latinos' Racial Attitudes toward Blacks (Priming)*

	Black Competition Black Candidate = Baseline	Black Discrimination Black Candidate = Baseline	Black Closeness Black Candidate = Baseline
Intercept	0.63 (0.04)***	0.49 (0.04)***	0.43 (0.04)***
Two White Candidates Treatment	0.05 (0.04)	−0.10 (0.06)	−0.07 (0.06)
Black Candidate with Latino Endorsement Treatment	0.05 (0.04)	−0.01 (0.06)	0.04 (0.05)
Black Candidate with Latino Endorsement and Coalition Treatment	0.07 (0.05)	0.06 (0.06)	0.07 (0.06)
N	197	199	198
R^2	0.013	0.025	0.029

Notes: + $p < 0.10$; * $p < 0.05$; ** $p < 0.01$; *** $p < 0.001$ for a two-tailed test, except for constant.
Black Competition: 0 = a sense of competition with Blacks, 1 = no sense of competition with Blacks.
Black Discrimination 0 = Blacks do not face discrimination, 1 = Blacks do face discrimination.
Black Closeness 0 = not close at all, 1 = very close to Blacks.

support for support for H_1: "Blacks and Latinos will express more positive feelings toward the out-group when co-ethnics endorse an out-group candidate" or H_2: "Blacks and Latinos will express more positive feelings toward the out-group when the out-group candidate is a part of an Elite Black–Latino Coalition." While Latinos did express more support for Black candidates with co-ethnic elite endorsements/in a Black–Latino coalition, these co-ethnic elite endorsements and calls to support a minority coalition do not change attitudes toward Blacks as a group. With the exception of the Black competition measures, the results are consistent with the previous literature that shows that Latinos express negative feelings about Blacks (McClain et al. 2006). Yet, these results do not support my hypotheses either, as Latinos in the sample did not express more positive feelings toward Blacks, even when they read about Blacks and Latinos working together in a coalition. One possibility is that racial

Latinos' Feelings toward Blacks

■ Black Competition   ■ Black Discrimination   ■ Black Closeness

White vs. Black (Reference)	Two White Candidates	White vs. Black, Latino Endorsement	White vs. Black, Latino Endorsement, Coalition
0.63 / 0.49 / 0.43	0.68 / 0.39 / 0.36	0.68 / 0.48 / 0.47	0.70 / 0.55 / 0.49

FIGURE 4.1 Latinos' Racial Attitudes towards Blacks (Priming) Comparison to White vs. Black: Notes: + p < 0.10;* p < 0.05; ** p < 0.01; *** p < 0.001 for a two-tailed test, except for constant. Black Competition: 0 = a sense of competition with Black s, 1 = no sense of competition with Blacks. Black Discrimination 0 = Blacks do not face discrimination, 1 = Blacks do face discrimination. Black Closeness 0 = not close at all, 1 = very close to Blacks. Marginal effects estimated from Table 4.1.

attitudes are too stable (Converse 1964). While the co-ethnic cues helped Latinos decide a Black candidate could represent them as mayor, the cues were not enough to change feelings about Blacks as a group.

CO-ETHNIC ELITE ENDORSEMENTS AND PRIMING AMONG BLACKS

Co-ethnic elite endorsements do not help Latinos express more positive feelings toward Blacks. In this section, I explore the relationship between Blacks' feelings about Latinos by treatment group, and determine if Black endorsements of Latinos prime Blacks to express more positive feelings toward Latinos. The White vs. Latino Candidate Treatment serves as the reference treatment here. The dependent variables are analogous to the ones I used in the previous analyses: Latino competition, Latino discrimination, and Latino closeness. The Latino competition variable comprises a series of questions about competition with Latinos over jobs, politics, and housing, where "0" indicates that respondents feel competitive with Latinos and "1" indicates that respondents do not feel competitive with Latinos. Latino discrimination is a variable made up of a series of questions about the extent to which Blacks think Latinos face discrimination in jobs and housing, where "0" indicates that respondents do not believe that Latinos face discrimination and "1" indicates that respondents do

TABLE 4.2 *Regression Analysis of Blacks' Racial Attitudes toward Latinos (Priming)*

	Latino Competition Latino Candidate = Baseline	Latino Discrimination Latino Candidate = Baseline	Latino Closeness Latino Candidate = Baseline
Intercept	0.66 (0.03)***	0.53 (0.04)***	0.53 (0.04)***
Two White Candidates Treatment	0.09 (0.04)*	−0.01 (0.05)	−0.02 (0.05)
Latino Candidate with Black Endorsement Treatment	0.07 (0.04)+	0.03 (0.05)	−0.06 (0.05)
Latino Candidate with Black Endorsement, Coalition Treatment	0.09 (0.04)*	0.15 (0.06)*	0.07 (0.05)
N	212	213	211
R^2	0.025	0.024	0.002

Notes: + $p < 0.10$; * $p < 0.05$; ** $p < 0.01$; *** $p < 0.001$ for a two-tailed test, except for constant.
Latino Competition: 0 = a sense of competition with Latinos, 1 = no sense of competition with Latinos.
Latino Discrimination 0 = Latinos do not face discrimination, 1 = Latinos do face discrimination.
Latino Closeness 0 = not close at all, 1 = very close to Latinos.

believe that Latinos face discrimination. Latino closeness is a measured by asking how close Blacks feel to Latinos, where "0" indicates not close at all and "1" indicates very close to Latinos.

In Table 4.2, I present the results of the regression analyses. The Latino Competition model shows that Blacks, regardless of treatment, were less willing to express a sense of competition with Latinos, relative to reading about a Latino candidate. That is, after reading about two White candidates, Blacks were nine percentage points less likely to express feelings of competition with Latinos in jobs, housing, and politics ($p < 0.05$). After reading about a Latino candidate with Black endorsements or in a Black–Latino coalition, they were also less likely to express feelings of competition with Latinos (seven percentage points, $p < 0.10$ and nine percentage points $p < 0.05$). Those who read about a Latino candidate

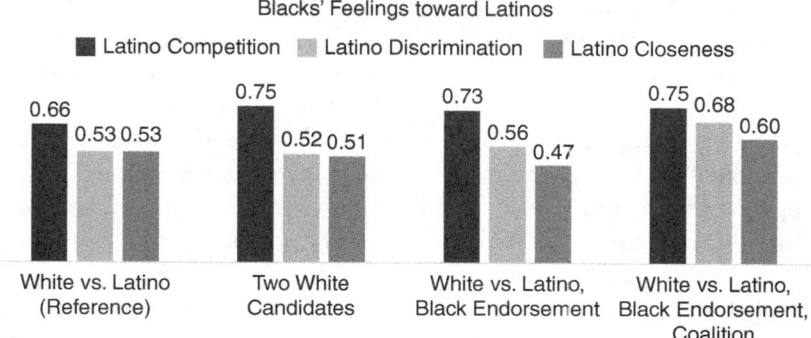

FIGURE 4.2 Blacks' Racial Attitudes towards Latinos (Priming)
Comparison to White vs. Latino: Notes: + p < 0.10; * p < 0.05; ** p < 0.01; *** p < 0.001 for a two-tailed test, except for constant. Latino Competition: 0 = a sense of competition with Latinos, 1 = no sense of competition with Latinos. Latino Discrimination 0 = Latinos do not face discrimination, 1 = Latinos do face discrimination. Latino Closeness 0 = not close at all, 1 = very close to Latino. Marginal effects estimated from Table 4.2.

alone were more likely to express feelings of competition with Latinos. Turning to the Latino discrimination model in column 2, we see that with a co-ethnic elite endorsement and a call to support the Elite Black–Latino Coalition, Blacks are 15 percentage points more likely to indicate that Latinos face discrimination (p < 0.05) than those who read about the Latino candidate alone. When we turn to feelings of closeness to Latinos, we see that regardless of the treatment, Blacks did not feel closer to Latinos.

Figure 4.2 illustrates these findings. Again, the treatment that featured the White vs. Latino candidates offers us an insight into the base levels of feelings toward Latinos among Blacks. Higher values indicate more positive feelings toward the out-group. Blacks who read about the Latino candidate alone did not feel very competitive with Latinos (66 percentage points). These feelings are much more positive when they read about two White candidates (75 percentage points, p < 0.05), when the Latino candidate receives an endorsement (73 percentage points, p < 0.10), and when the Latino candidate is in a Black–Latino coalition (75 percentage points, P < 0.05). When it comes to expressing that Latinos face discrimination, there is an increase in that feeling only when Blacks read about the Latino candidate in a Black–Latino coalition (68 percentage points, p < 0.05 compared to 53 percentage points in the reference treatment).

Finally, there is no evidence that co-ethnic elite endorsements or the Black–Latino coalition help Blacks feel closer to Latinos, relative to the Latino candidate treatment. The results about competition with Latinos provides evidence for H_1: "Blacks and Latinos will express more positive feelings toward the out-group when co-ethnics endorse an out-group candidate" and H_2: "Blacks and Latinos will express more positive feelings toward the out-group when the out-group candidate is a part of an Elite Black–Latino Coalition." However, we only find support for the second hypothesis for Latino discrimination. There is not support for either hypotheses in terms of Latino closeness. The results among Blacks also highlight the stability of racial attitudes. Blacks are willing to support Latino candidates when co-ethnic cues are present, but the cues do not work quite as well in the context of feelings toward Latinos as a group.

WHITES, RACIAL ATTITUDES, AND CONTEXT

There is no shortage of research on White racial attitudes toward Blacks and other minorities. Researchers have explored the relationship between Whites' racial attitudes and preferences for candidates and racial policies (Kinder and Sanders 1996; Mendelberg 2001; Sears, Sidanius, and Bobo 2000; Taylor 2000). Still other scholars note the strong connection between ideology and racial attitudes (Carmines and Stimson 1989). Not everyone thinks that policy preferences are closely tied to racial attitudes. Some scholars attribute policy preferences to nonracial values such as individualism and the ideal size of government (Hurwitz and Peffley 1998; Sniderman and Piazza 2002). The data in this chapter create a unique opportunity to explore Whites' attitudes toward Blacks and Latinos when they are presented with contextual information that suggests that those two minority groups are working together. As such, I predict that Whites' racial attitudes will be more negative when there are co-ethnic elite endorsements and when there is a call to support an Elite Black–Latino Coalition. This should be especially true when the candidate is Black, because previous research on White attitudes about Blacks shows that negative feelings about Whites are associated with decreased support for Black candidates or policies that are beneficial to Blacks (Kinder and Sanders 1996; Valentino et al. 2002).

In order to test these claims, I replicate the analyses from Table 4.2 among White respondents. First, I consider feelings toward Latinos in the presence of Latino candidates. I use the same dependent variables as

TABLE 4.3 *Regression Analysis of Whites' Racial Attitudes towards Latinos (Priming)*

	Latino Competition Latino Candidate = Baseline	Latino Discrimination Latino Candidate = Baseline	Latino Closeness Latino Candidate = Baseline
Intercept	0.60 (0.02)***	0.38 (0.02)***	0.42 (0.04)***
Two White Candidates Treatment	−0.02 (0.04)	−0.05 (0.04)	0.03 (0.04)
Latino Candidate with Black Endorsement Treatment	0.01 (0.04)	0.06 (0.04)+	−0.01 (0.03)
Latino Candidate with Black Endorsement, Coalition Treatment	−0.01 (0.02)	0.03 (0.04)	−0.04 (0.04)
N	361	363	365
R^2	0.001	0.005	0.005

Notes: + p < 0.10; * p < 0.05; ** p < 0.01; *** p < 0.001 for a two-tailed test, except for constant.
Latino Competition: 0 = a sense of competition with Latinos, 1 = no sense of competition with Latinos.
Latino Discrimination 0 = Latinos do not face discrimination, 1 = Latinos do face discrimination.
Latino Closeness 0 = not close at all, 1 = very close to Latinos.

before: Latino competition, Latino discrimination, and Latino closeness, where higher values are associated with more positive feelings and lower values are associated with more negative feelings toward the group. The reference treatment group is the Latino candidate treatment.

Table 4.3 shows that Whites do not seem to feel more positively or more negatively toward Latinos, regardless of the treatments. The one exception is that White respondents are more likely to say that Latinos face discrimination when they read about a Latino candidate with a Black endorsement (six percentage points, p < 0.10). Turning to Figure 4.3, I illustrate these results. As we can see, White respondents do not feel competitive with Latinos (as evidenced by the high values on Latino competition). The low values for Latino discrimination and Latino closeness indicate that Whites do not think that Latinos face much discrimination, nor do they feel

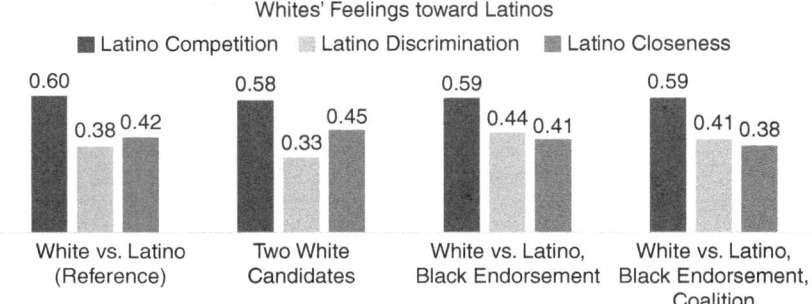

FIGURE 4.3 Whites' Racial Attitudes towards Latinos (Priming) Comparison to White vs. Latino: Notes: + p < 0.10;* p < 0.05; ** p < 0.01; *** p < 0.001 for a two-tailed test, except for constant. Latino Competition: 0 = a sense of competition with Latinos, 1 = no sense of competition with Latinos. Latino Discrimination 0 = Latinos do not face discrimination, 1 = Latinos do face discrimination. Latino Closeness 0 = not close at all, 1 = very close to Latinos. Marginal effects estimated from Table 4.3.

particularly close to them. When Whites read the Latino candidate with a Black endorsement treatment, they are more likely (44 percentage points p < 0.10, compared to 38 percentage points) to say Latinos face discrimination. These results do not provide support for H_3, that Whites will be more likely to express negative feelings toward Blacks/Latinos when exposed to a context in which Blacks and Latinos endorse minority candidates or H_4, that Whites will be more likely to express negative feelings toward Blacks/Latinos when exposed to a context in which Blacks and Latinos have formed an Elite Black–Latino Coalition.

Overall, the data suggest that Whites do not express different racial attitudes toward Latinos, even when Latino candidates are endorsed by a Black organization or part of an Elite Black–Latino Coalition. That is, when the candidate is Latino and the media highlights a context in which Blacks and Latinos are working together, Whites do not express more negative feelings toward Latinos. Results from Chapter 3 show that Whites in the study do not treat Latino candidates differently than White candidates. On par, though the attitudes are not that positive, regardless of treatment. The values on Latino competition indicate that Whites do not feel competitive with Latinos and this is true across all treatments. The values on Latino discrimination and Latino closeness are all relatively low, indicating that across all treatments, Whites do not think Latinos face discrimination nor do they feel close to them, the one

TABLE 4.4 *Regression Analysis of Whites' Racial Attitudes toward Blacks (Priming)*

	Black Competition Black Candidate = Baseline	Black Discrimination Black Candidate = Baseline	Black Closeness Black Candidate = Baseline
Intercept	0.63 (0.02)***	0.42 (0.02)***	0.45 (0.02)***
Two White Candidates Treatment	−0.01 (0.04)	−0.05 (0.04)	0.01 (0.04)
Black Candidate with Latino Endorsement Treatment	0.03 (0.03)	0.01 (0.04)	−0.01 (0.04)
Black Candidate with Latino Endorsement and Coalition Treatment	−0.05 (0.04)	−0.08 (0.04)*	−0.06 (0.04)+
N	362	365	365
R^2	0.011	0.007	0.004

Notes: + $p < 0.10$; * $p < 0.05$; ** $p < 0.01$; *** $p < 0.001$ for a two-tailed test, except for constant.
Black Competition: 0 = a sense of competition with Blacks, 1 = no sense of competition with Blacks.
Black Discrimination 0 = Blacks do not face discrimination, 1 = Blacks do face discrimination.
Black Closeness 0 = not close at all, 1 = very close to Blacks.

exception being that they do think Latinos face discrimination when the Latino candidate received a Black endorsement. These results show that when Latino candidates work with Blacks, White attitudes toward Latinos as a group do not change.

In Table 4.4, I explore the relationship between White respondents' exposure to Black candidates and feelings toward Blacks. The dependent variables are the same variables I used in Table 4.1: Black competition, Black discrimination, and Black closeness. The reference treatment here is the Black candidate treatment. First, we can see that for the most part, Whites do not express more positive or more negative feelings toward Blacks, regardless of the treatment. There are two notable exceptions: when they read about a Black candidate with Latino endorsements in the context of an Elite Black–Latino Coalition, White respondents are eight

136   The Co-ethnic Elite Cues Theory and Racial Attitudes

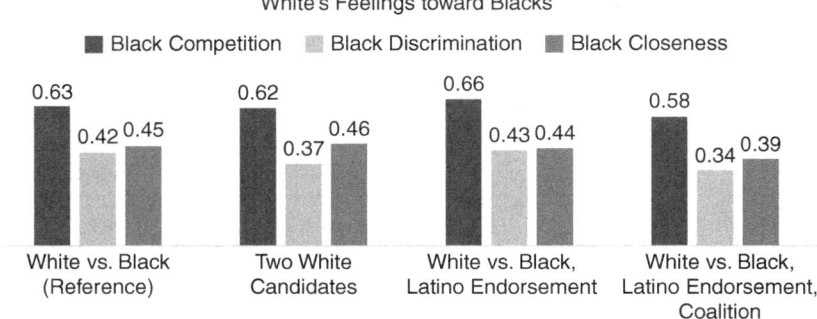

FIGURE 4.4 Whites' Racial Attitudes towards Blacks (Priming)
Comparison to White vs. Black: Notes: + p < 0.10;* p < 0.05; ** p < 0.01;
*** p < 0.001 for a two-tailed test, except for constant. Black Competition: 0 = a sense of competition with Black s, 1 = no sense of competition with Blacks. Black Discrimination 0 = Blacks do not face discrimination, 1 = Blacks do face discrimination. Black Closeness 0 = not close at all, 1 = very close to Blacks. Marginal effects estimated from Table 4.4.

percentage points less likely to say that Blacks face discrimination (p < 0.05) and six percentage points less likely to indicate they feel close to Blacks (p < 0.10). That is, exposure to a Black candidate with a Latino endorsement in the context of an Elite Black–Latino Coalition leads Whites to express negative feelings about Blacks, relative to just reading about a Black candidate alone. When Whites were exposed to Black candidates with Latino endorsements, we find no support for the hypotheses: H_3, that Whites will be more likely to express negative feelings toward Blacks/Latinos when exposed to a context in which Blacks and Latinos endorse minority candidates. There is support for H_4, that Whites will be more likely to express negative feelings toward Blacks/Latinos when exposed to a context in which Blacks and Latinos have formed an Elite Black–Latino Coalition. The lack of results on Black discrimination are consistent with previous research, which shows that Whites do not feel a sense of competition with Blacks (Bobo and Hutchings 1996; Glaser 1994; Oliver 2012).

In Figure 4.4, I illustrate this relationship. The Black discrimination and Black closeness variables are not very high, but they are even lower among those who read about the Black candidate with a Latino endorsement and the Black candidate with a Latino endorsement in the context of the Elite Black–Latino Coalition (34 percentage points, p < 0.10 and 39 percentage points, p < 0.05, respectively). This suggests that reading about a Black candidate who is working with Latinos leads Whites to express more negative feelings toward Blacks.

These results have broad implications for our thinking about racial attitudes among Whites. Whites do not feel competitive toward Latinos or Blacks. These results confirm previous research, providing evidence that this is still the case, even as Black and Latino populations continue to grow. The results also reveal that Whites do not think Latinos or Blacks face much discrimination. For both groups, these numbers are low, ranging from 34 percentage points to 45 percentage points, where higher values indicate the belief that the group faces discrimination in housing and jobs. Only when a Black candidate has formed an alliance with Latinos do Whites express different racial attitudes compared to the reference treatment, and those attitudes are more negative in terms of discrimination and closeness. When a Latino candidate has a Black endorsement, Whites express more positive feelings about Latino discrimination (though these feelings are not overwhelmingly positive). The results among Whites confirm the stability of racial attitudes. Research on intergroup relations suggests that proximity to out-groups is not enough to change feelings about out-groups (Valentine 2008). Valentine suggests that only through meaningful interactions might we find changes in feelings toward the out-group. Further, co-ethnic elite cues do not help ease the tensions between groups either. These results show that cues cannot change attitudes toward an out-group.

SHIFTING THE TARGET: ALTERNATIVE PRIMING AMONG WHITES

As a final test of White respondents' reaction to Blacks and Latinos working together, I consider the possibility that the endorsements themselves provide a cue to Whites in the sample. When Whites read about Blacks and Latinos working together in an Elite Black–Latino Coalition, they were more likely to express negative feelings about Blacks (discrimination and closeness). But in the experimental treatments that featured Black candidates, two treatments included information about Latino endorsements. Therefore, it is possible that reading about Latino endorsements for Black candidates may foster negative feelings toward Latinos. The goal is to determine how reading about Black candidates with Latino endorsements influences Whites' attitudes toward Latinos. The dependent variables are: Latino competition, Latino discrimination, and Latino closeness, where higher values are associated with more positive feelings and

TABLE 4.5 *Regression Analysis of Whites' Racial Attitudes towards Latinos when Reading about Black Candidates (Priming)*

	Latino Competition Black Candidate = Baseline	Latino Discrimination Black Candidate = Baseline	Latino Closeness Black Candidate = Baseline
Intercept	0.60 (0.02)***	0.42 (0.02)***	0.41 (0.02)***
Two White Candidates Treatment	−0.02 (0.04)	−0.09 (0.04)*	0.04 (0.04)
Black Candidate with Latino Endorsement Treatment	0.04 (0.04)	−0.04 (0.04)	0.01 (0.04)
Black Candidate with Latino Endorsement and Coalition Treatment	−0.06 (0.04)+	−0.08 (0.04)*	0.04 (0.04)
N	361	363	365
R^2	0.001	0.018	0.004

Notes: + $p < 0.10$; * $p < 0.05$; ** $p < 0.01$; *** $p < 0.001$ for a two-tailed test, except for constant.
Latino Competition: 0 = a sense of competition with Latinos, 1 = no sense of competition with Latinos.
Latino Discrimination 0 = Latinos do not face discrimination, 1 = Latinos do face discrimination.
Latino Closeness 0 = not close at all, 1 = very close to Latinos.

lower values are associated with more negative feelings toward the group. The reference treatment here is the Latino candidate treatment.

In Table 4.5, I estimate these regression models. The data show that when Whites read about Black candidates with a Latino endorsement in the context of an Elite Black–Latino Coalition, they are more likely to indicate a sense of competition with Latinos (-6 percentage points, $p < 0.10$) and to say that Latinos do not face discrimination (-8 percentage points, $p < 0.10$). Whites also say that Latinos do not face discrimination when they read about two White candidates (-9 percentage points, $p < 0.05$). In Figure 4.5, I illustrate the magnitude of these effects. Again, Whites do not express different feelings toward Latinos, except when Latinos endorse the Black candidate and are part of an Elite Black–Latino Coalition. When Whites read that treatment, they report

Shifting the Target

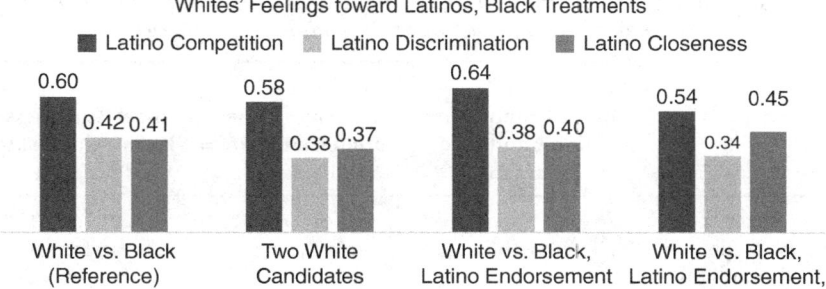

FIGURE 4.5 Whites' Racial Attitudes towards Latinos when Reading about Black Candidates (Priming)
Comparison to White vs. Black: Notes: + p < 0.10;* p < 0.05; ** p < 0.01; *** p < 0.001 for a two-tailed test, except for constant. Latino Competition: 0 = a sense of competition with Latinos, 1 = no sense of competition with Latinos. Latino Discrimination 0 = Latinos do not face discrimination, 1 = Latinos do face discrimination. Latino Closeness 0 = not close at all, 1 = very close to Latinos. Marginal effects estimated from Table 4.5.

a sense of competition with Latinos (54 percentage points, p < 0.10) and they report that Latinos do not face discrimination (35 percentage points, p < 0.10). Taken together, Whites express more negative feelings toward Latinos for working with Blacks, but only in the coalition treatment. When Latinos endorse Black candidates, Whites' feelings toward Latinos do not change, relative to the Latino candidate treatment. When it comes to feelings of closeness to Latinos among Whites, there are no differences by treatment, though these feelings are largely negative (ranging from 41 percentage points in the Latino candidate treatment to 45 percentage points in the Black–Latino coalition treatment).

As we saw in Table 4.3, Whites did not seem to express any negative feelings toward Latinos when exposed to Latino candidates. But two of the three treatments that feature Latino candidates also include information about Black endorsements. To determine how reading about Latino candidates with endorsements from Black leaders in the context of an Elite Black–Latino Coalition influences Whites' racial attitudes toward Blacks, I use the following dependent variables: Black competition, Black discrimination, and Black closeness, where higher values are associated with more positive feelings and lower values are associated with more negative feelings toward the group (Table 4.6).

TABLE 4.6 *Regression Analysis of Whites' Racial Attitudes towards Blacks when reading about Latino Candidates (Priming)*

	Black Competition Latino Candidate = Baseline	Black Discrimination Latino Candidate = Baseline	Black Closeness Latino Candidate = Baseline
Intercept	0.63 (0.02)***	0.38 (0.02)***	0.45 (0.02)***
Two White Candidates Treatment	−0.01 (0.04)	−0.02 (0.04)	0.01 (0.04)
Latino Candidate with Black Endorsement Treatment	−0.01 (0.03)	0.07 (0.04)+	−0.04 (0.04)
Latino Candidate with Black Endorsement, Coalition Treatment	−0.01 (0.04)	0.06 (0.04)	0.01 (0.04)
N	362	365	365
R^2	0.001	0.014	0.002

Notes: + $p < 0.10$; * $p < 0.05$; ** $p < 0.01$; *** $p < 0.001$ for a two-tailed test, except for constant.
Black Competition: 0 = a sense of competition with Blacks, 1 = no sense of competition with Blacks.
Black Discrimination 0 = Blacks do not face discrimination, 1 = Blacks do face discrimination.
Black Closeness 0 = not close at all, 1 = very close to Blacks.

The results here show that White respondents did not express more or less positive feeling about Blacks, regardless of the treatment. With one exception, when White respondents read about a Latino candidate with a Black endorsement, they were more likely to say that Blacks face discrimination (seven percentage points, $p < 0.10$). In Figure 4.6, I illustrate the magnitude of these results. When Whites read about the Latino candidate with a Black endorsement, they were more likely to say that Blacks face discrimination (45 percentage points, $p < 0.10$), compared to the reference treatment. Overall, Whites do not feel competitive with Blacks, even when they read about Latino candidates. They do not think Blacks face discrimination and they do not feel close to Blacks. Taken together, the results show that regardless of the candidates or the endorsers, Whites' attitudes toward Blacks and Latinos are largely negative and stable. These

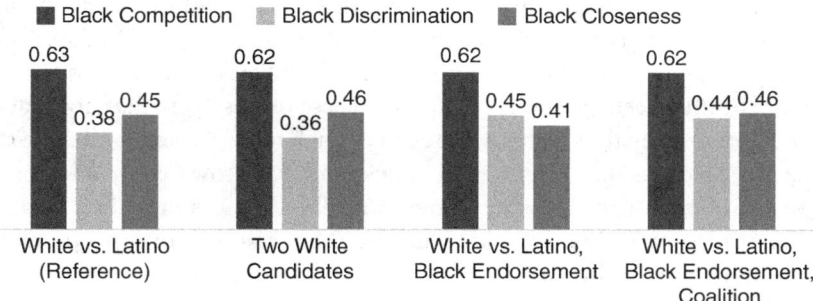

FIGURE 4.6 Whites' Racial Attitudes towards Blacks when Reading about Latino Candidates (Priming)
Comparison to White vs. Latino: Notes: + p < 0.10;* p < 0.05; ** p < 0.01; *** p < 0.001 for a two-tailed test, except for constant. Black Competition: 0 = a sense of competition with Black s, 1 = no sense of competition with Blacks. Black Discrimination 0 = Blacks do not face discrimination, 1 = Blacks do face discrimination. Black Closeness 0 = not close at all, 1 = very close to Latinos. Marginal effects estimated from Table 4.5.

do not change even when Blacks and Latinos are working together, which suggests that previous scholars are correct to rely on the context – the size and scope of minority populations at the county, city, and state levels – to investigate these relationships (Oliver and Mendelberg 2000; Taylor 1998).

CONCLUSIONS

The goal of this chapter was to determine if co-ethnic elite cues can change racial attitudes. Previous research demonstrated that, under some conditions, Latinos express negative feelings toward Blacks, while Blacks often express fairly positive feelings toward Latinos (Kaufmann 2003a; McClain et al. 2006). Given that some co-ethnic elite endorsements moved Blacks' and Latinos' candidate preference, I set out to determine if co-ethnic elite endorsements prime Blacks and Latinos to express more positive feelings toward the minority out-group as well. The evidence presented in this chapter supports some of my hypotheses, but largely, the results confirm that racial attitudes are fairly stable, even when co-ethnics endorse a member of the group in the local election.

Among Latinos, there are no differences by treatment with respect to attitudes toward Blacks. Blacks, on the other hand, indicate less competition with Latinos across all treatments, relative to reading about a Latino candidate alone. Blacks are more likely to indicate that Latinos face discrimination in the context of the Elite Black–Latino Coalition (Table 4.2). On the whole, co-ethnic elite endorsements do not seem to help Blacks and Latinos express more positive feelings about each other. These results show that, for Blacks and Latinos, co-ethnic elite cues are not enough to help voters overcome the negative feelings that Blacks and Latinos often have toward one another.

I also set out to determine how minority alliances influence Whites' feelings toward Blacks and Latinos. The results confirm previous research that Whites do not feel a sense of competition with Latinos or Blacks (Tables 4.3 and 4.4). When we considered other feelings toward Latinos, when a Latino candidate was endorsed by a Black organization, Whites were more likely to think Latinos face discrimination, compared to the reference treatment. When it comes to feelings toward Blacks (Black discrimination and Black closeness), Whites were less likely to think Blacks face discrimination or to feel close to Blacks when they read about Black candidates in the context of an Elite Black–Latino Coalition, compared to the reference treatment. Also, learning that the Black candidate is working in an Elite Black–Latino Coalition leads to less positive feelings toward Blacks (Table 4.4). When it comes to racial attitudes toward Blacks, there is still some tension there.

In Tables 4.5 and 4.6, I considered feelings toward the minority group providing an endorsement to an Elite Black–Latino Coalition candidate. When Whites read about a Black candidate with a Latino endorsement in the context of an Elite Black–Latino Coalition, they reported a greater sense of competition with Latinos and they were less likely to think that Latinos face discrimination, compared to the reference treatment (Table 4.5). Contrast this with the finding that they did not express these feelings about Latinos when there was a Latino candidate present in the treatment, but they did express negative feelings toward Latinos when they read about a Black candidate in one condition: When they read about a Latino candidate with Black endorsements, they are more likely to say Blacks face discrimination (Table 4.6). The main takeaway for Whites is that there is not much change in racial attitudes toward Blacks or Latinos.

While co-ethnic elite cues may help lessen negative feelings among Blacks under certain conditions, this is not the case for Latinos. Their attitudes toward Blacks did not change, even when Latinos endorsed Black candidates. These results have real implications for biracial coalitions, more broadly. For the most part, the co-ethnic cues did not foster more positive feelings toward the out-group for Latinos or Blacks, even though the cues did help them vote for the out-group candidates. As I will discuss in the Conclusion, the new biracial coalition may look different, but it can succeed.

NEXT STEPS

In the Conclusion, I summarize the results from the previous chapters and ask what is the status of the biracial electoral coalition today. I also ask what the previous chapters mean for democracy, racial and ethnic politics, and the importance of cues in elections.

NOTE

1. This survey experiment was conducted in August 2012 by GfK (formerly Knowledge Networks) which recruits participants using an address-based probability sampling frame. In exchange for responding to various surveys, participants receive free Internet access and a computer if they need them. This results in high-quality national probability samples and even includes households that may not have had Internet access or a computer initially.

Conclusion

– "Tuesday's election was a test of whether the activism and advocacy for change sparked by the killing of 18-year-old Michael Brown last August would translate into action at the ballot box. Turnout was just under 30 percent, still far shy of presidential races but nearly three times the turnout for the last Council election, two years ago."[1]

INCORPORATION AND REPRESENTATION

Recently, people have taken to the streets to protest about negative community and police relations in many cities across the United States. Following the deaths of several men of color, questions emerged about who has a seat in the mayor's office and on the city council. These questions serve as a reminder that in cities, descriptive representation is still important. In some cities, even as protestors organized to express discontent, volunteers started registering voters. Their goal was to change the composition of the local government – to demand higher levels of political incorporation for minority groups in those cities. This two-pronged approach demanding change in these cities had some success. For example, in Ferguson, Missouri, two new Black city councilmembers were elected to office in the spring of 2015. The council was tasked with hiring a new city manager and police chief. For Blacks who were once underrepresented on the council, the new council is expected to consider Black preferences in ways the previous council did not. These protest demands and electoral strategies remind us that political incorporation is still relevant in cities today.

This book builds on the seminal works *Protest Is Not Enough: The Struggle of Blacks and Hispanics for Equality in Urban Politics* (Browning, Marshall, and Tabb 1984), *Politics in Black and White:*

Race and Power in Los Angeles (Sonenshein 1993), and *Who Governs? Democracy and Power in an American City* (Dahl 1962). The issue of political incorporation – the process by which groups enter the political arena and have a seat at the table – is an important part of this book. As cities grow more diverse, new racial and ethnic groups will demand a seat at the table in order to implement policies that benefit them. For example, Oakland and San Francisco recently elected Asian American mayors for the first time in 2011 and 2010, respectively, while cities like New York, Chicago, and Houston still have not elected Latino mayors. New York and Chicago have elected Black mayors only once. The evidence I assemble in the preceding chapters tells us that co-ethnic elite cues provide voters with low-cost information about which candidates to support. While voters may prefer an in-group member and the descriptive representation that comes with it, a co-ethnic candidate is not always an option. In those cases, substantive representation is the next best option. In this way, leaders and organizations do the heavy lifting for voters. Voters, in turn, learn which candidate will provide them with substantive representation from these co-ethnic endorsements. The results from this book help us understand the conditions under which co-ethnic elite cues help voters select the best candidate to represent them when a co-ethnic candidate is not on the ballot.

THE IMPLICATIONS OF CO-ETHNIC ELITE CUES THEORY

The importance of diversity in cities goes beyond Chicago, Houston, Los Angeles, and New York. As new immigrants arrive in our country, they are driving past traditional immigrant destinations and making new cities their homes (Massey 2008). Upon arrival, they must decide how and when they want to participate in their new cities. Research on race, ethnicity, and local elections shows the strong relationship between co-ethnic candidates and support from co-ethnic voters (Barreto 2009; Dahl 1962) and the strength of racial and ethnic group voting blocs (Hajnal and Trounstine 2014). While this broad understanding of the role of race in local elections is useful, it fails to isolate *why* Blacks, Latinos, and Whites vote the way they do in any given election. This book contends that the race and ethnicity of endorsers is also very important, as they help voters know which candidate to support. That there are some instances in which Blacks and Latinos support the same candidates and other instances in which they do not suggests there is more to the story than just the race of the candidate. Co-ethnic elite cues help tell that story more fully.

Through the Co-ethnic Elite Cues Theory, I bring these different literatures into conversation, explaining *why* Blacks, Latinos, and Whites vote the way they do in local elections. The Co-ethnic Elite Cues Theory posits that cues (endorsements) from local racial/ethnic leadership and organizations influence Black and Latino voters – this is especially true when voters are thinking about their own racial and ethnic identities, but elite cues alone are not enough to change candidate preference. The racial/ethnic context of the campaign and the race of the candidate also matter. When the candidate is Latino, regardless of racial salience, co-ethnic elite cues explain vote choice among Black voters quite well. When the candidate is Black, regardless of ethnic salience, Latinos rely on co-ethnic elite cues and perceive some candidates as sympathetic to Latino issues. For both Blacks and Latinos, the fact that a White candidate has a minority endorsement is not enough to make them prefer that candidate. For White candidates, race and ethnicity need to be salient for the co-ethnic elite cues to matter. I find that both Blacks and Latinos are receptive to calls to support minority candidates in Elite Black–Latino Coalitions. These findings have important implications for the study of race and politics. That Blacks and Latinos are willing to support out-group minority candidates provides some evidence that these groups are willing to work together. While, the data also show that they harbor some negative feelings toward one another, these feelings do not prevent Blacks from supporting Latino candidates and Latinos from supporting Black candidates.

Although Whites are not the focus of this book, they cannot be ignored, as they are active voters in most municipal elections (Hajnal and Trounstine 2005). One goal of this project is to determine how White voters respond to minority candidates and coalitions. For example, how do White voters react to a Latino candidate who has been endorsed by a Black organization or a Black candidate who has been endorsed by a Latino organization? As it turns out, White voters do not care much. That is, they do not punish minority candidates for receiving endorsements from other minority groups or for being part of an Elite Black–Latino Coalition. Only the Black candidate (with no endorsement or coalition) received lower support among Whites, compared to the White liberal candidate. These results also have important implications for the study of race and politics. Previous research suggests that minority candidates should not make explicit appeals to race and ethnicity, as those appeals may scare off White voters (Hero 1992). The data presented in this book suggest this might no longer be the case. This is good news for minority candidates, because it shows that this fear may be unfounded.

This finding, coupled with the results that that Latino and Black voters respond positively to candidates when they form Elite Black–Latino Coalitions, means that <u>minority candidates</u> may have more flexibility <u>than we previously believed</u>. The new biracial coalition can be led by minority candidates, and they can reach out to other minority groups without losing White voters.

BEYOND PARTISANSHIP: THE NEW CUE

The findings in this book have important implications for the way we think about cues, racial and ethnic politics, and representation more broadly. That Blacks and Latinos rely on co-ethnic cues when casting their ballots is an important finding that has implications for democracy. There has been a decline in partisanship – identifying with one of the two major parties in the United States. With the increase in 'independents' or non-identifiers, there are real questions about the health of our democracy (Hajnal and Lee 2011). We know that partisans are more likely to participate, so to the extent that people no longer identify with a political party, we might see less interest in politics and voting. However, if co-ethnic cues provide information to voters, we may not need to worry as much. That is, just as the partisan cue tells partisans which candidates to support, even when voters do not have much information about the candidates, these co-ethnic cues allow voters to vote as though they were fully informed.

INCORPORATION IN THE 100 LARGEST CITIES IN THE UNITED STATES

According to a report from the 2010 Census, Latinos make up 16% of the population, Blacks make up 13% of the population, Asians make up 5% of the population, and Whites make up 72% of the population.[2] While some larger cities have elected minority mayors, there is still much work to be done in achieving racial parity in executive positions. In the 100 largest cities in the United States, as of 2016, there are two Asian American mayors, eight Latino mayors, and 18 Black mayors (Table C.1). The other 72 largest cities in the United States currently have White mayors. In four cities – Baltimore, Maryland; Newark, New Jersey; Baton Rouge, Louisiana; and Birmingham, Alabama – Black majorities elected Black mayors. In five locales – Miami, Florida; Corpus Christ, Texas; Chula Vista, California; Laredo, Texas; and Hialeah, Florida – Latino majorities elected Latino mayors. In the other 18 cities, minority

TABLE C.1 *Current minority mayors in the 100 largest U.S. cities by population*

City	State	Name	Race	Population in 2010	Percent Same Race as Mayor	Next Election
Los Angeles	CA	Eric Garcetti	Latino	3,792,621	47%	2017
Houston	TX	Sylvester Turner	Black	2,109,372	23%	2017
San Antonio	TX	Ivy Taylor	Black	1,327,407	7%	2015
Jacksonville	FL	Alvin Brown	Black	821,784	31%	2015
San Francisco	CA	Edwin M. Lee	Asian American	805,235	33%	2020
Denver	CO	Michael Hancock	Black	600,158	10%	2019
Washington, D.C.		Muriel Bowser	Black	601,723	49%	2019
Baltimore	MD	Stephanie Rawlings-Blake	Black	620,961	63%	2016
Sacramento	CA	Kevin Johnson	Black	466,488	14%	2016
Long Beach	CA	Robert Garcia	Latino	462,257	40%	2018
Kansas City	MO	Sly James	Black	459,787	26%	2019
Atlanta	GA	Kasim Reed	Black	420,003	30%	2018
Miami	FL	Tomás Regalado	Latino	399,457	66%	2017
Santa Ana	CA	Miguel A. Pulido	Latino	324,528	78%	2016
Corpus Christi	TX	Nelda Martinez	Latino	305,205	59%	2017
Stockton	CA	Michael Tubbs	Black	291,707	12%	2020
Toledo	OH	Paula Hicks-Hudson	Black	287,208	27%	2018
Newark	NJ	Ras J. Baraka	Black	277,140	52%	2018

City	State	Mayor	Race	Population	%	Year
Plano	TX	Harry LaRosiliere	Black	259,841	8%	2017
Buffalo	NY	Byron Brown	Black	261,310	39%	2017
Norfolk	VA	Kenny Alexander	Black	246,393	42%	2018
Chula Vista	CA	Mary Salas	Latino	243,916	58%	2018
Laredo	TX	Peter Saenz	Latino	236,091	95%	2018
Durham	NC	Bill Bell	Black	228,330	41%	2017
Irvine	CA	Steven S. Choi	Asian American	212,375	39%	2020
Hialeah	FL	Carlos Hernández	Latino	224,669	94%	2017
Baton Rouge	LA	Kip Holden	Black	229,493	54%	2016
Birmingham	AL	William A. Bell	Black	212,237	73%	2017

Indicates Cities where largest racial and ethnic group is the same as the Mayor.

Population Data (census.gov), Ethnicity/Race Data (http://quickfacts.census.gov), List of Mayors (http://ballotpedia.org/List_of_current_mayors_of_the_top_100_cities_in_the_United_States). All accessed August 10, 2016.

candidates needed to look beyond their co-ethnic voters in order to win the election. That candidates need to make broad racial and ethnic appeals is promising, and I take it to mean that the winning candidates did their best to appeal to voters beyond their own racial and ethnic groups. Even as some cities elect their second and third minority candidates to the mayor's office, San Francisco just reelected its first Asian American mayor. According to the data assembled by Hajnal and Trounstine in their Mayoral Data Set, Whites and Latinos vote for the same candidate quite often – and these candidates usually win (2014). Those data also show that Elite Black–Latino Coalitions generally support minority candidates, while White–Latino coalitions generally elect White candidates. To the extent that we still care about minority incorporation, the Elite Black–Latino Coalition may still be the best route for minority candidates. Incorporation, then, is still an important question as access to the political arena for minority groups is still tenuous in many cities. Descriptive representation – having a representative that looks like you – can lead to an increased participation rate for Latinos and Blacks (Barreto, Segura, and Woods 2004; Bobo and Gilliam 1990). While we may be more excited to think about the first Latino president or the second Black president, there are still plenty of "firsts" that can happen at the mayoral level.

THE NEW BIRACIAL COALITION

As we turn to the next round of mayoral elections in the United States, we should pay careful attention to the ways in which candidates look to members of other ethnic and racial groups to help them win. The data presented in the preceding chapters suggest that by reaching out to leaders and organizations that represent racial and ethnic groups, candidates can gain support from voters who are members of those groups. For Latino candidates, the best strategy is to reach out to Black leaders and organizations for endorsements, as this seems to help Blacks vote for them and does not reduce the likelihood of White voter support. The results from Chapter 3 show us that openly talking about Elite Black–Latino Coalitions does not lead White voters to punish Latino candidates. For Black candidates, the data from Chapter 2 show there is a greater hurdle to earn Latino votes, but the potential is there, as evidenced by the data in Chapter 3 where Latino voters supported the Black candidate at higher levels with endorsements and the coalition. Additionally, the Latino endorsements and the Elite Black–Latino Coalition helped White voters treat Black candidates the same as the White candidate who held the same issue position. The new biracial coalition can be led by either Latino candidates or Black candidates, but the candidates will need co-ethnic endorsements from the out-group to succeed.

LOOKING FORWARD: BUILDING A MORE DIVERSE COALITION

To the extent that Blacks and Latinos want to elect mayors that look like them, co-ethnic elite endorsements provide a cheap, but very useful signal that a minority candidate is in line with their interests. One benefit of the experimental data presented here was that the candidates all held the same issue positions. The candidates' issue positions did not change in any of the experiments. If respondents were selecting the candidates based on the issues, we should have seen no differences across treatments. For White voters who share issue preferences with minorities in the local context, these findings indicate that supporting minority candidates is one route to electing a mayor that shares their vision of the city.

As to the normative question about diversity in the mayor's office, this book offers a useful guide to getting those candidates into office. While the data show that co-ethnic elite endorsements for minority candidates are quite persuasive for Blacks, they are less so for Latino voters. However, they can be persuasive to both groups under the right conditions. The fact that White voters are also on board when minority candidates receive endorsements is also promising for these candidates. This is especially true for Latino candidates. In this way, the new biracial coalition may be helmed by Latino candidates with Black leader and organization support. The face of the new biracial coalition is likely a Latino face. The prognosis for White candidates is less optimistic. While it is clear that White candidates can represent minority interests well, the data shown here indicate that they need to discuss racial issues in order for the endorsements to be persuasive to both Black and Latino voters. This seems like a risky strategy as it may drive non-sympathetic Whites to the ballot box.

Finally, this book focuses only on Blacks, Latinos, and Whites. Given that the Asian American population is growing at a fast rate, future research should consider how they respond to co-ethnic cues. It is not clear which endorsements will be most effective to this group, as they have several identity options. They may prefer their national origin identity to the term *Asian American*. Only future research can address this question. Additional research is also needed to determine which group or groups Asian Americans want to coalesce with. They may decide to join Blacks and Latinos, join forces with only Blacks or Latinos, join Whites, or go it alone. The next round of mayoral elections may bring us one step closer to a better understanding of minority political incorporation in our increasingly diverse cities and towns.

NOTES

1. Eligon, John. "Ferguson elects 2 Blacks to city council, but rejects activist candidates." *New York Times*. April 7, 2015.
2. www.census.gov/2010census/news/releases/operations/cb11-cn125.html.

Elections Appendix

EA TABLE O.1 *Los Angeles Election Results (% Vote)*

	White	Black	Latino	Asian American
1997				
Riordan (White)	71*	19	60**	62**
Hayden (White)	26	75**	33	35
2001				
Villaraigosa (Latino)	41	20	82*	35
Hahn (White)	59*	80**	18	65**
2005				
Villaraigosa (Latino)	57**	58**	86*	42
Hahn (White)	43	42	14	59**
2013				
Garcetti (Latino)	59**	31	60*	55**
Greuel (White)	41	69**	40	45

1993–2001 Sonenshein and Pinkus[1], 2005 The Center for the Study of Los Angeles, 2013 Guerra and Gilbert[2]

Winner

 * Majority Co-ethnic Support
 ** Majority Cross-Ethnic Support

[1] Sonenshein, Raphael J. and Susan H. Pinkus. 2005. "Latino Incorporation Reaches the Urban Summit: How Antonio Villaraigosa Won the 2005 Los Angeles Mayor's Race." PS October 2005, pp. 713–21.

[2] Guerra, Fernando J. and Brianne Gilbert. 2013. Los Angeles Votes 2013: Mayoral General Election Exit Poll. Thomas and Dorothy Leavey Center for the Study of Los Angeles, Loyola Marymount University, Los Angeles, California.

EA TABLE O.2 *New York Election Results (% Vote)*

	White	Black	Latino
1997			
Giuliani (White)	76*	20	43
Messinger (White)	21	79**	57**
2001			
Bloomberg (White)	60*	25	47
Green (White)	38	75**	49
2005			
Bloomberg (White)	67*	46	34
Ferrer (Latino)	30	53**	63*
2009			
Bloomberg (White)	67*	23	43
Thompson (Black)	29	76*	55**
2013 Dem Primary			
de Blasio (White)	41	42	38
Thompson (Black)	19	42	27
Quinn (White)	22	6	14
Liu (Asian American)	4	4	7
Weiner (White)	3	5	8
2013 General			
de Blasio (White)	52*	95**	85**
Lhota (White)	43	4	10

1993–2001 Kaufmann[1], 2005 New York City Mayoral Election Study, 2009 *New York Times*,[2] 2013 Primary *New York Times* Exit Poll[3]
2013 *New York Times* Exit Poll[4]

Winner
*   Majority Co-ethnic Support
** Majority Cross-Ethnic Support

[1] Kaufmann, Karen M. 2004. *The Urban Voter: Group Conflict and Mayoral Voting Behavior in American Cities*. Ann Arbor: University of Michigan Press.
[2] "Profile of New York City Voters." *New York Times*. November 4, 2009.
[3] www.nytimes.com/projects/elections/2013/nyc-primary/mayor/exit-polls.html
[4] www.nytimes.com/projects/elections/2013/general/nyc-mayor/exit-polls.html

EA TABLE O.3 *Houston Election Results (% Vote)*

	White	Black	Latino
1997 General			
Mosbacher (White)	51*	1	3
Brown (Black)	14	97*	16
Saenz (Latino)	4	1	69*
Greanias (White)	30	1	12
1997 Runoff			

(continued)

EA TABLE 0.3 (continued)

	White	Black	Latino
Mosbacher (White)	77*	3	34
Brown (Black)	23	97*	66**
1999			
Brown (Black)	N/A	N/A	N/A
No Real Contenders	N/A	N/A	N/A
2001			
Brown (Black)	N/A	90*	28
Sanchez (Latino)	N/A	10	72*
2003 General			
White (White)	55*	17	35
Sanchez (Latino)	41	4	55**
Turner (Black)	1	70**	1
2013 Runoff			
White (White)	51*	85**	39
Sanchez (Latino)	47	11	56*
2005			
White (White)	N/A	N/A	N/A
No Real Challengers	N/A	N/A	N/A
2007			
White (White)	N/A	N/A	N/A
No Real Challengers	N/A	N/A	N/A
2009			
Parker (White)	69*	13	63**
Locke (Black)	29	86*	25
2011			
Parker (White)	N/A	N/A	N/A
No Real Challengers	N/A	N/A	N/A
2013			
Parker (White)	N/A	N/A	N/A
No Real Challengers	N/A	N/A	N/A

1997 McKeever[1], 2001 Vaca,[2] 2003 Hajnal and Trounstine[3], 2009 de Leon[4]

Winner
* Majority Co-ethnic Support
** Majority Cross-Ethnic Support

[1] McKeever, Matthew. 2001. "Interethnic Politics in the Consensus City." In *Governing American Cities.* Michael Jones-Correa (Ed.). New York: Russell Sage Foundation. pp. 240–43.
[2] Vaca, Nicolas. 2004. *The Presumed Alliance. The Unspoken Conflict between Latinos and Blacks and What It Means for America.* New York. Harper Collins Press. p. 168.
[3] Hajnal, Z. and J. Trounstine. 2014. "What Underlies Urban Politics? Race, Class, Ideology, Partisanship, and the Urban Vote." *Urban Affairs Review,* 50, 63–99.
[4] "How Major Voting Groups Voted in December 12, 2009 Runoff Election." Hector de Leon.

EA TABLE O.4 *Chicago Election Results (% Vote)*

	White	Black	Latino
1999			
Daley (White)	95*	45	85**
Rush (Black)	5	55*	15
2003			
Daley (White)	85*	55**	79**
Jakes (Black)	6	22	7
2007			
Daley (White)	N/A	N/A	N/A
Walls (Black)	N/A	N/A	N/A
Brown (Black)	N/A	N/A	N/A
2011			
Emanuel (Jewish)	N/A	N/A	N/A
Chico (Latino)	N/A	N/A	N/A
deValle (Latino)	N/A	N/A	N/A
Braun (Black)	N/A	N/A	N/A
2015 General			
Emanuel (Jewish)	N/A	N/A	N/A
Garcia (Latino)	N/A	N/A	N/A
Walls (Black)	N/A	N/A	N/A
Wilson (Black)	N/A	N/A	N/A
Fioretti (White)	N/A	N/A	N/A
2015 Runoff			
Emanuel (Jewish)	66	58**	32
Garcia (Latino)	34	42	68*

1999 and 2003 Hajnal and Trounstine[1]

Winner
* Majority Co-ethnic Support
** Majority Cross-Ethnic Support

[1] Hajnal, Z. and J. Trounstine. 2014. "What Underlies Urban Politics? Race, Class, Ideology, Partisanship, and the Urban Vote." *Urban Affairs Review*, 50, 63–99.

EA TABLE O.5 *Los Angeles Poll*

March 8, 2005 Primary Exit Poll
Which actions taken by Hahn contributed to your vote today?

	Blacks	Latinos	Whites
Appointing Bratton over Parks	48	25	22
Secession of SFV and Hollywood	20	25	37
Neither	39	56	53

Los Angeles Times Poll

NEW YORK CITY: RACIAL AND ETHNIC POLITICS IN THE BIG APPLE

In New York City in 1997, Rudolph Giuliani, a White candidate, received four endorsements from Black leaders, including Representatives Edolphus Towns and Floyd Fluke and city councilmembers Priscilla Wooten and Thomas White Jr. Ruth Messinger, another White candidate, received six endorsements from Black leaders: Assemblyman Clarence Norman Jr., Representative Charles B. Rangel, former mayor of New York City David Dinkins, State Comptroller H. Carl McCall, activist Al Sharpton, and reverend of the Canaan Baptist Church in Harlem Wyatt Tee Walker. Giuliani received a Latino endorsement from Councilman Adam Clayton Powell IV. The newspapers reported 28 endorsements in this contest. In the election, Giuliani received 20% of the Black vote and 43% of the Latino vote. Messinger received 70% of the Black vote and 57% of the Latino vote. Both Blacks and Latinos provided Messinger with cross-ethnic voting support. In this election, 35% of the newspaper articles discussed race and ethnicity, which means racial and ethnic salience was high or above average. Additionally, during the 1997 New York campaign, Messinger had to balance her relationship with Black civil rights leader Reverend Al Sharpton and his relationship with some community leaders who were accused of anti-Semitism.[1] This put Messinger in the awkward position of trying to appease White voters and Black voters at the same time. By connecting her to a Black community leader, race was made salient in the campaign. In this case, Messinger received more Black endorsements and a majority of the Black vote. Among Latinos, there was only one endorsement, but in the end Messinger received more support from this group. Race and ethnicity were salient in the election and the endorsements were influential when it came to Black votes. The 1997 mayoral election in New York City is categorized as high coverage of race and ethnicity in the presence of racial and ethnic issues in EA Table 0.6.

In the Democratic runoff election in New York in 2001, Fernando Ferrer, a Latino candidate, received four endorsements from Black leaders and organizations (Representative Charles B. Rangel; the Grand Council of Guardians, a fraternal organization of black police officers, state troopers, correction officers and other law enforcement officials; Reverend Al Sharpton; and activist Sonny Carson). Mark Green, a White candidate, received only one endorsement from a Black leader: former mayor of New York City David Dinkins. Ferrer also received one

EA TABLE O.6 *Relationship between Endorsements and Vote Choice by Racial/Ethnic Salience in Mayoral Elections*

Media Coverage of Race/Ethnicity	Presence of Racial and Ethnic Issues in the Election	
	No	Yes
Low	Low Impact Chicago 1999 Houston 2013 Los Angeles 1997 Los Angeles 2009 New York 2001	Moderate Impact Houston 1997 Los Angeles 2013 New York 2013
High	Moderate Impact Chicago 2003* New York 2009*	High Impact Chicago 2015* Houston 2001 Houston 2003 Los Angeles 2001* Los Angeles 2005 New York 1997 New York 2005

Bold = Co-ethnic Elite Cues Theory explains vote choice
* = Co-ethnic Elite Cues Theory does not explain vote choice
Elections where there were no exit poll data or no endorsement data (Chicago 2007, 2011; Houston 1999, 2005, 2007, 2009, 2011).
Low coverage of race and ethnicity and no racial/ethnic issues: Low Impact
Low coverage of race and ethnicity in the presence of racial/ethnic issues
High coverage of race and ethnicity and no racial or ethnic issues
High coverage of race and ethnicity in the presence of racial and ethnic issues

endorsement from a Black and Latino organization – the Service Employees' Union, while Green did not receive any endorsements from Black–Latino organizations. Ferrer received one endorsement from Latino leaders and organizations (the New York Police Department Hispanic Detectives Society), while Green did not receive any endorsements from Latino leaders and organizations. The newspapers reported 17 endorsements in the primary. In the election, Ferrer received 71% of the Black vote (cross-ethnic voting), while Green received only 29%. Ferrer also received 84% of the Latino vote to Green's 16%. Race and ethnicity were also salient in the 2001 Democratic New York runoff campaign, as Green sent out negative campaign literature that seemed to question Ferrer's ability to be the mayor of New York given his background as a Puerto Rican.[2] Green later apologized for this and, in the end, Ferrer offered Green his endorsement during the general election.

In this case, the candidate with the most endorsements from Black and Latino leaders and organizations also received the most votes from these groups. The Co-ethnic Elite Cues Theory predicts that Ferrer would receive the majority of the votes from Latino voters (co-ethnic voting), as he is a Latino candidate.

In 2013, Bill Thompson was back and he faced Bill de Blasio, a White candidate with a Black wife and two biracial children, in the Democratic primary. It was an interesting primary election in that Bill de Blasio took a strong stance against the "stop and frisk" policy, which made race and ethnicity an important part of the campaign.[3] The racial and ethnic coverage of the campaign was just below the threshold of 31%. It was not just the racial and ethnic issue of stop and frisk that contributed to race and ethnicity being salient in this campaign. The media also brought race into the campaign in another way: the de Blasio family.[4] By using his family in many of his campaign ads, he sent a signal to voters about race. While previous research has cautioned minority voters from making too many racial appeals in campaigns, de Blasio made these appeals explicitly (Hero, 1992). Ultimately, Thompson received three endorsements from Black leaders (Representative Charles B. Rangel, former mayor David N. Dinkins, and Representative Hakeem Jeffries), while de Blasio received only one (Harry Belafonte). Bill Thompson also received one endorsement from a Latino leader, Fernando Ferrer, while de Blasio did not receive any. The newspapers reported 20 endorsements in the primary. Although Blacks had the option to select a Black candidate in the Democratic primary, the Black vote was split (42% going to both candidates according to the *New York Times* exit poll). No one candidate received a majority of the Latino vote in the primary. Thirty-eight percent of Latinos voted for de Blasio and 27% voted for Thompson.[5] The vote was close between Thompson and de Blasio, but Thompson conceded defeat and de Blasio won the primary. Bill de Blasio went on to win the election to become New York's first Democratic mayor since Dinkins.

In the general election, de Blasio faced Joe Lhota. There were not many new endorsements announced, but de Blasio received two more Black endorsements: one from the local African American newspaper, the *Amsterdam News*, and one from President Obama. There were not any Latino endorsements announced for either candidate in the *New York Times*. The paper reported 20 endorsements in the general election. The stop and frisk issue remained salient in the general election and de Blasio captured 95% of the Black votes and 85% of the Latino votes (both groups engaged in cross-ethnic voting). This provides some support for the Co-ethnic Elite Cues Theory. In summary, the recent elections in New York City highlight the conditions under which the race and ethnicity of the candidates and the racial and ethnic salience can make co-ethnic elite endorsements more persuasive to Black and Latino voters. The New York 2013 election is categorized as low coverage of race and ethnicity in the presence of racial/ethnic issues in EA Table 0.6.

LOS ANGELES: RACIAL AND ETHNIC POLITICS IN THE CITY OF ANGELS

Now let's turn our attention to Los Angeles in 1997 where incumbent mayor Richard Riorden faced California State Senator Tom Hayden. In this election, race and ethnicity were not salient. The media mentioned race and ethnicity in only 28% of the coverage and there were no racial issues (low or below average). Riorden racked up an impressive list of Black endorsements from Magic Johnson, the Reverend Cecil "Chip" Murray, County Supervisor Yvonne Brathwaite Burke, U.S. Representative Julian C. Dixon, and State Senator Teresa Hughes. He also received an endorsement from a Latino city councilman, Richard Alatorre. Hayden received only one Black endorsement from Reverend Jesse Jackson. The *Los Angeles Times* reported 26 endorsements during the campaign. The vote return data show that Hayden received 75% of the Black vote and Riorden received 60% of the Latino vote. While both groups engaged in cross-ethnic voting, they did not support the same candidate. Given that race and ethnicity coverage was below average in this campaign and there were no racial or ethnic issues, I expected endorsements to matter less here. This election is considered low coverage of race and ethnicity and no racial/ethnic issues in EA Table 0.6.

During the 2005 election in Los Angeles, the same candidates, Hahn and Villaraigosa, faced one another again. This time, Villaraigosa received six Black leader and organization endorsements from city councilmember and former police chief Bernard Parks, Los Angeles County Supervisor Yvonne Brathwaite Burke, Representative Maxine Waters, Magic Johnson, the *Sentinel*, and Reverend Cecil Murray First African Methodist Episcopal Church (retired). Villaraigosa received four Latino leader and organization endorsements (Senator Richard Alarcon, Councilman Tony Cardenas, City Council President Alex Padilla, and Los Angeles County Supervisor Gloria Molina). Hahn received two Black endorsements (Assemblymen Mervyn Dymally and Jerome Horton) and two Latino endorsements (State Assembly Member Rudy

Bermudez and Councilmember Ed Reyes). The *Los Angeles Times* reported 54 endorsements while covering this election. In the election, Villaraigosa received 58% of the Black vote, while Hahn received 42%. Villaraigosa received 82% of the Latino vote to Hahn's 14% (co-ethnic voting). In the 2005 Los Angeles campaign, race was made salient after the second African American police chief in the history of the city, Bernard Parks, was fired. *Los Angeles Times* poll data suggest a plurality (48%) of Blacks voted for Villaraigosa because of the Parks incident. Although many Blacks preferred Villaraigosa on policy grounds, it might be that Black leaders wanted to punish Hahn for firing Parks and this is why they offered their endorsements to Villaraigosa. In this case, the candidate with the majority of the Black endorsements did receive a majority of the Black votes (cross-ethnic voting). Villaraigosa received a majority of the Latino vote and the majority of the Latino endorsements. The news coverage of the campaign mentioned racial and ethnic terms 32% of the time, which is just above the average. When coupled with the Bernard Parks issue, we expect that in the absence of a Black candidate, Black voters voted for the candidate with the most Black endorsements. This was the case in the 2005 election. This election provides support for the Co-ethnic Elite Cues Theory. This is a case when a Black–Latino electoral coalition emerged as Blacks and Latinos elected their preferred candidate. This election is categorized as high coverage of race and ethnicity in the presence of racial and ethnic issues in EA Table 0.6.

The Los Angeles 2009 election represents an election when there was not much coverage on the election nor did the election generate many racial and ethnic endorsements. Only 10% of the coverage was racial or ethnic in nature and there were so few endorsements, the *Los Angeles Times* reported on its own endorsement for Villaraigosa (with three more endorsements mentioned overall). While the incumbent mayor faced nine challengers, none of them stood out and the media barely reported on them. Villaraigosa won the election without a runoff. Given that racial and ethnic salience was low or below average in this campaign, the Co-ethnic Elite Cues Theory suggests that endorsements should matter less to voters. In this election, the only endorsements mentioned were from the *Los Angeles Times*, so there is not enough endorsements data to assess the Co-ethnic Elite Cues Theory. This election is categorized as low coverage of race and ethnicity and no racial/ethnic issues in EA Table 0.6.

The Los Angeles 2013 election provides an interesting look at the notion of identity and the race of the candidate. During the general election, we saw evidence of co-ethnic voting, with a majority of Blacks voting for the Black candidate, Jan Perry, and a majority of Latinos voting for the Latino candidate, Eric Garcetti (Guerra and Gilbert 2013). However, Garcetti's identity was complicated by the fact that he also identifies as Jewish.[6] Jan Perry did not earn enough support to move on to the runoff election, so Garcetti faced Wendy Greuel, a White candidate. Greuel amassed six endorsements from Black leaders and organization in Los Angeles (Magic Johnson; Representative Maxine Waters; Lorraine Bradley, daughter of Tom Bradley; Supervisor Mark Ridley Thomas; Charles E. Blake, West Angeles Church of God in Christ Bishop; Reverend Cecil "Chip" Murray; and *Sentinel* publisher Danny J. Bakewell Sr.), while Garcetti received five (the Black Community Clergy and Labor Alliance (BCCLA); the New Frontier Democratic Club, the preeminent African American Democratic organization in Los Angeles; Councilmembers Jan Perry and Bernard Parks, and the Los Angeles African American Women Political Action Committee). In the end, 69% of Blacks voted for Greuel (cross-ethnic voting). Both candidates also received endorsements from Latino elites and organizations, but the theory predicts that Latinos may support the co-ethnic candidate, Garcetti. By Election Day, Garcetti received only five Latino endorsements, compared to Greuel's seven, but 60% of Latinos voted for Garcetti in the election. The *Los Angeles Times* reported 65 endorsements. The mentions of race and ethnicity in the *Los Angeles Times*' coverage of race and ethnicity in the campaign was low, with only 26% of the articles mentioning race or ethnicity. However, there were racial issues in that there were political ads that indicated that Wendy Greuel voted yes on Proposition 187 (which is an anti-immigrant law).[7] The Co-ethnic Elite Cues Theory did work well here, just not for an Elite Black–Latino Coalition, as Blacks supported the White candidate with the majority of the Black endorsements and Latinos supported Garcetti. In summary, the recent elections in Los Angeles highlight when the race and ethnicity of the candidates and the racial and ethnic salience may make co-ethnic elite endorsements more persuasive to Black and Latino voters. The election is categorized as low coverage of race and ethnicity in the presence of racial/ethnic issues in EA Table 0.6.

HOUSTON: THE CONSENSUS CITY

The 2001 election in Houston was a contest between Lee Brown, a Black candidate, and Orlando Sanchez, a Latino candidate. There is no expectation of an Elite Black–Latino Coalition here, as each group is expected to vote for the candidate from its own racial/ethnic group. Brown received six Black leader and organization endorsements and four Latino leader and organization endorsements. Brown received endorsements from the following Black leaders and organizations: the Harris County Council of Organizations, Dallas Mayor Ron Kirk, Councilmembers Carol Mims Galloway and Don Boney, the International Association of Black Professional Firefighters, and the Gulf Coast AME Ministerial Alliance, which is an alliance that represents almost 36,000 members of 66 African Methodist Episcopal Churches in the Houston area. His Latino endorsers included the former mayor of San Antonio Henry Cisneros, Democratic gubernatorial candidate Tony Sanchez, and Councilmembers Gabriel Vasquez and John Castillo. Sanchez received no Black leader and organization endorsements and two Latino organization endorsements (one from the Latina P.A.C., which is a political committee of Hispanic women, and one from the Houston Hispanic Chamber of Commerce Policy Committee a Hispanic Business Organization). The *Houston Chronicle* reported on 31 endorsements in this campaign. In the election, Brown received 90% of the Black vote and 28% of the Latino vote. Sanchez received 10% of the Black vote and 72% of the Latino vote. Both Blacks and Latinos engaged in co-ethnic voting during this election. Race and ethnicity were salient in this campaign, as both Sanchez and Brown sought out their racial/ethnic voter base, thus highlighting race and ethnicity in the campaign. The coverage of the election in the *Houston Chronicle* confirms this as it mentioned race and ethnicity in 66% of the articles, which is high or above average. The Co-ethnic Elite Cues Theory predicts that Blacks and Latinos will support their respective co-ethnic candidates. The 2001 mayoral election in Houston provides strong evidence of this as Blacks supported the Black candidate and Latinos supported the Latino candidate. The election is categorized as high coverage of race and ethnicity in the presence of racial and ethnic issues in EA Table 0.6.

In the 2003 Houston mayoral election, Lee Brown was unable to run again due to term limits. Orlando Sanchez was back and he faced Bill White, a White candidate, and Sylvester Taylor, a Black candidate, in the general election. Race and ethnicity were salient in this campaign as the *Houston Chronicle* coverage mentioned race and ethnicity in 35% of the election coverage, which is above average or high. In addition to the racial and ethnic mentions, the candidates discussed immigration because a grassroots organization pushed for reform in the city. The Spanish newspaper *El Dia* reported that Sanchez supported licenses for undocumented immigrants. However, Sanchez denied making such statements.[8] In addition to this, a mailer was sent to Black voters that implied that White was opposed to African Americans in office.[9] In the general election, White received four endorsements from Black leaders and Organizations: Texas State Representatives Garnet Coleman and Senfronia Thompson, Texas State Senator Rodney Ellis, Councilwoman Ada Edwards, and Mayor of Houston Lee Brown. Sylvestor Turner also received endorsements from Black leaders and organizations. His endorsers included U.S. Representative Sheila Jackson Lee and a group of local clergy that included Kirbyjon Caldwell of Windsor Village United Methodist Church, Bill Lawson of Wheeler Avenue Baptist Church, Ralph West of Church Without Walls, James Dixon of Northwest Community Baptist Church, and Roy Love of Gulf Meadows Church. Sanchez did not receive any racial or ethnic endorsements in the general election. Only White and Sanchez advanced to the runoff election. In that election, White added to his list of Black endorsers, picking up endorsements from Harris County Commissioner El Franco Lee and Fort Bend County Constable Ruben Jones. He also added three Latino endorsements from Councilwoman Carol Alvarado, Harris County Commissioner Sylvia Garcia, and members of the Tejano Democrats. Sanchez received an endorsement from the Hispanic Chamber of Commerce. The *Houston Chronicle* reported 35 endorsements in the general election and 22 in the runoff election. The election results show that the candidate with the most Black endorsements, Bill White, received 85% of the Black vote, which provides some support for the Co-ethnic Elite Cues Theory. Blacks also engaged in cross-ethnic voting. Among Latinos, the Latino candidate received 56% of the Latino vote, which provides evidence of co-ethnic voting. The Houston 2003 election is categorized as high coverage of race and ethnicity in the presence of racial and ethnic issues in EA Table 0.6.

The Houston 2005 and 2007 mayoral elections were very similar to the Los Angeles 2009 election. White ran in both elections and was easily reelected with 91% and 87% of the votes, respectively. A survey of the election coverage in the *Houston Chronicle* in each of these contests shows that there were very few endorsements mentioned (two in 2005 and one in 2007) and race and ethnicity were not mentioned (none of the articles in 2005 mentioned race and only 6% of the coverage focused on race or ethnicity in 2007, which is low or below average). There are no exit poll data by race and ethnicity for this election, so I cannot assess the Co-ethnic Elite Cues Theory for this contest.

The Houston 2009 mayoral election featured Annise Parker, a White candidate; Gene Locke, a Black candidate; and Councilmember Peter Brown, also White. Despite there being a minority candidate on the ballot, race and ethnicity were not salient in the election because the election also featured the first openly gay mayoral candidate and as a result, sexuality and morality became the focus of the election. This is confirmed by the *Houston Chronicle* coverage, in which only 28% of the articles mentioned race. There were some endorsements mentioned in the coverage of this election, but many of them came from religious organizations. Peter Brown did receive endorsements from two Black clergy: the Reverend Bill Lawson of Wheeler Avenue Baptist Church and Dr. D. Z. Cofield. Black voters overwhelmingly supported Locke. The *Houston Chronicle* mentioned 14 endorsements. No Latino endorsements were mentioned, though Parker received 63% of the Latino vote. Annise Parker was easily reelected to the mayor's office in 2011 and 2013 (low coverage of race and ethnicity and no racial/ethnic issues in EA Table 0.6). In both of these contests, racial and ethnic coverage was low (5% and 29%, respectively) and the campaign coverage focused more on LGBT issues.[10] The number of endorsements reported was also low: (one in 2011 and three in 2013). In summary, the recent elections in Houston show that when race and ethnicity are salient, the race of the candidate and co-ethnic elite endorsements may help explain vote choice, but this is not always the case.

CHICAGO: RACIAL AND ETHNIC POLITICS IN THE WINDY CITY

Mayoral elections in Chicago provide a unique view of racial and ethnic politics. In the 1999, 2003, and 2007 elections, Richard M. Daley won the mayoral elections with more than 70% of the vote. Daley faced Black candidates in each of these elections and I expect Black voters to support a Black candidate. I find evidence of co-ethnic voting among Blacks in the 1999 election when Daley faced Bobby Rush, a Black candidate and a majority of Blacks supported him, as expected by the Co-ethnic Elite Cues Theory. The *Chicago Tribune* reported 22 endorsements in this election. The 1999 election is categorized as low coverage of race and ethnicity and no racial/ethnic issues in EA Table 0.6. However, in the 2003 election, a majority of Blacks, Latinos, and Whites in the city supported Daley. This does not provide support for the Co-ethnic Elite Cues Theory among Blacks, as the theory predicts Black voters will support the Black candidate. The newspapers reported 16 endorsements while covering this election. The 2003 election is categorized as High coverage of race and ethnicity and no racial or ethnic issues in EA Table 0.6. In 2007, Daley faced two Black candidates, but there are no exit poll data by group to see if Blacks supported one of these candidates. The number of endorsements reported in 2007 was five. Racial and ethnic saliency were high or above average in the 2003 and 2007 campaigns (48% and 33% of the articles covered race and ethnicity, respectively), with the *Chicago Tribune* mentioning race and ethnicity quite a bit, but the candidates did not discuss racial issues in the 1999, 2003, or 2007 campaigns. Given the high mentions of race and ethnicity and the lack of racial or ethnic issues, I expect endorsements to have a moderate influence on vote choice among Latinos, but the *Chicago Tribune* reported only one Latino endorsement for Daley in 2007 from U.S. Representative Luis Gutierrez. This makes it difficult to assess the Co-ethnic Elite Cues Theory among Latinos in Chicago. Further, there are no exit poll data available by racial and ethnic group to test this claim. It was not until 2011, when Daley did not run and a Latino candidate ran, that several Latino endorsements were mentioned in the newspaper.

The 2011 Chicago election featured one Jewish candidate, Rahm Emmanuel, two Latino candidates, Gery Chico and Miguel del Valle, and a Black candidate, Carol Moseley Braun. Race and ethnicity were not salient in the campaign as the news coverage reported on race and ethnicity in only 31% of the stories – just below average. Additionally, no racial or ethnic issues were highlighted in that campaign. In this election, we would expect endorsements to have little influence on the vote choice among Blacks and Latinos. Further, I expect Blacks to support a Black candidate (co-ethnic voting). Chico received 12 endorsements from Latino leaders and organizations, including endorsements from the Hispanic American Labor Council, Laborers, U.S. Representative Luis V. Gutierrez, State Senator Tony Munoz, State Representative Edward Acevedo, Former Cook County Commissioner Joseph Mario Moreno, Aldermen Danny Solis and Proco "Joe" Moreno, Paul Vallas former CEO of Chicago Public Schools, the Mexican American Politic Organization, and the Latin American Police Association. Chico also received one endorsement from a Black leader (Reverend B. Herbert Martin of the Progressive Community Church). No other Latino endorsements were mentioned for the other three candidates. Braun received five Black endorsements from the Clergy Coalition, a group of nearly 50 black ministers, Representative Bobby Rush, and Alderwomen Fredrenna Lyle and Michelle Harris. The *Chicago Tribune* reported 34 endorsements in this campaign. Unfortunately, exit poll data from this election did not report vote choice by race/ethnicity. A report of vote choice by wards coupled with a map of race and ethnicity by wards shows that Chico did well in four wards, two of which were majority Latino wards (Green 2011).[11] Emanuel earned more than 50% of the vote in 36 wards, many of them with a majority of Black and Latino voters. Braun and del Valle did not receive a majority of the votes in any single ward. There were nine wards where there was no candidate received a majority of the vote. Emanuel won the election with 55% of the vote. These ward-level data provides some information, but we cannot fully assess the theory among Black and Latino voters.

NOTES

1. "The mayor mars Columbus Day." *New York Times*, October 15, 1997, A22.
2. Murphy, Dean E. and Michael Cooper. "Bloomberg sees overtones of race in final days of green effort." *New York Times*, October 17, 1997, D5.
3. "Last call in the race for mayor." *New York Times*, September 5, 2013, A24.
4. "The Two Bloombergs." *New York Times*, September 17, 2013, A22.
5. www.nytimes.com/projects/elections/2013/nyc-primary/mayor/exit-polls.html
6. Rainey, James and Seema Mehta. "Finish line is in sight; Garcetti and Greuel crisscross the city in a last attempt to connect with voters before the election." *Los Angeles Times*, May 20, 2013, A1.
7. Lopez, Steve. "Is L.A. too cool to vote? It shouldn't be. Crank up Randy Newman and head to the polls." *Los Angeles Times*, May 19, 2013, A2.
8. Graves, Rachel. "From West Side to East End, Sanchez courts his old allies." *Houston Chronicle*, September 28, 2003. Edition: 4 STAR Section: A Page: 01.
9. Rodriguez, Lori. "Race resurfaces as election issue – fliers play trump card in mayoral contest." *Houston Chronicle*, October 26, 2003 Edition: 4 STAR Section: A Page: 29.
10. Olson, Bradley. "Ministers motivated for defeat of Parker conservative group opposing lesbian in office Parker: city charter concerns." *Houston Chronicle*, November 14, 2009 Edition: 3 STAR Section: B Page: 1.
11. http://media.apps.chicagotribune.com/ward-redistricting/index.html#41.88656001350776,-87.67107009887695,11,0

References

The American National Election Studies (ANES; www.electionstudies.org). The ANES 2008 Time Series Study [data set]. Stanford University and the University of Michigan [producers]. These materials are based on work supported by the National Science Foundation under grants SES-0535334, SES-0720428, SES-0840550, and SES-0651271, Stanford University, and the University of Michigan. Any opinions, findings, and conclusions or recommendations expressed in these materials are those of the author(s) and do not necessarily reflect the views of the funding organizations.

Abrajano, M., J. Nagler, and R. M. Alvarez (2005). A natural experiment of race-based and issue voting: The 2001 city of Los Angeles elections. *American Politics Quarterly*, 58(2), 203–18.

Anderson, B. (1991). *Imagined Communities*. London: Verso Press.

Ansolabehere, S. and S. Iyengar (1997). *Going Negative: How Political Advertisements Shrink and Polarize the Electorate*. New York: Free Press.

Arceneaux, K. and R. Kolodny (2009). Educating the least informed: Group endorsements in a grassroots campaign. *American Journal of Political Science*, 53(4), 755–70.

Barreto, M. (2007). Si Se Puede! Latino candidates and the mobilization of Latino voters. *American Political Science Review*, 101(3), 425–41.

  (2009). *Ethnic Cues: The Role of Shared Ethnicity in Latino Political Participation*. Ann Arbor: University of Michigan Press.

Barreto, M. A., L. R. Fraga, S. Manzano, V. Martinez-Ebers, and G. M. Segura et al. (2008). *Should They Dance with the One Who Brung 'Em?: Latinos and the 2008 Presidential Election*. PS: Political Science and Politics. October: 753–60.

Barreto, M. A., G. M. Segura, and N. D. Woods. (2004). The mobilizing effect of majority-minority districts on Latino turnout. *American Political Science Review*, 98, 65–75.

Bean, F. D., K. Brown, and R. G. Rumbaut (2006). Mexican immigrant political and economic incorporation. *Perspectives on Politics*, 4(02), 309–13.

Beltran, C. (2010). *The Trouble with Unity: Latino Politics and the Creation of Identity*. Oxford: Oxford University Press.

Berelson, B. R., P. E. Lazarsfeld, and W. N. McPhee (1954). *Voting*. Chicago: University of Chicago Press.

Bobo, L. and F. Gilliam Jr. (1990). Race, sociopolitical participation and Black empowerment. *American Political Science Review*, 84(2), 377–94.

Bobo, L. and V. L. Hutchings (1996). Perceptions of racial group competition extending Blumer's theory of group position to a multiracial social context. *American Sociological Review*, 61(6), 951–72.

Brader, T., N. A. Valentino, and E. Suhay (2008). What triggers public opposition to immigration? Anxiety, group cues, and immigration threat. *American Journal of Political Science*, 52(4), 959–78.

Brady, H. E. and P. M. Sniderman (1985). Attitude attribution: A group basis for political reasoning. *American Political Science Review*, 79(4), 1061–78.

Browning, R. P., D. R. Marshall, and D. H. Tabb (1984). *Protest Is Not Enough: The Struggle for Blacks and Hispanics for Equality in Urban Politics*. Berkeley: University of California Press.

  (2003). *Racial Politics in American Cities*. 3rd edn. New York: Longman Publications.

Bullock, C. S., III, and B. A. Campbell (1984). Racist or racial voting in the 1981 Atlanta municipal elections. *Urban Affairs Quarterly*, 20(2), 149–64.

Burns, N., K. L. Schlozman, and S. Verba (2001). *The Private Roots of Public Action: Gender, Equality, and Political Participation*. Cambridge, MA: Harvard University Press.

Campbell, A., P. Converse, W. Miller, and D. Stokes (1960). *The American Voter*. New York: Wiley.

Campos-Flores, A. and H. Fineman (2005). A Latin power surge. *Newsweek*, 145(22), 24–32.

Carmines, E. G. and J. A. Stimson (1989). *Issue Evolution: Race and the Transformation of American Politics*. Princeton, NJ: Princeton University Press.

Cho, W. K. T. (1999). Naturalization, socialization, participation: Immigrant and (non-)voting. *Journal of Politics*, 61(4), 1140–55.

Chong, D. (1991). *Collective Action and the Civil Rights Movement*. Chicago: University of Chicago Press.

  (1993). How people think, reason, and feel about rights and liberties. *American Journal of Political Science*, 37(3), 867–99.

Chong, D. and J. M. Druckman (2007). Framing theory. *Annual Review of Political Science*, 10, 103–26.

Cohen, C. J. (1999). *The Boundaries of Blackness: AIDS and the Breakdown of Black Politics*. Chicago: University of Chicago Press.

Cohen, G. L. (2003). Party over policy: The dominating impact of group influence on political beliefs. *Journal of Personality and Social Psychology*, 85(5), 808–22.

Colby, S. L. and J. M. Ortman (2014). *Projections of the Size and Composition of the U.S. Population: 2014 to 2060*, Current Population Reports, P25-1143, U.S. Census Bureau, Washington, DC.

Conover, P. J. (1988). The role of social groups in political thinking. *British Journal of Political Science*, 18(1), 51–75.

Conover, P. J. and S. Feldman (1989). Candidate perception in an ambiguous world: Campaigns, cues, and inference processes. *American Journal of Political Science*, 33(4), 912–40.

Converse, P. E. (1964). The nature of belief systems in mass publics. In David E. Apter (Ed.), *Ideology and Discontent* (pp. 206–59). New York: Free Press.

Dahl, R. (1962). *Who Governs? Democracy and Power in an American City*. New Haven, CT: Yale University Press.

Dawson, M. (1994). *Behind the Mule: Race and Class in African American Politics*. Princeton, NJ: Princeton University Press.

Delli Carpini, M. X. and S. Keeter (1996). *What Americans Know about Politics and Why It Matters*. New Haven, CT: Yale University Press.

DeSantis, V. S. and T. Renner (1991). Contemporary patterns and trends in government structure. In *The Municipal Year Book*. Municipal Washington, DC: International City/County Management Association.

  (2002). City government structures: An attempt at clarification. *State & Local Government Review*, 34(2), 95–104.

Deutsch, K. (1966). *Nationalism and Social Communication*. Cambridge: MIT Press.

Downs, A. (1957). *An Economic Theory of Democracy*. New York: Harper Collins.

Druckman, J. N. (2001). On the limits of framing effects: Who can frame? *The Journal of Politics*, 63(4), 1041–66.

Druckman, J. N. and K. R. Nelson (2003). Framing and deliberation: How citizens' conversations limit elite influence. *American Journal of Political Science*, 47(4), 729–45.

Enten, H. J. LA mayoral race: Garcetti leads Greuel as runoff election enters final month. *The Guardian*, April 22, 2013. Web. November 17, 2014.

Erikson, R. S. (1976). The influence of newspaper endorsements in presidential elections: The case of 1964. *American Journal of Political Science* 20(2), 207–33.

Fraga, L. R., J. A. Garcia, R. Hero, M. Jones-Correa, V. Martinez-Ebers, and G. M. Segura Latino National Survey (LNS) (2006). [Computer file]. ICPSR20862-v4. Ann Arbor, MI: Inter-university Consortium for Political and Social Research [distributor], 2010-05-26. doi:10.3886/ICPSR20862.

Frey, W. H. (2006, March). Diversity spreads out: Metropolitan shifts in Hispanic, Asian, and Black populations since 2000. In *Living Cities Census Series* (pp. 1–28). Washington, DC: Brookings Institution.

  (2014). *Diversity Explosion: How New Racial Demographics Are Remaking America*. Washington, DC: Brookings Institution.

Garcia, J. A. and C. H. Arce (1988). Political orientations and behaviors of Chicanos: Trying to make sense out of attitudes and participation. In F. Chris Garcia (Ed.), *Pursuing Power: Latinos and the Political System* (pp. 125–51). Notre Dame, IN: University of Notre Dame Press.

Gay, C. (2006). Seeing difference: The effect of economic disparity on Black attitudes toward Latinos. *American Journal of Political Science*, 50(4), 982–97.

Gellner, E. (1983). *Nations and Nationalism*. Oxford: Blackwell Press.

Gerber, E. R. and J. H. Phillips (2003). Development ballot measures, interest group endorsements, and the political geography of growth preferences. *American Journal of Political Science*, 47(4), 625–39.

Gilens, M. (1999). *Why Americans Hate Welfare*. Chicago: University of Chicago Press.

Glaser, J. M. (1994). Back to the Black Belt: Racial environment and white Racial attitudes in the south. *Journal of Politics* 56(1), 21–41.

Gold, M. (2001). Kenneth Hahn's legacy serves his son well in mayor's race. *The Los Angeles Times*.

Green, P.M. (2011). The Chicago Municipal Election February 22, 2011 A Vote Analysis. http://sites.roosevelt.edu/pgreen/files/2014/05/OFFICIALChicago2011MunicipalElection2.pdf.

Grenier, G. J., and M. Castro (2001). Blacks and Cubans in Miami: The negative consequences of the Cuban enclave on ethnic relations. In *Governing American Cities*. Michael Jones-Correa (Ed.). New York: Russell Sage Foundation.

Grenier, G. J. and L. Pérez (2003). *The Legacy of Exile: Cubans in the United States* Boston: Pearson Education.

Grofman, B., L. Handley, and R. G. Niemi (1994). *Minority Representation and the Quest for Voting Equality*. Cambridge: Cambridge University Press.

Grossman, G. M. and E. Helpman (1999). Competing for endorsements. *The American Economic Review*, 89(3), 501–24.

Guerra, F. J. and Gilbert, B. (2013). Los Angeles Votes 2013: Mayoral General Election Exit Poll. Thomas and Dorothy Leavey Center for the Study of Los Angeles, Loyola Marymount University, Los Angeles, California.

Hajnal, Z. L. (2001). White residents, Black incumbents, and a declining racial divide. *American Political Science Review*, 95(3), 603–17.

Hajnal, Z. and T. Lee (2011). *Why Americans Don't Join the Party: Race, Immigration, and the Failure (of Political Parties) to Engage the Electorate*. Princeton, NJ: Princeton University Press.

Hajnal, Z. and J. Trounstine (2005). Why turnout does matter. *Journal of Politics*, 67(2), 515–35.

(2014). What underlies urban politics? Race, class, ideology, partisanship, and the urban vote. *Urban Affairs Review*, 50(1), 63–99.

Hanmer, M. J. and K. O. Kalkan (2012). Behind the curve: clarifying the best approach to calculating predicted probabilities and marginal effects from limited dependent variable models. *American Journal of Political Science*, 57(1), 263–77.

Harris-Lacewell, M. (2004). *Barbershops, Bibles, and B.E.T.: Everyday Talk and Black Political Talk*. Princeton, NJ: Princeton University Press.

Hero, R. E. (1989). Multiracial coalitions in city elections involving minority candidates: some evidence from Denver. *Urban Affairs Review*, 25, 342–51.

(1992). *Latinos and the U.S. Political System. Two-Tiered Pluralism*. Philadelphia: Temple University Press.

Hero, R. E. and R. R. Preuhs (2013). *Black–Latino Relations in U.S. National Politics: Beyond Conflict or Cooperation*. Cambridge: Cambridge University Press.

Horowitz, D. (1991). *A Democratic South Africa? Constitutional Engineering in a Divided Society*. University of California Press.
  (1985). *Ethnic Groups in Conflict*. Berkeley: University of California Press.
Huber, G. A. and J. S. Lapinski (2006). The "race card" Revisited: Assessing racial priming in policy contests. *American Journal of Political Science*, 50(2), 421–40.
Hurwitz, J., and M. Peffley (1998). *Perception and Prejudice: Race and Politics in the United States*. New Haven, CT: Yale University Press.
Hutchings, V. L. (2003). *Public Opinion and Democratic Accountability: How Citizens Learn about Politics*. Princeton, NJ: Princeton University Press.
Hutchings, V. L., N. Valentino, T. Philpot, and I. White. (2004). The compassion strategy: Race and the gender gap in American politics. *Public Opinion Quarterly*, 68(4), 512–41.
Hutchings, V. L., C. Wong, J. Jackson, and R. E. Brown (2011). Explaining perceptions of competitive threat in a multiracial context. In Guy-Uriel E. Charles, Heather K. Gerken, and Michael S. Kang (Eds.) *Race, Reform, and Regulation of the Electoral Process* (pp. 52–74). Cambridge University Press.
Iyengar, S. and D. R. Kinder (1987). *News That Matters*. Chicago: University of Chicago Press.
Jackson, B. O., E. Gerber, and B. E. Cain (1994). Coalitional prospects in a multi-racial society: African-American attitudes towards other minority groups. *Political Research Quarterly*, 47(2), 277–94.
Jones-Correa, M. (1998). *Between Two Nations: The Political Predicament of Latinos in New York City*. Ithaca, NY: Cornell University Press.
Kam, C. D. (2005). Who toes the party line? Cues, values, and individual differences. *Political Behavior*, 27(2), 163–82.
Kaufmann, K. M. (2003a). Cracks in the rainbow: Group commonality as a basis for Latino and African-American political coalitions. *Political Research Quarterly*, 56(2), 199–210.
  (2003b). Black and Latino voters in Denver: Responses to each other's political leadership. *Political Science Quarterly*, 118(1), 107–25.
  (2004). *The Urban Voter: Group Conflict and Mayoral Voting Behavior in American Cities*. Ann Arbor: University of Michigan Press.
Keiser, R. A. (2003). Philadelphia's evolving biracial coalition. In Browning, Marshall, and Tabb (Eds.). *Racial Politics in American Cities*. 3rd edn. (pp. 97–113). New York: Longman Publications.
Key, V. O. (1949). *Southern Politics in State and Nation*. New York: Knopf.
Kinder D. R. and T. R. Palfrey (1993). On behalf of an experimental political science. In Donald R. Kinder and Thomas R. Palfrey(Eds.) *Experimental Foundations of Political Science* (pp. 1–39). Ann Arbor: University of Michigan Press.
Kinder, D. R., and L. Sanders (1996). *Divided by Color*. Chicago: University of Chicago Press.
Krebs, T. B. (1998). The determinants of candidates' vote share and advantages of incumbency in city council elections. *American Journal of Political Science*, 42(3), 921–35.

Kuklinksi, J. H. and N. L. Hurley (1994). On hearing and interpreting political messages: A cautionary tale of citizen cue-taking. *Journal of Politics*, 56(3), 729–51.

Latino Decisions. 2008. www.pacificmarketresearch.com/ld/pdfs/latinodecisions_california_0807.pdf.

Lau, R. R. and D. P. Redlawsk (2001). Advantages and disadvantages of cognitive heuristics in political decision making. *American Journal of Political Science*, 45(4), 951–71.

Leal, D. (2002). Political participation by Latino non-citizens in the United States. *British Journal of Political Science*, 32(2), 353–70.

Lee, T. (2002). *Mobilizing Public Opinion: Black Insurgency and Racial Attitudes in the Civil Rights Era*. Chicago: University of Chicago Press.

    (2008). Race, immigration, and the identity-to-politics link. *Annual Review of Political Science*, 11, 457–78.

Leighley, J. E. (2001). *Strength in Numbers? The Political Mobilization of Racial and Ethnic Minorities*. Princeton, NJ: Princeton University Press.

Leighley, J. E. and A. Vedlitz (1999). Race, ethnicity and political participation: Competing models and contrasting explanations. *Journal of Politics*, 61(4), 1092–114.

Lewis-Beck, M., W. G. Jacoby, H. Norpoth, and H. F. Weisberg (2008). *The American Voter Revisited*. Ann Arbor: University of Michigan Press.

Lieske, J. (1989). The political dynamics of urban voting behavior. *American Journal of Political Science*, 33(1), 150–74.

Lijphart, A. (1999). *Patterns of Democracy: Government Forms & Performance in Thirty-Six Countries*. New Haven, CT: Yale University Press.

Liu, B. (2001). Racial context and White interests: Beyond black threat and racial tolerance. *Political Behavior*, 23(2), 157–80.

    (2003). Deracialization and urban racial context. *Urban Affairs Review* 38(4), 572–91.

Lodge, M., M. Steenbergen, and S. Brau (1995). The responsive voter: Campaign information and the dynamics of candidate evaluation. *American Political Science Review*, 89(2), 309–26.

Lupia, A. (1994). Shortcuts versus encyclopedias: Information and voting behavior in California insurance reform elections. *American Political Science Review*, 88(1), 63–76.

Maddaus, G. (2013). Wendy Greuel and Eric Garcetti have the same position on pensions; so what's this fight about? *LA Weekly*, May 22, 2013. Web. July 21, 2015.

Massy, D. (2008). *New Faces in New Places: The Changing Geography of American Immigration*. New York: Russell Sage Foundation Publications.

Masuoka, N. (2006). Together they become one: Examining the predictors of pan-ethnic group consciousness among Asian Americans and Latinos. *Social Science Quarterly*, 87, 993–1011.

Masuoka N. (2008). Defining the group: Latino identity and political participation. *American Politics Research*, 36(1), 33–61.

McClain, P. D. (1993). The changing dynamics of urban politics: Black and Hispanic municipal employment – is there competition? *Journal of Politics*, 55(2), 399–414.

McClain, P. D., N. M. Carter, V. M. DeFrancesco Soto, J. D. Grynaviski, S. C. Nunnally, T. J. Scotto, J. A. Kendrick, G. F. Lackey, and K. D. Cotton (2006). Racial distancing in a southern city: Latino immigrants' views of Black Americans. *Journal of Politics*, 68(3), 571–84.

McClain, P. D. and A. K. Karnig (1990). Black and Hispanic socioeconomic and political competition. *American Political Science Review*, 84(2), 535–45.

McConnaughy, C. M., I. K. White, D. L. Leal, and J. P. Casellas (2010). A Latino on the ballot: Explaining coethnic voting among Latinos and the response of White Americans. *The Journal of Politics*, 72(4), 1199–211.

McDermott, M. L. (1997). Voting cues in low-information elections: Candidate gender as a social information variable in contemporary United States elections. *American Journal of Political Science*, 41(1), 270–83.

(1998). Race and gender cues in low-information elections. *Political Research Quarterly*, 51(4), 895–918.

(2006). Not for members only: Group endorsements as electoral information cues. *Political Research Quarterly*, 59(2), 249–57.

McIlwain C. D. and S. M. Caliendo (2011). *Race Appeal: How Candidates Invoke Race in U.S. Political Campaigns*. Philadelphia: Temple University Press.

McKeever, M. (2001). Interethnic politics in the consensus city. In Michael Jones-Correa (Ed.) *Governing American Cities* (pp. 230–48). New York: Russell Sage Foundation.

Medina, J. (2013a). A race of "firsts" for Los Angeles voters, but many seem to take it in stride. *New York Times*, May 20, 2013. Web. July 21, 2015.

(2013b). Garcetti is elected mayor of Los Angeles, thwarting opposition of labor unions. *New York Times*, May 22, 2013. Web. July 21, 2015.

Mendelberg T. (2001). *The Race Card: Campaign Strategy, Implicit Messages, and the Norm of Equality*. Princeton, NJ: Princeton University Press.

Michelson, M. (2006). Mobilizing the Latino youth vote: Some experimental results. *Social Science Quarterly* 87(5), 1188–206.

Miller, A., P. Gurin, G. Gurin, and O. Malanchuk (1981). Group consciousness and political participation. *American Journal of Political Science*, 25(3), 494–511.

Mollenkopf, J. H. (2003). New York: Still the great anomaly. In Browning, Marshall, and Tabb (Eds.). *Racial Politics in American Cities*. 3rd edn. (pp. 115–41). New York: Longman Publications.

Muñoz, C., Jr. and C. Henry (1986). Rainbow coalitions in four big cities: San Antonio, Denver, Chicago and Philadelphia. *PS: Political Science & Politics*, 19(3), 598–609.

Nelson, T. E. and D. R. Kinder. (1996). Issue frames and group-centrism in American public opinion. *Journal of Politics*, 58, 1055–78.

Nicholson, S. P. (2011). Dominating cues and the limits of elite influence. *The Journal of Politics*, 73, 1165–77.

O'Keefe, D. J. (1990). *Persuasion. Theory and Research*. Newbury Park: Sage Publications

Oliver, J. E. (2012). *Local Elections and the Politics of Small-Scale Democracy*. Princeton, NJ: Princeton University Press.

Oliver, J. E. and S. Ha (2007). Vote choice in suburban elections. *American Political Science Review*, 101(3), 393–408.

Oliver, J. E. and T. Mendelberg (2000). Reconsidering the environmental determinants of White racial attitudes. *American Journal of Political Science*, 44(3), 574–89.

Orr, M. and D. M. West (2006). Power and race in cross-group coalitions. *National Political Science Review*, 11, 207–20.

Page, B. and R. Shapiro. (1992). *The Rational Public*. Chicago: University of Chicago Press.

Pantoja, A. D., R. Ramirez, and G. M. Segura (2001). Citizens by choice, voters by necessity: Patterns in political mobilization by naturalized Latinos. *Political Research Quarterly*, 54(4), 729–50.

Perry, H. L. (1991). Deracialization as an analytical construct in American urban politics. *Urban Affairs Quarterly*, 27(2), 181–91.

Philpot, T. and H. Walton Jr. (2007). One of our own: Black female candidates and the voters who support them. *American Journal of Political Science*, 51(1), 49–62.

Pinderhughes, D. M. (2003). Chicago politics: Political incorporation. In Browning, Marshall, and Tabb (Eds.) *Racial Politics in American Cities*. 3rd edn. New York: Longman Publications.

Rahn, W. M. (1993). The role of partisan stereotypes in information processing about political candidates. *American Journal of Political Science*, 37(2), 472–96.

Rappaport, R. B., W. J. Stone, and A. I. Abramowitz. (1991). Do endorsements matter? Group influence in the 1984 Democratic caucuses. *American Political Science Review*, 85(1), 193–203.

Reeves, K. (1997). *Voting Hopes or Fears? White Voters, Black Candidates & Racial Politics in America*. Oxford: Oxford University Press.

Rogers, R. R. (2006). *Afro-Caribbean Immigrants and the Politics of Incorporation: Ethnicity, Exception, or Exit*. Cambridge: Cambridge University Press.

Rosenstone, S. J. and J. M. Hansen (1993). *Mobilization, Participation, and Democracy in America*. New York: Macmillan Publishing Company.

Sanchez, G. R. (2006). The role of group consciousness in Latino public opinion. *Political Research Quarterly*, 59(3), 435–46.

Sanchez, G. R. and N. Masuoka (2010). Brown-utility heuristic? The presence and contributing factors of Latino linked fate. *Hispanic Journal of Behavioral Sciences*, 32(4), 519–31.

Schaffner, B. F., M. Streb, and G. Wright (2001) Teams without uniforms: The nonpartisan ballot in state and local elections. *Political Research Quarterly*, 54(1), 7–30.

(2002). The partisan heuristic in low-information elections. *Public Opinion Quarterly*, 66(4), 559–81.

Sears, D. O., J. Sidanius, and L. Bobo (2000). *Racialized Politics: The Debate about Racism in America*. Chicago: University of Chicago Press.

Segura, G. M. and H. A. Rodrigues (2006). Comparative ethnic politics in the United States. *Annual Review of Political Science*, 9, 375–95.
Shcattschneider, E. E. (1960). *The Semi-Sovereign People: A Realist's View of Democracy in America*. New York: Holt, Rinehart, and Winston.
Sniderman, Paul M. and T. L. Piazza. (2002). *Black Pride and Black Prejudice*. Princeton, NJ: Princeton University Press.
Sonenshein, R. J. (1993). *Politics in Black and White: Race and Power in Los Angeles*. Princeton, NJ: Princeton University Press.
  (2003a). Post incorporation politics in Los Angeles. In Browning, Marshall, and Tabb (Eds.) *Racial Politics in American Cities*. 3rd edn. (pp. 51–76). New York: Longman Publications.
  (2003b). The prospects for multiracial coalitions: Lessons from America's three largest cities, in Browning, Marshall, and Tabb (Eds.) *Racial Politics in American Cities*. 3rd edn. New York: Longman Publications.
Sonenshein, R. J. and S. H. Pinkus (2002). The dynamics of Latino incorporation: The 2001 Los Angeles mayoral election as seen in *Los Angeles Times* exit polls. *PS: Political Science & Politics*, 35(1), 67–74.
  (2005). Latino incorporation reaches the urban summit: How Antonio Villaraigosa won the 2005 Los Angeles mayor's race. *PS: Political Science & Politics*, 38(4), 713–21.
Squire, P. and E. R. A. N. Smith (1988). The effect of partisan information on voters in nonpartisan elections. *Journal of Politics*, 50(1), 169–79.
Tajfel, H. and J. C. Turner (1979). An integrative theory of intergroup conflict. In W. G. Austin and S. Worchel (Eds.) *The Social Psychology of Intergroup Relations* (pp. 34–47). Monterey, CA: Brooks/Cole.
Tate, K. (1993). *From Protest to Politics: The New Black Voters in American Elections*. Cambridge, MA: Russell Sage and Harvard University Press.
Taylor, M. C. (1998). How White attitudes vary with the racial composition of local populations: Numbers count. *American Sociological Review*, 63(4), 512–35.
Ture, K. and C. Hamilton ([1967] 1992). *Black Power: The Politics of Liberation*. New York: Vintage Books.
Turner, J. (2007). The messenger overwhelming the message: Ideological cues and perceptions of bias in television news. *Political Behavior*, 29, 441–64.
U.S. Census Bureau, 2004, U.S. Interim Projections by Age, Sex, Race, and Hispanic Origin. www.census.gov/ipc/www/usinterimproj/. Internet Release Date: March 18, 2004.
Vaca, N. (2004). *The Presumed Alliance: The Unspoken Conflict between Latinos and Blacks and What It Means for America*. New York: Harper Collins Press.
Valentine, G. (2008). Living with difference: Reflections on geographies of encounter. *Progress in Human Geography*, 32, 321–35.
Valentino, N. A., V. L. Hutchings, and I. K. White (2002). Cues that matter: How political ads prime racial attitudes during campaigns. *American Political Science Review*, 96(1), 75–90.
Varshney, A. (2002). *Ethnic Conflict and Civil Strife: Hindus and Muslims in India*. New Haven, CT: Yale University Press.

Verba, S. and W. H. Nie (1987). *Participation in America: Political Democracy and Social Equality*. Chicago: University of Chicago Press.
Verba, S., K. Schlozman, and H. Brady (1996). *Voice and Equality Civic Voluntarism in American Politics*. Cambridge, MA: Harvard University Press.
Walsh, K. C. (2004). *Talking about Politics: Informal Groups and Social Identity in American Life*. Chicago: University of Chicago Press.
Walton, H., Jr. (1972). *Black Politics. A Theoretical and Structural Analysis*. Philadelphia, PA: Lippencott Press.
  (1984). *Invisible Politics: Black Political Behavior*. New York: State University of New York Press.
  (1997). *African American Power and Politics: The Political Context Variable*. New York: Columbia University Press.
Waters, M. (1999). *Black Identities: Immigrant Dreams and American Realities*. Cambridge, MA: Harvard University Press.
White, I. K. (2007). When race matters and when it doesn't: Racial group differences in response to racial cues. *American Political Science Review*, 101 (2), 339–54.
Wolfinger, R. E. (1965). The development and persistence of ethnic voting. *The American Political Science Review*, 59(4), 896–908.
Wong, J. S. (2006). *Democracy's Promise: Immigrants and American Civic Institution*. Ann Arbor: University of Michigan Press.
Zaller, J. (1992). *The Nature and Origins of Mass Opinion*. Cambridge; New York: Cambridge University Press.

Index

Abramowitz, A. I., 29, 102
Abyssinian Baptist Church (New York), 44–46
Acevedo, Edward, 166–67
Acevedo Vilá, Aníbal, 44–45
Affirmative action
   candidate preference and, 58
   in experimental test of theory, 61–63, 64–69, 95–96
   in Houston, 43–44, 56
African-American candidates. *See* Black candidates
African-American voters. *See* Black voters
Afro-American Police Officers League (Houston), 43–44
Afro American Sheriff's Deputy League (Houston), 43–44
Alarcon, Richard, 160–64
Alatorre, Richard, 160
Alvarado, Carol, 161–63
American Federation of Labor–Congress of Industrial Organizations (AFL–CIO), 30, 62
American National Election Study (2008), 64
Amsterdam News (New York), 42–43, 44–45
Asian American candidates
   in Oakland, 145
   in San Francisco, 12, 145, 150
Asian American voters, 22, 23, 151–52

Bakewell, Danny J., Sr., 161–62
Baltimore, Black candidates in, 147

Baptist Ministers Alliance of Houston & Vicinity Religious Organization, 43–44
Barreto, M., 30, 35–36, 56–57, 59
Baton Rouge, Black candidates in, 147
Bean, F. D., 35
Belafonte, Harry, 159
Berkeley, California, minority coalitions in, 6–7
Bermudez, Rudy, 160–64
Birmingham, Alabama, Black candidates in, 147
Black candidates
   in Baltimore, 147
   in Baton Rouge, 147
   in Birmingham, Alabama, 147
   in Chicago, 5–6, 145
   in Houston, 5
   in largest US cities, 147–49
   Latino support for
      in Black–Latino coalitions, 107–8
      endorsements and, 106
   in Los Angeles, 3–4
   in Newark, 147
   in New York, 4–5, 145
   White voters, racial attitudes among, 135–37, 138–39, 140
Black Community Clergy and Labor Alliance (Los Angeles), 161–62
Black–Latino coalitions
   overview, 19, 20, 99–101, 113–14
   barriers to, 24–26

Black voters
  logistic regression analysis of, 115–16
  support for Latino candidates, 108
  in Chicago
    overview, 99–101
    endorsements, importance of, 112–13
    potential for, 15–16, 19, 24
  in Co-ethnic Elite Cues Theory, 36–37
  conditions for, 101
  cross-ethnic voting and, 112
  empirical analysis of (See Empirical analysis)
  endorsements and
    overview, 102–3
    Black support for Latino candidates, 108
    in Chicago, 112–13
    experimental research, 106
    in Los Angeles, 85–86, 112
    in New York, 85, 112–13
    White voters, effect on, 109–12
  experimental research
    overview, 113–14
    data collection, 103–6
    endorsements and, 106
    experimental treatments, 105
    fictional news stories, 117–22
    Latino support for Black candidates, 107–8
    methods, 103–6
    next steps regarding, 114
  historical background, 12–13
  in Houston
    overview, 99–101
    potential for, 15–16, 19, 24
  hypotheses regarding, 103
  ideology and, 24–26, 101
  incorporation, implications for, 145–47, 150–51
  Latino voters
    logistic regression analysis of, 115
    support for Black candidates, 107–8
  in Los Angeles
    overview, 99–101
    endorsements, importance of, 85–86, 112
    experimental test of theory compared, 86–87
    potential for, 15–16, 19, 24
  in New York
    overview, 99–101
    endorsements, importance of, 85, 112–13

  potential for, 15–16, 19, 24
  White voters and, 102
  out-group candidates, support for, 19, 20
  minority candidates, 20, 87
  racial/ethnic salience and, 103
  shifts in, 29
  viability, testing of, 106
  White voters
    avoiding alienation of, 112–13
    effect on, 100, 101–2, 109–12
    logistic regression analysis of, 115–16, 117
    in New York, 102
Black voters
  Black–Latino coalitions and (See also Black–Latino coalitions)
  logistic regression analysis of, 115–16
  support for Latino candidates, 108
  candidates, importance of race/ethnicity, 56–57, 69
  co-ethnic voting among, 41
  cohesiveness of, 34–35
  cross-ethnic voting among, 8–9, 38, 41, 81, 100, 108–9
  cues and, 27
  elites and, 27
  endorsements, importance of
    overview, 29–30, 57–58, 69
    in experimental test of theory, 64–69
    Latino voters compared, 85–87
    in Los Angeles, 80–81
    priming, co-ethnic endorsements and, 129–32, 142–43
  experimental test of theory and
    demographics in, 65
    Garcetti, logistic regression analysis of support for, 92
    logistic regression analysis of, 87–88
    in Los Angeles, 92
    results regarding, 64–69
  group identity, importance of, 58–59
  ideology and, 58
  Latino candidates, support for in Black–Latino coalitions, 108
  in Los Angeles
    endorsements, effect of, 80–81
    experimental test of theory and, 92
    out-group candidates, support for, 100, 108–9, 131–32
  perceived candidate sympathy among, 69–71

Black voters (cont.)
  political behavior of, 34–35
  potential for electoral coalitions among, 69–71
  priming and, 129–32
  racial attitudes among
    overview, 123–24, 141–42
    priming and, 129–32
    regression analysis of, 130
  racial/ethnic salience, importance of, 32, 64–69
Blake, Charles E., 161–62
Bloomberg, Michael, 1, 4–5, 42–43, 44–46, 48, 56, 154
Bobo, L., 34
Boney, Don, 162–63
Booker, Cory, 45–46
Bradley, Ethel, 46–47
Bradley, Lorraine, 161–62
Bradley, Tom, 46–47, 161–62
Braun, Carol Moseley, 5–6, 156, 166–67
Brewer, Henry (fictional candidate), 64–65, 69–70, 72, 74, 95–97
Broadman, Jeremy (fictional candidate), 64–65, 69–70, 72, 98
Bronx Dominican Coalition, 42–43
Brown, Dorothy A., 156
Brown, Jack (fictional candidate), 103–6, 117–22, 143
Brown, Lee, 5, 43–44, 56, 161–63
Brown, Peter, 154–55, 165
Browning, R. P., 6–7
Brown Memorial Baptist Church (New York), 44–45
Bryant, John, 46–47
Burke, Bill, 46–47
Burke, Yvonne Brathwaite, 46–47, 160–64
Bustamante, Cruz, 46–47
Butts, Calvin O., III, 44–46

Caldwell, Kirbyjon, 161–63
Caliendo, S. M., 32, 53
California Proposition 187, 77
Campbell, A., 30, 58, 102
Canaan Baptist Church (New York), 157
Candidates, race/ethnicity of
  Asian American candidates
    in Oakland, 145
    in San Francisco, 12, 145, 150
  Black candidates (*See* Black candidates)
  Black voters, importance to, 56–57, 69
  characteristics of, 32–33
  Co-ethnic Elite Cues Theory, implications for, 145–47
  electoral coalitions, importance to, 14, 16
  endorsements, relationship to, 58
  in experimental design of test, 61–62, 97
  experimental test of theory, importance in, 19, 53, 54, 56–57
  in Houston, 165
  hypotheses regarding, 60–61
  Latino candidates (*See* Latino candidates)
  Latino voters, importance to, 72–74, 85–87
  local elections, importance in, 37–38, 56–57, 99
  in Los Angeles, 161–62
  in New York, 45–46
  out-group candidates (*See* Out-group candidates)
    minority candidates (*See* Out-group minority candidates)
  racial/ethnic salience, relationship to, 32, 58
  White candidates (*See* White candidates)
Cardenas, Tony, 160–64
Carson, Sonny, 157–59
Castillo, John, 162–63
Caucasian candidates. *See* White candidates
Caucasian voters. *See* White voters
Census Bureau, 9
Chicago
  amendments to theory based on elections in, 48–49
  Black candidates in, 145
  Black–Latino coalitions in
    overview, 99–101
    endorsements, importance of, 112–13
    potential for, 15–16, 19, 24
  Co-ethnic Elite Cues Theory, application of, 165–67
  co-ethnic voting in, 165–67
  election results in, 156
  empirical analysis of elections, 47–48
  endorsements in, 48
  factors in selection of cities for study, 2–3
  Latino candidates in, 145
  minority coalitions in, 7
  race, ethnicity, and voting behavior in, 5–6
  racial/ethnic salience in, 41, 49
Chicago Tribune, 38, 39, 47–48, 165–67
Chico, Gery, 5–6, 156, 166–67

Chula Vista, California, Latino candidates in, 147
Church of God in Christ Texas, South Central Jurisdiction, 43–44
Church Without Walls (Houston), 161–63
Cisneros, Henry, 162–63
Citizenship in cities, 17
Clemente, Roberto Jr., 44–45
Clergy Coalition (Chicago), 166–67
Clinton, Hillary, 30, 36, 59
Coalition of Black Women (Chicago), 47–48
Coalitions. *See* Electoral coalitions
Co-ethnic Elite Cues Theory
  overview, 8–10, 19, 24–26
  amendments to, 48–49
  Black–Latino coalitions in, 36–37 (*See also* Black–Latino coalitions)
  candidates, race/ethnicity of (*See* Candidates, race/ethnicity of)
  Chicago, application to, 165–67
  co-ethnic voting in, 36–37
  comparative perspective, 33–34
  cross-ethnic voting in, 36–37
  cues in, 27 (*See also* Cues)
  elites in, 27–28
  empirical analysis of (*See* Empirical analysis)
  endorsements and (*See* Endorsements)
  evolution of, 7–8
  exceptions to, 45–48
  experimental test of (*See* Experimental test of theory)
  group politics and, 26
  high coverage of race
    with no racial/ethnic issues, 45–46
    with racial/ethnic issues, 44–45, 46–48
  Houston, application to, 162–65
  hypotheses of, 60–61
  implications of, 145–47
  incorporation, implications for, 145–47
  Los Angeles, application to, 77–78, 160–62
  low coverage of race
    with no racial/ethnic issues, 42–43
    with racial/ethnic issues, 43–44
  New York, application to, 157–60
  partisanship, implications for, 147
  racial attitudes and (*See* Racial attitudes)
  racial/ethnic salience in (*See* Racial/ethnic salience)

Co-ethnic voting
  overview, 1–2
  Black voters, among, 41
  in Chicago, 165–67
  in Co-ethnic Elite Cues Theory, 36–37
  in Houston, 161–63
  Latino voters, among, 41, 56–57, 77–78, 79–80
  in Los Angeles, 161–62
Cofield, D. Z., 165
Cohen, C. J., 35
Coleman, Garnet, 161–63
Comerciantes Latinos Unidos de Houston, 43–44
Comparative perspective, 33–34
Conover, P. J., 58–59
Corpus Christi, Texas, Latino candidates in, 147
Council of Black Elected Democrats (New York), 42–43
Cross-ethnic coalitions, 3, 14
Cross-ethnic voting
  overview, 6
  Black–Latino coalitions and, 112
  Black voters, among, 8–9, 38, 41, 81, 100, 108–9
  in Co-ethnic Elite Cues Theory, 36–37
  endorsements, effect of, 54
  group politics and, 26
  in Houston, 41, 44, 100, 164
  Latino voters, among, 8–9, 38, 41, 86, 100
  in Los Angeles, 41, 46–47, 78, 81, 86, 160–62
  in New York, 41, 42–43, 45, 100, 157–60
Cues. *See also* Endorsements
  overview, 27
  Black voters and, 27
  Latino voters and, 27

Daley, Richard M., 5–6, 156, 165–66
Dallas, local elections in, 13
Davis, Jim (fictional candidate), 103–6, 107–8, 112, 117–18, 143
de Blasio, Bill, 5, 154, 159–60
del Valle, Miguel, 5–6, 156, 166–67
Demographics of cities. *See* Population in cities
Denver, local elections in, 60
Dinkins, David N., 44–46, 157–59
Diversity in local elections, 14
Dixon, James, 161–63

Dixon, Julian C., 160
Downs, A., 29
Dymally, Mervyn, 160–64

Edwards, Ada, 161–63
El Dia (Houston), 161–63
El Diario/La Prensa (New York), 42–43, 44–45
Electoral coalitions
　Asian American voters in, 151–52
　Black–Latino coalitions (*See* Black–Latino coalitions)
　Black voters, potential among, 69–71
　building diversity in, 151
　candidates, importance of race/ethnicity, 14, 16
　cross-ethnic coalitions, 3, 14
　endorsements, importance of, 16
　Latino voters, potential among, 74–76
　minority coalitions, 6–7
　White-Black coalitions, 12–13
　White-Latino coalitions, 12–13
Elite Black–Latino coalitions. *See* Black–Latino coalitions
Elite cues. *See* Endorsements
Elites
　overview, 27–28
　Black voters and, 27
　Latino voters and, 27
　priming and, 126
Ellis, Rodney, 161–63
Emanuel, Rahm, 5–6, 47–48, 156, 166–67
Empirical analysis. *See also* Experimental test of theory
　overview, 37–38
　of Chicago elections, 47–48
　data in, 38–39
　of endorsements, 42, 50
　high coverage of race
　　with no racial/ethnic issues, 45–46
　　with racial/ethnic issues, 44–45, 46–48
　of Houston elections, 43–44
　of Los Angeles elections, 46–47
　low coverage of race
　　with no racial/ethnic issues, 42–43
　　with racial/ethnic issues, 43–44
　methodology of, 38–39
　newspapers, use of, 38–39
　of New York elections, 42–43, 44–46
　of racial/ethnic salience, 37–38, 39–40, 49

Endorsements
　overview, 20, 29–30
　Black–Latino coalitions and
　　overview, 102–3
　　Black support for Latino candidates, 108
　　in Chicago, 112–13
　　experimental research, 106
　　in Los Angeles, 85–86, 112
　　in New York, 85, 112–13
　　White voters, effect on, 109–12
　Black voters, importance to
　　overview, 29–30, 57–58, 69
　　in experimental test of theory, 64–69
　　Latino voters compared, 85–87
　　in Los Angeles, 80–81
　　priming, co-ethnic endorsements and, 129–32, 142–43
　candidates, relationship of race/ethnicity to, 58
　in Chicago, 48
　cross-ethnic voting, effect on, 54
　effectiveness of, 29
　electoral coalitions, importance to, 16
　empirical analysis of, 42, 50
　in experimental design of test, 62, 97
　experimental test of theory, importance in, 19, 53, 54, 57–58
　in Houston, 50
　importance of, 29–30, 50–51
　Latino voters, importance to
　　overview, 29–30, 57–58, 72–74
　　Black voters compared, 85–87
　　in experimental text of theory, 71–73
　　in Los Angeles, 82–85
　　priming, co-ethnic endorsements and, 126–29, 142–43
　in Los Angeles, 48–49, 50, 76–77, 80–81
　non-racial/ethnic endorsements, 29–30
　out-group candidates and, 142–43
　racial/ethnic salience, relationship with, 158
　by unions, 29–30
　use in empirical analysis, 38–39, 62–63
　White voters, importance to, 137–41
English-only laws in experimental test of theory, 61–63, 96–97
Erickson, R. S., 30
Ethnic attitudes. *See* Racial attitudes
Ethnicity
　Chicago, voting behavior in, 5–6
　group politics and, 15

Houston, voting behavior in, 5
  ideology versus, 11
  Los Angeles, voting behavior in, 3–4
  New York, voting behavior in, 4–5
  partisanship versus, 11, 34
Ethnic salience. *See* Racial/ethnic salience
Experimental test of theory. *See also*
    Empirical analysis
  overview, 19, 54–56
  affirmative action in, 61–63, 64–69, 95–96
  Black voters and
    demographics of, 65
    Garcetti, logistic regression analysis of
      support for, 92
    logistic regression analysis of, 87–88
    in Los Angeles, 92
    results regarding, 64–69
  campaign context, importance of, 59–60
  candidates, importance of race/ethnicity,
    19, 53, 54, 56–57
  data collection, 63
  endorsements, importance of, 19, 53, 54,
    57–58
  English-only laws in, 61–63, 96–97
  experimental design, 61–63
  fictional news stories, 95–97
  group identity, importance of, 58–59
  hypotheses derived from, 60–61
  Latino voters and
    demographics of, 66
    Garcetti, logistic regression analysis of
      support for, 94
    Greuel, logistic regression analysis of
      support for, 93
    logistic regression analysis of, 88–89
    in Los Angeles, 93, 94
    results regarding, 71–73
  Los Angeles compared
    overview, 19, 76
    Black–Latino coalitions and, 86–87
    context of, 68–69
    Garcetti, logistic regression analysis of
      support for, 89–90, 92, 94
    Greuel, logistic regression analysis of
      support for, 91, 93
  methods, 61
  next steps regarding, 87
  procedures, 61
  racial/ethnic salience, importance
    of, 53, 54
  sample information, 64

Farrar, Jessica, 43–44
Federation of Hispanic Chambers
  of Commerce (New York),
  42–43
Ferguson, Missouri, police-community
  relations in, 144
Ferrer, Fernando, 4–5, 42–43, 44–45, 53,
  56, 85, 99, 100, 154, 157–59
"50% + 1" rule, 11, 12–13
Fioretti, Robert, 47–48
First African Methodist Episcopal Church
  (Los Angeles), 160–64
Flake, Floyd H., 45–46
Fluke, Floyd, 157
Foreign populations in cities, 16

Gallegos, Mario, 43–44
Galloway, Carol Mims, 162–63
Garcetti, Eric, 4, 48–49, 76–77, 78, 79–81,
  82–85, 89–90, 92, 94, 112, 153,
  161–62
Garcia, Jesus "Chuy," 5–6, 47–48, 156
Garcia, Juan (fictional candidate), 103–6,
  108, 111–12, 118–20, 143
Garcia, Sylvia, 161–63
GfK, 122, 143
Gilbert, Brianne, 78
Gilliam, F., Jr., 34
Giuliani, Rudolph, 154, 157
Gonzalez, Anthony (fictional candidate),
  64–65, 69–70, 95–97
Grand Council of Guardians (New York),
  157–59
Greanias, George, 5, 154–55
Greater Allen A. M. E. Cathedral
  (New York), 45–46
Green, Mark, 4–5, 42–43, 56, 154,
  157–59
Greuel, Wendy, 4, 48–49, 76–77, 78, 80–81,
  82–85, 91, 93, 153, 161–62
Group identity
  ideology and, 6–7
  importance of, 58–59
Group politics, 26
Guardians Association (New York), 42–43
Guerra, Fernando, 78
Gulf Coast AME Ministerial Alliance
  (Houston), 43–44, 162–63
Gulf Meadows Church (Houston),
  161–63
Gutierrez, Luis V., 165–67

Hahn, Jim, 3–4, 22, 46–47, 55, 68, 85–86, 97, 153, 160–64
Hairston, Leslie, 47–48
Hajnal, Z., 11, 17, 19, 34, 35, 36, 57, 97, 101, 110, 150
Hall, Anthony, 43–44
Harris, Michelle, 166–67
Harris County Council of Organizations (Houston), 43–44, 162–63
Harris-Lacewell, M., 28
Hayden, Tom, 153, 160
Hayek, Salma, 78, 83–85
Hero, R. E., 28
Hialeah, Florida, Latino candidates in, 147
Hispanic American Labor Council (Chicago), 166–67
Hispanic Business Organization (Houston), 43–44
Hispanic candidates. *See* Latino candidates
Hispanic Clergy Association (New York), 42–43
Hispanic Detectives Society (New York), 157–59
Hispanic voters. *See* Latino voters
Horton, Jerome, 160–64
Houston
 affirmative action in, 43–44, 56
 Black–Latino coalitions in
  overview, 99–101
  potential for, 15–16, 19, 24
 candidates, importance of race/ethnicity, 165
 Co-ethnic Elite Cues Theory, application of, 162–65
 co-ethnic voting in, 161–63
 cross-ethnic voting in, 41, 44, 100, 164
 election results in, 154–55
 empirical analysis of elections, 43–44
 endorsements in, 50
 factors in selection of cities for study, 2–3
 Latino candidates in, 145
 patterns in local elections, 13
 race, ethnicity, and voting behavior in, 5
 racial/ethnic salience in, 40, 41, 49
Houston Black American Democrats, 43–44
Houston Black Firefighters Association, 43–44
Houston Chronicle, 38, 39, 43–44, 162–65
Houston Hispanic Chamber of Commerce, 43–44, 161–63
Houston Hispanic Coalition, 43–44
Hoy (New York), 42–43, 44–45

Hughes, Teresa, 160
Hurley, N. L., 27, 30, 58, 68, 123
Hutchings, V. L., 63, 124
Hypotheses
 Black–Latino coalitions, regarding, 103
 candidates, regarding race/ethnicity of, 60–61
 Co-ethnic Elite Cues Theory, derived from, 60–61
 out-group candidates, regarding, 124
  minority candidates, 103, 106
 racial attitudes, regarding, 124, 125

Ideology
 Black–Latino coalitions and, 24–26, 101
 Black voters and, 58
 candidate preference and, 58
 group identity and, 6–7
 Latino voters and, 56–57
 race and ethnicity versus, 11
 White voters, and racial attitudes among, 132
Incorporation
 overview, 144–45
 Black–Latino coalitions, implications of, 145–47, 150–51
 Co-ethnic Elite Cues Theory, implications of, 145–47
 in largest US cities, 147–49
Inner City Broadcasting Corporation, 44–45
International Association of Black Professional Firefighters (Houston), 162–63

Jackson, Andre (fictional candidate), 72, 74
Jackson, Jesse, 44–45, 47–48, 160
Jakes, Paul, 156
James, Kevin, 4
James, Letitia, 45–46
Jeffries, Hakeem, 159
Johnson, Earvin "Magic," 44–45, 46–49, 78, 80–81, 160–64
Johnson, Lyndon B., 30
Jones, Emil Jr., 47–48
Jones, Ruben, 161–63

Kaufmann, K. M., 31–32, 69, 102
Kirk, Ron, 162–63
Knowledge Networks, 122, 143
Krebs, T. B., 57
Kuklinski, J. H., 27, 58, 68, 123

La Opinion (Los Angeles), 78, 83–85, 86
Latin American Police Association
 (Chicago), 166–67
Latina P. A. C. (Houston), 162–63
Latina Political Action Committee
 (New York), 44–45
Latino candidates
 Black support for in Black–Latino
  coalitions, 108
 in Chicago, 5–6, 145
 in Chula Vista, California, 147
 in Corpus Christi, Texas, 147
 in Hialeah, Florida, 147
 in Houston, 5, 145
 in largest US cities, 147–49
 in Los Angeles, 3–4
 in Miami, 147
 in New York, 4–5, 145
 White voters, racial attitudes among,
  132–35, 139–41
"Latino identity," 37
Latino National Survey, 64
Latino voters
 Black candidates, support for
  in Black–Latino coalitions,
   107–8
  endorsements and, 106
 Black–Latino coalitions and (*See also*
  Black–Latino coalitions)
  logistic regression analysis of, 115
  support for Black candidates, 107–8
 candidates, importance of race/ethnicity,
  56–57, 72–74, 85–87
 co-ethnic voting among, 41, 56–57,
  77–78, 79–80
 cohesiveness of, 35–36
 cross-ethnic voting among, 8–9, 38, 41,
  86, 100
 cues and, 27
 elites and, 27
 endorsements, importance of
  overview, 29–30, 57–58, 72–74
  Black voters compared, 85–87
  in experimental text of theory, 71–73
  in Los Angeles, 82–85
  priming, co-ethnic endorsements and,
   126–29, 142–43
 experimental test of theory and
  demographics in, 66
  Garcetti, logistic regression analysis of
   support for, 94
  Greuel, logistic regression analysis of
   support for, 93
  logistic regression analysis of,
   88–89
  in Los Angeles, 93, 94
  results regarding, 71–73
 group identity, importance of, 58–59
 ideology and, 56–57
 in Los Angeles
  co-ethnic voting among, 79–80
  endorsements, effect of, 82–85
  experimental test of theory and,
   93, 94
 out-group candidates, support for,
  74–76, 100, 127–29
 perceived candidate sympathy among,
  74–76
 political behavior of, 35–36
 potential for electoral coalitions among,
  74–76
 priming and, 126–29
 racial attitudes among
  overview, 123–24, 141–42
  priming and, 126–29
  regression analysis of, 128
 racial/ethnic salience, importance of, 32,
  71–74
Lau, R. R., 102
Lawson, Bill, 161–63, 165
Leal, D., 35
Lee, El Franco, 161–63
Lee, Sheila Jackson, 43–44, 161–63
Lee, T., 28, 35
Lewis, Karen, 47–48
Lhota, Joe, 154, 159–60
Lieske, J., 57
Liu, John, 5, 30, 154
Local elections. (*See also specific city*)
 broad patterns in, 11–13
 candidates, importance of race/ethnicity,
  37–38, 56–57, 99
 diversity in, 14
 ethnicity, voting behavior and, 2–6
 nonpartisan elections, 5, 24, 57
 partisanship in, 22, 24, 57
 race, voting behavior and, 2–6
 racial/ethnic salience in, 41
 thresholds, choice of, 11, 23
 voter turnout in, 18
Locke, Gene, 154–55, 165
Lopez, Margarita, 44–45

Los Angeles
  Black–Latino coalitions in
    overview, 99–101
    endorsements, importance of, 85–86, 112
    experimental test of theory compared, 86–87
    potential for, 15–16, 19, 24
  Black voters in, effect of endorsements, 80–81
  candidates, importance of race/ethnicity, 161–62
  Co-ethnic Elite Cues Theory, application of, 77–78, 160–62
  co-ethnic voting in, 161–62
  cross-ethnic voting in, 41, 46–47, 78, 81, 86, 160–62
  election results in, 153
  empirical analysis of elections, 46–47
  endorsements in, 48–49, 50, 76–77, 80–81
  exit polls in, 78–79, 98, 156
  experimental test of theory compared
    overview, 19, 76
    Black–Latino coalitions and, 86–87
    context of, 68–69
    Garcetti, logistic regression analysis of support for, 89–90, 92, 94
    Greuel, logistic regression analysis of support for, 91, 93
  factors in selection of cities for study, 2–3
  Latino voters in
    co-ethnic voting among, 79–80
    endorsements, effect of, 82–85
    experimental test of theory and, 93, 94
    minority coalitions in, 7
    race, ethnicity, and voting behavior in, 3–4
    racial/ethnic salience in, 41, 49, 76–77, 160–62
Los Angeles African American Women Political Action Committee, 161–62
Los Angeles Times, 38, 39, 46–47, 160–62
Love, Roy, 161–63
Loyola Marymount University, Thomas and Dorothy Leavey Center for the Study of Los Angeles, 78
Luebke, Paul, 31
Lupinski, J. S., 30
Lyle, Fredrenna, 166–67

Marshall, D. R., 6–7
Martin, B. Herbert, 166–67
Masuoka, N., 59
Mayoral Elections Data Set (Hajnal and Trounstine), 11, 19, 75, 97, 150
McCall, H. Carl, 157
McDermott, M. L., 30, 62, 102
McGowen, Ernest, 43–44
McIlwain, C., 32, 53
Meeks, James, 47–48
Mendelberg, T., 32
Mendez, Olga, 42–43
Messinger, Ruth, 154, 157
Mexican American Political Organization (Chicago), 166–67
Mexican-American Sheriff's Organization (Houston), 43–44
Miami, Latino candidates in, 147
Michelson, M., 36
Miller, A., 34
Miller, Clinton, 44–45
Minority coalitions, 6–7
Molina, Gloria, 46–47, 78, 82–83, 160–64
Moreno, Joseph Mario, 166–67
Moreno, Proco "Joe," 166–67
Mosbacher, Rob, 5, 43–44, 56, 154–55
Mother AME Zion Church (New York), 44–45
Munoz, Tony, 166–67
Murray, Cecil "Chip," 160–64

National Latino Officers Association (New York), 44–45
Newark, Black candidates in, 147
New Frontier Democratic Club (Los Angeles), 161–62
New Orleans, endorsements in, 30
Newspapers
  circulation of, 39
  empirical analysis, use in, 38–39, 62
  racial/ethnic issues, coverage of, 51–52
New York
  amendments to theory based on elections in, 48–49
  Black candidates in, 145
  Black–Latino coalitions in
    overview, 99–101
    endorsements, importance of, 85, 112–13
    potential for, 15–16, 19, 24
    White voters and, 102

candidates, importance of race/ethnicity, 45–46
Co-ethnic Elite Cues Theory, application of, 157–60
cross-ethnic voting in, 41, 42–43, 45, 100, 157–60
election results in, 154
empirical analysis of elections, 42–43, 44–46
factors in selection of cities for study, 2–3
Latino candidates in, 145
minority coalitions in, 7
race, ethnicity, and voting behavior in, 4–5
racial/ethnic salience in, 41, 49
New York Daily News, 99
New York One (television channel), 53
New York Times, 38, 39, 42–43, 44–45, 159–60
Nicholson, S. P., 123
Nie, W. H., 34
Nonpartisan elections, 5, 24, 57
Norman, Clarence, Jr., 157
Northwest Community Baptist Church (Houston), 161–63

Oakland
Asian American candidates in, 145
minority coalitions in, 7
Obama, Barack, 45–46, 47–48, 159–60
100 African-American Leaders (Chicago), 47–48
100 Blacks in Law Enforcement Who Care (New York), 44–45
Out-group candidates
Black–Latino coalitions and, 19, 20
Black voters supporting, 100, 108–9, 131–32
endorsements and, 142–43
hypotheses regarding, 124
Latino voters supporting, 74–76, 100, 127–29
Out-group minority candidates
Black–Latino coalitions and, 20, 87, 107–8, 112
hypotheses regarding, 103, 106

Pacheco, Nick, 46–47
Padilla, Alex, 46–47, 160–64
Parker, Annise, 5, 154–55, 165
Parker, Kevin, 44–45
Parks, Bernard, 3–4, 22, 48–49, 55, 160–64

Partisanship
Co-ethnic Elite Cues Theory, implications of, 147
group politics and, 15
in local elections, 22, 24, 57
race and ethnicity versus, 11, 34
Paterson, David, 44–45
Peña, Federico, 60
Perry, Jan, 4, 48–49, 78, 80–81, 161–62
Perry, Susan (fictional mayor), 117–22
Philadelphia
minority coalitions in, 7
patterns in local elections, 13
Polanco, Richard, 46–47
Police-community relations, 20, 144
Police violence, 144
Population in cities
of Blacks, 9, 12, 21
of Blacks and Latinos combined, 21
changes in, 15–16
citizenship, 17
foreign populations, 16
of Latinos, 9, 12, 20–21
projections, 22
of Whites, 12
Powell, Adam Clayton, IV, 157
Powell, Colin, 45–46
Preuhs, R. R., 28
Priming
Black voters, co-ethnic endorsements and, 129–32
elites and, 126
Latino voters, co-ethnic endorsements and, 126–29
White voters
alternative priming, 137–41
Black candidates and, 135–37
co-ethnic endorsements and, 137–41
Latino candidates and, 132–35
Progressive Community Church (Chicago), 166–67
Protest is Not Enough: The Struggle for Blacks and Hispanics for Equality in Urban Politics (Browning, Marshall, and Tabb), 144–45

Quinn, Christine, 5, 154

Race
Chicago, voting behavior in, 5–6
group politics and, 15

Race (cont.)
  Houston, voting behavior in, 5
  ideology versus, 11
  Los Angeles, voting behavior in, 3–4
  New York, voting behavior in, 4–5
  partisanship versus, 11, 34
Racial attitudes
  overview, 20, 123–24, 141–43
  Black voters, among
    overview, 123–24, 141–42
    priming and, 129–32
    regression analysis of, 130
  experimental research
    data collection, 125–26
    methods, 125–26
  hypotheses regarding, 124, 125
  Latino voters, among
    overview, 123–24, 141–42
    priming and, 126–29
    regression analysis of, 128
  next steps regarding, 143
  priming and
    Black voters, 129–32
    elites, role of, 126
    Latino voters, 126–29
    White voters, 132–37
  White voters, among
    overview, 132–37, 142
    Black candidates, toward, 135–37, 138–39, 140
    Black–Latino coalitions, effect of, 134–41, 142
    ideology and, 132
    Latino candidates, toward, 132–35, 139–41
    minority candidate support and, 124–25
    regression analysis of, 133, 135–37, 138, 140
Racial/ethnic salience
  overview, 19, 20, 30–32
  Black–Latino coalitions and, 103
  Black voters, importance to, 32, 64–69
  campaign context, importance of, 59–60
  candidates, relationship of race/ethnicity to, 32, 58
  in Chicago, 41, 49
  empirical analysis of, 37–38, 39–40, 49
  endorsements, relationship with, 158
  in experimental design of test, 62, 97
  experimental test of theory, importance in, 53, 54
  in Houston, 40, 41, 49
  importance of, 50–51
  Latino voters, importance to, 32, 71–74
  local elections and, 41
  in Los Angeles, 41, 49, 76–77, 160–62
  measurement of, 53
  in national elections, 32
  in New York, 41, 49
Ramirez, Roberto, 44–45
Rangel, Charles B., 44–45, 157–59
Rappaport, R. B., 29, 102
Redlawsk, D. P., 102
Reyes, Ed, 160–64
Richardson, Bill, 59
Ridley-Thomas, Mark, 46–47, 48–49
Riorden, Richard, 153, 160
Rogers, R. R., 35
Rush, Bobby, 156, 165–67

Saenz, Gracie, 5, 43–44, 154–55
Salience of race and ethnicity. See Racial/ethnic salience
Sanchez, Orlando, 5, 43–44, 154–55, 161–63
Sanchez, Tony, 162–63
San Diego, local elections in, 13
San Francisco
  Asian American candidates in, 12, 145, 150
  minority coalitions in, 7
Santini Padilla, Jorge, 44–45
The Sentinel (Los Angeles), 160–64
Service Employees International Union (SEIU) (New York), 42–43, 44–45, 157–59
Sharpton, Al, 44–45, 157–59
Simmons, Russell, 44–45
Smith, Michele, 47–48
Solis, Danny, 166–67
Steele, Bobbie, 47–48
Stevenson, Adlai, 58
Stone, W. J., 29, 102
Sutton, Percy E., 44–45
Sutton, Pierre, 44–45

Tabb, D. H., 6–7
Tajfel, H., 58
Tejano Democrats (Houston), 161–63
Thomas, Mark Ridley, 161–62
Thompson, Bill, 5, 41, 45–46, 53, 56, 154, 159

Thompson, Senfronia, 161–63
Torres, Gerard, 43–44
Towns, Edolphus, 157
Trounstine, J., 11, 17, 19, 34, 36, 57, 97, 101, 150
Turner, J. C., 58
Turner, Sylvester, 154–55, 161–63
Tyson, Albert, 47–48

Valentine, G., 137
Valentino, N. A., 32
Vallas, Paul, 166–67
Vasquez, Gabriel, 162–63
Velez, Dasdil, 42–43
Verba, S., 34
Villaraigosa, Antonio, 3–4, 22, 46–47, 48–49, 55, 68, 85–86, 97, 153, 160–61
Voter turnout in local elections, 18

Walker, Wyatt Tee, 157
Wallis, William "Dock" III, 47–48, 156
Walters, Rita, 46–47, 48–49
Walton, H., Jr., 15, 34
Washington, Harold, 5–6
Washington, James (fictional candidate), 103–6, 107–8, 109–11, 112, 120–22, 143
Waters, Maxine, 46–47, 48–49, 160–64
Weiner, Anthony, 5, 154
West, Ralph, 161–63
West Angeles Church of God in Christ (Los Angeles), 161–62
Wheeler Avenue Baptist Church (Houston), 161–63, 165
White, Bill, 5, 161–63
White, I. K., 59
White, Thomas, Jr., 157
White-Black coalitions, 12–13
White candidates
    in Chicago, 5–6
    in Houston, 5
    in largest US cities, 147–49
    in Los Angeles, 3–4
    in New York, 4–5
White-Latino coalitions, 12–13
White voters
    Black–Latino coalitions and
        avoiding alienation of, 112–13
        effect of, 100, 101–2, 109–12
        logistic regression analysis of, 115–16, 117
        in New York, 102
    endorsements, importance of, 137–41
    minority candidate support among, 124–25
    priming and
        alternative priming, 137–41
        Black candidates and, 135–37
        co-ethnic endorsements and, 137–41
        Latino candidates and, 132–35
    racial attitudes among
        overview, 132–37, 142
        Black candidates, toward, 135–37, 138–39, 140
        Black–Latino coalitions, effect of, 134–41, 142
        ideology and, 132
        Latino candidates, toward, 132–35, 139–41
        minority candidate support and, 124–25
        regression analysis of, 133, 135–37, 138, 140
Who Governs? Democracy and Power in an American City (Dahl), 144–45
Wilson, Willie, 47–48
Windsor Village United Methodist Church (Houston), 161–63
Wooten, Priscilla A., 42–43, 157

Zaller, J., 27–28